Edward Thomas and Wales

Jeff Towns is an antiquarian book-dealer, writer and documentary maker. His Dylan Thomas collections have been acquired by museums and institutions around the world. His fascination with Edward Thomas lies deep in a London childhood with holiday visits to Wales and a passion for poetry.

Edward Thomas and Wales

Make me content
With some sweetness
From Wales
Whose nightingales
Have no wings
from *Words*

Edited with an Introduction, Chronology
and Afterword by Jeff Towns

Wales in the Poetry of Edward Thomas
an essay by Dr Andrew Webb

Parthian, Cardigan SA43 1ED
www.parthianbooks.com
First published in 2018
© Jeff Towns 2018
© Andrew Webb 2018
ISBN 978-1-912681-12-9
Edited by Barbara Whitfield
The Modern Wales series receives support from the Rhys Davies Trust
Cover design: www.theundercard.co.uk
Typeset by Elaine Sharples
Printed by Pulsio
Published with the financial support of the Welsh Books Council
British Library Cataloguing in Publication Data
A cataloguing record for this book is available from the British Library.
Every attempt has been made to secure the permission of copyright
holders to reproduce archival and printed material.

This book is dedicated to my mother, Lavinia May Parry,

who made me 'five eighths Welsh' – and – Sylvie Martha

Lloyd-Towns – Welcome to Wales

ACKNOWLEDGMENTS

To Peter Stead who started this book with me, sadly he had to leave the project, but has stayed interested and has been as generous as ever; to Katie Bowman for her tireless typing, transcribing and support; to Andy Webb for all his insights into the life and work of Edward Thomas and his contribution to this book; to M. Wynn Thomas for advice and support especially regarding Owen M. Edwards; to Wyn Thomas for translating the Gwili extract from the original Welsh; to Alison Harvey at Cardiff University Special Collections and Archives; to Kate Aslett & Joe Towns for their encouragement; to Julia Maxted and Richard Emeny from the Edward Thomas Fellowship; to Veronica Watts for her constant help; to all at Parthian – Richard Lewis, Maria ZygogiannI and Barbara Whitfield; and finally to John Idris Jones and Mrs Jessie Thomas who first introduced me to Edward Thomas.

CONTENTS

CONTENTS

INTRODUCTION

Had Edward Thomas written in Welsh he would now be a National Figure. But as he was born in London of Welsh parents and was bred and lived in England, and wrote in English, the essentially Celtic qualities of his spirit have been strangely veiled both from his audience and his critics.

Edward Garnett, in his 'Introduction' to the
Gregynog *Chosen Essays*, 1926

As this quotation shows, less than a decade after Edward Thomas's death, his close friend and literary adviser, Edward Garnett was questioning the apparent neglect of Thomas's 'Welshness'. The extracts presented here from Edward Thomas's prose works, and the life events listed in the 'Chronology', have been chosen not only to show how important Wales, the place, its people and its literature, were to Thomas, but to indicate how deeply Wales permeated Thomas's life and writings. The extracts and life events are presented in chronological order and without comment to enable the reader to judge for themselves the extent to which Thomas's 'essentially Celtic qualities', as Garnett would have it, shine through. This is not prompted by any xenophobia or jingoism on my part; I consider most kinds of Nationalism dangerous and unpleasant. The South African poet and critic Peter Sacks writes that Thomas 'claimed his truest co-nationals were the birds...' and Thomas himself makes his position clear

1

when, as a soldier he wrote in *This is no case of petty right or wrong;*

> I hate not Germans, nor grow hot
> With love of Englishmen, to please newspapers.
> Beside my hate for one fat patriot
> My hatred of the Kaiser is love true...

I empathise with these sentiments but also with the Welsh writer and critic Sally Roberts Jones, who begins her 1987 essay, 'Edward Thomas and Wales', in *The Art of Edward Thomas*, with this disclaimer:

> At one time it was the custom to claim any writer with even the slightest connection with Wales as a Welsh writer, and the fledgling Anglo-Welsh tradition acquired such figures as John Donne, George Meredith and Wilfred Owen. In some cases further investigation does suggest a genuine claim to a place in the succession, but far more often over-enthusiastic support of dubious candidates has led to a rejection of others with much more valid claims.

My own readings of Thomas's work, and my knowledge of his life, lead me to conclude that Edward Thomas, although born in London, is a writer with those 'genuine' and 'valid claims', and this book is an attempt, therefore, to gather together, textual and biographical evidence to support this claim. Maybe I feel compelled to attempt this because I first encountered Edward Thomas when I arrived in Wales, aged 18, to continue my education and my introduction to Thomas was necessarily Welsh in flavour, as I was taught about him by Welsh lecturers. Then, as a bookseller, one of my best customers was a Welsh relative of Thomas's close friend John Jenkins (known by his bardic name Gwili), who was proud to share with me his knowledge of Thomas's frequent visits to South Wales. But this was fifty years ago when Thomas's reputation was quite different and over the last two decades Edward Thomas's reputation both as a prose writer and poet have been growing. The approach of his Centenary in 2017 was marked by a flurry of new books, both biographical and critical, but on reading them I noticed a marked absence of references to Wales.

My earlier interest in Thomas had been rekindled when in the course of my work as a rare book dealer I acquired two significant Edward Thomas collections and started a friendship with a fanatical Edward Thomas collector. Sadly, at the same time I began to notice headlines and titles such as these:

'Edward Thomas: an acute depressive who loved the English Countryside', *Daily Telegraph*
'Edward Thomas and the English countryside', a Cambridge Conference title
'Edward Thomas: A Mirror of England', a book title
'Poetry and the English countryside', the title of speech given by Sir Andrew Motion, Poet Laureate

Further, during Thomas's centenary year, I attended several conferences on his work becoming increasingly uneasy with how little he was talked about in the context of his Welsh heritage. Thankfully, at a Cardiff University conference I encountered Dr Andrew Webb of Bangor University, whose lecture, based on his book *Edward Thomas and World Literary Studies: Wales, Anglocentrism and English Literature,* eloquently articulated much of what I was feeling. We met, talked, became friends, and he encouraged me to put this book together even agreeing to contribute an essay, 'Wales in the Poetry of Edward Thomas', in which he gives a close reading of Thomas's poetry, examining structural elements, language and thematic usage, which expose Thomas's relationship with the literature of the land of his heritage.

In 1949 Dylan Thomas compiled a broadcast for the BBC on Edward Thomas. He was a huge admirer of his work and included Edward Thomas's poems in many of his readings. By then Dylan Thomas was established at the height of his fame but he had also become somewhat embroiled in the rise and flowering of Anglo-Welsh writing which had begun in the mid-thirties with the advent of a number of new Welsh-writing-in English periodicals and magazines. He began his broadcast thus:

I do not know how much of a Welshman Edward Thomas was, and it does not matter. He was a poet which means he is a poet still, and always will be.

My belief is that it does matter, but I think it must be kept in perspective and even Dylan Thomas later in his script declares;

I said I did not know how Welsh he was, but we know he loved Wales. Walter de la Mare says of him, 'his voice was

4

low and gentle, but musical, with a curious sweetness and hollowness when he sang his old Welsh songs to his children'.

I am happy to give Dylan Thomas the last word.

WALES IN THE PROSE OF EDWARD THOMAS: SELECTED EXTRACTS

Shadows of the Hills, 1897

'Shadows of the Hills' was first published on October 23rd, 1897 in The Speaker. This appears to be Thomas's earliest published piece of prose set in Wales. It was written when he had not yet turned twenty. It contains many of his early themes – natural history, Welsh history, Arthurian and mystical elements, and all written in a somewhat stilted and gothic prose.

The red whinberry heights sound with the patter of sheep-bells and the hill river's hoarse shouting to the valley. Sheep-bells and stream find an answer in a roaring from the windy firs that bloom the opposite hill with green haze, and in the calling of a deeper water that creeps to the sea, past scornful factory chimneys and below the wood, in meadowed meanders between the alder and hazel of tall banks. And mountain, and vale and village, are all held by the peace of a vast silence which the murmur of the sea or the moan of toil can never break. Only when the soul has dropped into a sympathy with the calm may the hearing seize a weak and uncertain lisping as of that tone which circulates in the dumb shell. Silence is the voice of God: but, thinking on the present sorrow of this vale, on the old sorrow of the barrows

7

beside the salt shore, that sound of the ocean touches like the moan of men. It informs the bardic harp and the songs of childhood with a sadness. Yet the finches fly and sing on the green bough; the weak-purple scabious flowers by the stony wayside, the foxglove in fern of the hills: and the singing lark bursts from under foot like fire. The noise of the sea is at hand evermore, like a stupendous bass hushing the myriad trebles of delight; whilst the lips of little streams are parched or frozen to quietness; tall ships move up the bay, to bar the sky of evening with masts, and to ride out once more below the purple promontory looking west – infinite labour, infinite disaster, infinite courage, infinite hope; men come and go about the House in the Hills, the Little Village, the Long Glen, and the Dumb Glen farther inland; and whilst the girls with names like those of the childhood of the world (White Flower, White Breast, which, in the language of these hills, also means the celandine of March; and many more) roam down rich hedges and down lanes crossed by the tinkling and glitter of baby streamlets, to seek blossom in spring, wild fruit in the red autumn.

Step by step, dwelling carefully on the ancient barrow, the musical shore beside whose wide lawns and the dead Black Castle that once stood on them looking seaward, the water swirls with level tide fast and steady, the Druid hills littered with crag amid the fern, step by step the soul touches back into far time. Now the hills tower darkly in sudden altitudes that seem to overhang the world like sunset cloud with an awe and grandeur more vast than truth. The sea speaks to all the hills as the waves burst bound, and hour by hour blind the high moon with their bristling manes. And the gales inland are full of the sea. Then in a calm the gulls float mirrored on placid tides, and the copses sing together. All combine in a peace which so contents that no fear is left lest it should ever break; the perfection of light and peace exalt everything with a divinity eye could not perceive just before. I see the tall knights troop under the crags with sheen of banners and music of the clashing harness; I hear Cymry meet Saxons in the long shock and roar of the breaking battle at the whitening of the mountain dawn, the foes part, the Cymry sing –

"The Roman dies, the Saxon dies"

and the hoar Druids come down companioned from the fern to the coast, where legions thunder and a wail goes up by the forest pass; then a great silence, a darkness, and no more seems to have known the sunlight, but lonely ernes pass from sea to sea.

Only the sorrows of things remain. River and coast and mountain preserve almost in its old first completeness the monument of effort and disaster and death. Only the sorrows of things remain, to find a voice in the eternal mourning of that west wind which seek pine and cliff and breaker as strings for the solace and utterance of its melancholy. As if only sorrow were divine and immortal! For of all that acute joy of the world's childhood, or of what seems the childhood to an old age whose memory grows weak, no song or other echo of its laughter survives. But that triple joy and pride of life have burned and gone out past return – the aspiration, the fervour, the abandon, the rage, the *ferocitas* of youth.

Long ago bards made the battle hymn, and warriors sang it among the swords; but they are gone. Cottage and church and castle were here; but they, although the gods do not lightly desert the hearth or the altar where they have once dwelt, they also are gone: and but seldom do voices call from them on coast or mountain. Yet a barren memory with its clawed brier and thorn clings to a few locks, caught long ago on the mountain, which are still fair enough and white enough to give us pleasure, though fairer were in the rich fleeces of that old day.

Merlin paced near this parapet of broken rock which looks southward and seaward from the hill summit, to watch the dragon clouds come over the ridge at dusk and to listen to the night. One also died, looking at the waters of this brown brook that turns pebble to gold in the sunshine, whose great soul split itself drop by drop in the despair of dreams, rather than ride to Camelot and join the momentary beauty that showed no love for child or wife or mother. And Cromwell was here. But how pale is the countenance of warrior or prince in this glory of the white pure noon. Notwithstanding, there are locks gathered here and there which have a melody for the heart when the summer wind blows through them, and when the sunbeam lightens them as it does the wool we lift to admire.

The autumn woods are blowing, the swallows have gone, the last foxglove is on the hill; the harmonies are mild and sumptuously sombre rather than sad. One recollection, indeed, there is, which is full of the spirit of this quiet sunset time of the year.

Steep, stony, and, like many of the roads, crossed by a

stream at several turns, below whisperings of elm, oak, and mountain ash, a lane rises from the meadows of the high, queenly fern toward white-fronted cottages at the foot of a steeper height; then, above, as the hill unbends its majesty to receive a hamlet, half the bay comes into sight: and the memory of an ancient home is here. An ancient home; they tell that a Knight – Basil of the Woods, or the Knight solitary – abode here within sight and sound of the hill river, where now sheepdogs call, herds low lazily, and the bard with the selfsame harp which his sires bore, comes in the time of snowdrops or yellow fruit and plucks now a finger of yew, now a daisy, for the same breast: such is chance. But no one stone rests now upon another in the olden place of turret and court and wall. Little but his name survives, and yet somewhat may be guessed after long gazing upon the hills that knew his voice and his footstep. The tale runs dimly seen, but not all unlike this.

Basil went out to the forest as he grew in youth; the ocean beach and high mountains knew him. And his mellow and euphonious life continued to flow on evenly below the hill. Now a flower and now dead foliage was brought home from the wood. His lips murmured unceasingly with songs learned in the hills. Until men at length began to speak of him among themselves as one who probably went to a strange worship and converse with strange divinities in the wild; they whispered also of crime, madness, and the foul fiend. The hermit related how he had met those in the East who had afterwards died from this solitariness or ill society; there, Alsop – one man had risen to heaven as he traced a shore and became a god to the prayers of a strange people. Sages concluded that he loved Nature. Was it love of Nature in Basil of the Woods? How could he be said to love her? Rather, if men had known, would they have called Basil her victim, as some in old times were victims of the gods. For Nature took him and held him fast like a jealous lover. He gave all his life to her in the loneliness of long and repeated communion. As he lay upon her breast, he had learned high and strange things that awed and silenced him, but could not content. But he might not always meet her calling or her waiting, for men, too, were bidding him to the sound of axe and plough and sword. The tryst saw darker and still darker embrace, and the mystery of their love touched the underworld even as its beauty still touched heaven with joyousness. Her face was clouded with a passion where love closed in strife with doubt. Then like a brute mother that tears her young in the forest, so towering in tumult of hate and love and doubt, she seized him and slew him in life with the frost of a great melancholy. After that one death, whether he passed away or stayed mysteriously as a memory stays, it is not known. Some tell that he still haunts a brown cavern in the mountains, wherefrom he can see ocean and land; and that still sweet it is night after night to watch from companionable shore that long hunting of belted Orion near Artemis and choirs of the starred nymphs, from his autumn rising in the steely eastern darkness to the last low melting purple of the March west and the stooping to pines and sea.

***

Horae Solitariae, 1902

The following extracts are from Horae Solitariae, a collection of essays first published 1902. Thomas said of the book that it was 'bound to Wales, because my visits to Wales have been in an obscure fashion their inspiration'. The Times reviewer said that its author possessed, 'an ear for the finer voices of nature and books, and a gift of happy, if somewhat elaborate, discourse'. R. George Thomas's later verdict was that it was 'a truly imaginative creation of Welsh character'.

Inns and Books
[first published in *Literature*, September, 1901]

An old Calendar may often be found at the Inn, and will be worth opening especially if enriched, alongside the weather forecast, by the first owner's notes. Among many I have seen the *British Merlin* of the eighteenth century, "adorned with many delightful and useful verities, fitting all capacities in the islands of Great Britain's monarchy," and compiled "for his country's benefit" by Cardanus Rider. Here too I have discovered the planets that rule over the names of children, and have smiled at the number of Colleys during Cibber's ascendancy. Yet I have rarely found the right book (an odd volume of Richardson or Sterne); less often have I brought it with me. I have read Browning where I longed for Prior. I have put up with Shakespeare where the ale, the signboard, and the host wanted Massinger. Now, I can only pray that I shall meet Jeremy Taylor not Bishop Hall – Smollett and not

Goldsmith's Natural History. It was perhaps my best fortune to fall in with a volume called *The Unknown Way*. Left behind by some tired reviewer, it may be, after a perusal that bred only a few jests, the book was still new. It was after midnight. The Welsh hills rose all around, their flanks vaster than the sky, and pricked, as it were, by cottage lights. Now and then the lightning snapped a fiery finger. At length enormous ridgy clouds moved along and encamped upon the summits of the range, and in the flashes they seemed to be castles that extended their towers like imprecating arms to heaven. The moon sailed up, and, no stronger than if she breathed into the night, a wind puffed amid a lane of poplars with a liquid whisper as I read many and many lovely verse, and lastly these:

"Now, till morn, remain our own
Magic shores of old surmise,
Peaks no morning can dethrone,
Lands that know no boundaries-
There the unfulfilled abides;
There the touch of night unbars
Gates of ways that noonday hides,
Paths that reach beyond the stars."

For criticism one may go to Fleet Street. For appreciation I am resolved to visit the Merlin Arms again.

***

Recollections of November
[first published in *The Atlantic Monthly*,
November, 1901]

A Welshman of the company declared that in speaking his own fine tongue he seemed to taste buttermilk and fruit at some mountain farm, a mile nearer heaven than one commonly lives.

***

Digressions on Fish and Fishing
(based on Thomas's Welsh friend Gwili)

Some objectors to the godliness of angling may be found. Many years ago, I remember to have met a superannuated preacher of some rigid sect in Wales, who had exchanged quite naturally his symbolical crook for rod and line. A fine patriarchal vision he was when going a-fishing. "Go to chapel, you young fool… go to chapel; you're no fisherman, though maybe you will become a fisher of men," was his pastoral advice to a Sunday sportsman who lost a good pike before his eyes. He himself grew into a famous Sabbath rod in his later days, "still," as he used to say, looking back on his long career, "still the only man that did not rest on the seventh day." His venerable aspect and great renown were long his protection in these offences. But one day, an "elder," a sitter for half a century in the "great seat" below the pulpit, and yet virgin as to Dennys and Walton, quietly hinted that old _____ might be better employed. The spring twilight was growing cold, and all the land, with its congresses of mighty trees, looked solemn in the silence that reaches the ear of God. A big trout was tumbling in the deeps. But the old man tucked his rod under his arm and left the bank. Placing his rod and his catch in the vestry, he entered the chapel, and, even truer to his craft than the excellent Dean Nowel, preached in his steaming boots. That sermon, with the text "He taketh up all of them with the angle," is famous still. But the old man was right. He should have been allowed to go on and "cast all his sins into the depths." He was too feeble for the excitements of the fierce Welsh oratory. Not very long after he "fell asleep in peace," threading a bait beside the waters. And another reverend angler I knew in Wales, whom I may not forget. There was a singular finish and cadence about the courses of his life. He himself would call it modestly "a beautiful blank, like a fair sheet of paper unsoiled by art." He was born in a cottage whose wall rose sheer from a bank where a little river died in the surges of a tumultuous estuary. His boyhood and manhood were spent partly in another cottage whose garden slopes to the same river, but chiefly in the river itself, he being a famous truant in those days. When he came to the years that bring ennui and the philosophic mind, he wrote verse; and when, according to the happy Cambrian custom, he used a bardic name, he took it from the stream whose sound was ever in his ears, and which – being no "swan," but just a merry sandpiper – he tamed to suit the dainty melodies of his verses. In one of his best lyrics – I think they are his; anyhow his frequent repetition made them his own – he put his own wild heart into the cry of the river, as it turned and seemed in places to lose its way, ever with its heart set towards the sea: "The sea! the sea evermore." He was, he said, no more than Carlyle's minnow, "Far from the maine-sea deepe." Yet his soul went out to the sea, to the great matters of the world, ever giving these reality and colour by references to the little river and its copses, that furnished his house of thought with the metaphors by which he lived. He was one of the few genuine fishing philosophers I ever knew. One who will sit through a shower under a tree, discoursing, "And on the world and his Creator think," is apt to catch no fish. Most of my angling philosophers bought their fish of the village barber, who kept them in a bucket.

***

Isoud with the White Hands

(the story of 'that sweet saint, Dwynwen of Wales')

Near the mill another path branched into a park. The sea of turf was occupied by great oaks and the shadows of oaks. In one part the gardener had planted cypress, justly confident in the effect of these pillars of darkness seen against a hot blue sky, auburn roofs and the pale grass. The shadows of the trees fell upon me as I entered the park, and filled me with solemn thought. I cannot walk under trees without a vague and powerful feeling of reverence. Calmly persuasive, they ask me to bow my head to the unknown god. In the evening, especially, when the main vocation of sight is to suggest what eyes cannot see, the spacious and fragrant shadow of oak or pine is a

17

temple which seems to contain the very power for whose worship it is spread.

For a time the sky was grey with thoughts of rain. The small birds twittered nervously in the wood below; the ring doves came home gleaming in the humid horizontal beams. But presently all that was left of the grey was a tenderness in the golden light. From among the trees I could see a pool at the foot of a sloping lawn, and a swan moving to and fro so nobly, that I should have thought she was borne by the water, if that had not been as still as ice. The colours of the sunset were doubled in the pool – with something added, as things are seen in dreams. The turf had a perfume particularly nourishing to the fancy, and which, giving contentment, is on the side of the old doctors who commended the alimentary "virtues" of scents.

As quietly as the night was coming, and as benignly, something floated under the trees, turning an unknown face towards me; then passed away as softly as the day was fading. I just saw the pale glorious face. A bevy of dainty spaniels followed her soberly, as if to make up for the state which did not encircle her out of doors. She herself was, like a cherub by Reynolds, only a perfect face flying in the air; and about her was a sense of inaudible harps. ... Could she be the face that had been as a benediction, when I stared and was baffled and stared again into the meaningless London crowd? For a day or two such a remembered face has sometimes been a guardian genius of my ways; the delirium of seeing the thousand faces again when I had fallen asleep was comforted by the one, though utterly unknown, and never in reality to reappear. Was she one of those holy ones met again by divine good chance? She, too, has revisited my closed eyes. Or perhaps she was the "angel" of a heroine from my childish books, one of those of whom I fancied that I should seek their faces in the shadows, and should not be happy, or contented with my sorrow, until I saw them once more. At times she has come to me as that sweet saint, Dwynwen of Wales. Unfortunate in her innocent passion, Dwynwen was restored to tranquillity in sleep. The friendly Deity also promised her the fulfilment of any three wishes. She chose therefore that the sentence against her hostile lover should be revoked; that all true lovers should triumph or be healed; and that she (it was her only ungenerous choice) should never wish to be married. She afterwards took the veil and became a saint, and if the true lover called upon her, he was cured or satisfied. She became traditionally an Aphrodite, beautiful and unpolluted. And a saint, gently befriending pure affection, my apparition certainly must have been. But although visionary smiles have answered me when I called upon her spirit as Dwynwen, she came in the end to embody perfectly my fancies of Isoud with the White Hands. In the "Morte D'arthur" she and her gallant, mournful brother, the knight Kehydius, are but as ghosts of desperate longing amid all those knights and queens, so brilliant even in their tragedies. Kehydius loved La Beale Isoud; but, if unsuccessful, he was happy in comparison with his white sister. "He," says Malory, "died for love." She lived on, as if death scorned such easy victory. In the "Morte D'arthur," she fades out of sight, and, like a revenant in her faint life, we may think of her as continuing so, and here crossing my path among these fields, in the likeness of a girl, merely pure and beautiful, and a little sad, like Isoud with the White Hands.

***

The Poems of John Dyer, 1903

Edward Thomas edited this selection and contributed the introduction. It is number 4 in The Welsh Library, a series established by Owen M. Edwards who was Thomas's tutor at Oxford and a key figure in Thomas's developing Welsh consciousness.

The Introduction
JOHN DYER, 1701-1757

John Dyer was born at Aberglasney, a considerable house, in the parish of Llangathen, in Caermarthenshire, in 1700 according to some, in 1701 according to others; more probably in 1701. The register which would have shown the date of his birth has been lost, and I can only learn that he was fifty-six years old when he died in 1757. He was the second son of a solicitor "of great reputation," and from father and mother had English blood. He was educated, first at a country school, then at Westminster School, under Dr Freind. Of his attainments we know nothing. It is likely that he painted and wrote verse at an early age; and he is said to have planned "Grongar Hill" when he was sixteen years old. Before he was ripe for a university, he was called from Westminster to his father's office. Having no taste for the law, he left it on his father's death, soon afterwards. His taste for painting led him to become a pupil of Jonathan Richardson, in Lincoln's Inn Fields. Richardson's written work inspired Reynolds, but his teaching would not seem to have matured Dyer's capacity to anything beyond a skilled mediocrity. According to one of his own published letters, the youth, on leaving Richardson, became "an itinerant painter" in South Wales and the neighbouring counties of England. He must have paid visits to London about this time. Savage and Aaron Hill were among his friends. From an epistle by the former, it appears that, like his master, he painted portraits. His character, gentle, amiable, independent and unworldly, endeared him to those whom he met, if it did not attract the literary world.

Probably in 1724, he went, still as a painter, to Italy. He spent two years in Rome and Florence and other cities that were a matter of course. Like some of the next century's poets, whom he faintly but certainly foreshadowed, he was delighted by the riches of Nature, the Renaissance, the Middle Ages, and antiquity, which he saw. With a milder rapture than Shelley's, he was happy in sight of the Baths of Caracalla and the Coliseum. He is said to have been more successful with pen and ink sketches than with crayon and oils; but it may be conjectured that his work in colour and line had little but the indirect value of training his eye in a way that afterwards served him as a poet of Nature. To "Clio", probably the "Clio" whom he is known to have painted, he addressed some trifling "Verses from Rome"; Clio sent back a set of verses of equal merit.

1726, the year of his return to England, was a year of some literary activity for Dyer. It was the year of the publication of Thomson's "Winter." Savage's *Miscellany* of that date contained five pieces from Dyer's pen, viz.: "The Inquiry," an unimportant composition that proves his rural contentment; "To Aaron Hill," a complimentary epistle; "An Epistle to a Painter," *i.e.* to Richardson; "The Country Walk," and "Grongar Hill." As then published, "Grongar Hill" was not significant. In form "an irregular ode," divided into stanzas, it displayed some unattractive Pindarism and the antics of that day. "The Country Walk," the one wild flower of the collection, slender but unique, in manner suggested the turn which was given later to "Grongar Hill." He was again an itinerant painter.

In 1727, "Grongar Hill" appeared in its final shape. The revision had been happy, but somewhat imperfectly inspired. Thus the opening lines are negligent and vague, and "unhappy fate," etc., is indefensible. But when we consider the fitness of the metre, and the skilful presentation of a mood so uncommon in his day, breathing in the first lines, and gracefully completed in the last, we must grant to the poem a very special claim. If we exclude consideration of the age in which it appeared, it has still a charm, if only for the small number of readers who care for all the poetry of nature. As a product of 1727, it must be allowed that it adds to the strength of a necessary link in the chain of English literature that deals poetically with Nature. It has been praised in English and Welsh, and in the last century was paraphrased in Welsh. The manner of Dyer's work, and the combination of personal fancy with accurate observation, make him a closer relative to Wordsworth than his bulky rival Thomson, who was in many ways far more richly gifted. It is necessary to add, since it has been wrongly located, that Grongar is in Caermarthenshire, and in sight of Aberglasney.

It is obvious that Dyer must have been much out of doors. He probably knew South Wales intimately. He had a short, practical experience of agriculture, and a love of animals. At the same time he was not a hearty out-door philosopher. His health was always indifferent, and the Campagna had injured it. He seems to have had an amiable, constitutional melancholy, and must have known the angrier moods of that "sweet enemy"; for, in 1729, he is said to have written his epitaph. He called himself "old and sickly" in middle age; for many years in later life he was deaf; yet remained true to the character which was given to him by Aaron Hill, who says,

'You look abroad serene
And marking both extremes, pass clear between.'

***

Bronwen: A Welsh Idyll, 1903

Although dated 1903 this piece was not published until it appeared in the posthumous collection, Cloud Castle and Other Papers, published in 1922. Thomas's second child and his first daughter had been born the year previous to Bronwen being written. He wrote of her birth to his friend Jessie Berridge, 'It is an ugly, healthy thing with a lot of hair and blue eyes. What shall we call it? ... I incline to

Rachel, Mary, Maudlin – or Megalostate!' In the end he would settle on the Welsh name Bronwen.

It was cool dawn on the summits of the hills. The daisy was unawakened yet in the glen, and a light mist slept across the fields beneath. Low down in the rosy drift of sunrise hung the new moon, on tip-toe, as it seemed, for flight; a brief time only it hung; and at length it dropped as the light added, on the purple peals of comfrey, bell to bell. Now, too, lark met nightingale for the last time of the year in song. For the season was the midst of June. It was the time of the white wild rose and the purple cranes-bill, and the streaked convolvulus braiding dry paths.

And already Bronwen is in the grass beside her home. Lonely and content, she leans with a whisper of singing over her sweet toil, looking up seldom, and then only to number the stars that die one by one in the hot sky, or to answer the honied tones of the swallows passing her head. Or she plucks a blossom for her brow. So, all the time, she is happy, thinking sweet thoughts in her loneliness, and in the shade of her own wild hair. For about her neck the weight of yellow hair dropped and spread, and upon the flowers, as she bent shoulder-deep in the June grass. Like marble is her form as she stoops still at her toil: like a cloud whenever she turns in her place. Her skin is like a lily; but the summer has found out the rosy life of her veins; and Bronwen is like the anemone of March. She is beautiful. But she is alone. Perhaps the light poplar-tree beside the mere longs to throw its shadow in the crystal; with her was it even so. And the agrimony wands have taken fire in the green grass.

So Bronwen sings and toils; and now, as she sits, a white star broadens and grows bright towards her out of the east, like Mercury kindling through a purple that deepens on to moonrise. She has seen this star and looks. What is it? Sometimes it burns, and sometimes it fades from sight; yet it is too constant for a sea wave catching the sunbeam at slowly returning intervals. A star of heaven it can scarce be. Nor certainly is it a swell of the crystal air of summer flashing as oftentimes it will like a shifted shield. How like it is to the shimmer of battle steel! But then it moves slowly and alone and steadily; and for a time there is peace between the Round Table and the world. A shield, nevertheless, it is, coming to her out of the silver distance of dawn.

Looking wistfully and placidly toward the shield, like a child staring at vacancy, Bronwen pauses but a moment; then gathers up the web and instruments of her toil into her grasp; and so vanishes through the purple gloom of the ivy at her porch. Nor does she stay at the wide opened door, though the shield flash to her from the foot of the hill.

Knight and steed and shield are crossing the grass beside the home.

A bough from the fresh wood is in his hand, drooping across the saddle. His lips murmur with song momentarily, but mostly are still. And he comes out of the fastnesses of dawn clad in a liquid splendour as if bathed in that pure light which made silver of the raindrops along the moss of the wall. Eager to taste the rich morning air, he has doffed his helmet, thus disclosing his face. Mark the placidity with which dawn has moulded it, and the keen lines drawn by the desire of all the features to drink to the uttermost what the hour gives. Save behind, where it will escape mercurially from the clasped helm, his gold hair is close. Black, however, is the hue of his brows, and arched in tranquil purity. At first glimpse, everything shows immense capacity for delight; at the next, a tyrannous self-mastery, a strenuous content with disappointment, which would be sad but at such an hour. But his face ripples and shifts with expression in the manner of pools where gusts chase the lines of waves with changing shade and light. By the fashion of it, he has listened to many sounds, bitter and sweet. Sights without number, too, he has seen, many a sunrising and sunsetting.

Now he halts with a happy sigh like one baiting at a well-known door.

So he stands beside Bronwen's home; he gazes, and for him the flowers are shining from the garden, for him the dark ivy leaf turns silver as it winks in its own massed glooms. Thus he waits. Waits? But he knows not that he waits, nor why he unlinks his steel and stops his horse.

Meantime, like one who goes on an errand long before appointed, Bronwen has stepped to her bower and laid by her toil. Quietly and without haste, carefully as if she robed herself for bridal, she has put off her antique silk in exchange for a festival raiment of white, drawing it from the spicy darkness with the joy of a village maiden on her rare holiday. For one minute only she stays proudly in her loneliness, without glass or mirror. Then she sweeps to the gate, to meet a guest that might have been accustomed and well known. She is there. And how her arms rise in unconscious welcome as she notes the smile meeting her own at their first sight! "A fair journey, Sir Knight!" cries Bronwen, "and may our country be kind to you." He laughs, and in reply, "Good day, lovely maiden!" cries he, "and may men be kind to you, as Heaven is kind. Wish you happy, I cannot; for I see you full of the summer and the fair weather and the dawn and this sweet place, happy thus beyond the might of my wish." Joyously she answers him. "It is fair, indeed, on my hillside this month, but lonely. Many days I see naught that moves. The knights are in the wars beyond Gwynedd. How, then, has a hoof from Camelot reached me and stayed even a moment? On our festival day, too, finding me thus alone, the festival at the quieting of the nightingale in the hazels beside the brown Gwili – the beautiful Gwili!" here she follows the swift's flight as it reels to the Gwili river in the south. "I am indeed from Camelot, and in peace, happily. On a blithe errand, too, I come: to carry a missive of betrothal between a lord of the white south shore and a princess of this land. I shall have toil to find her; I have seen none for leagues. Lovely she must be, if you are one of her maidens." So speaks Sir Agravaine. "Come! You will never find her. Let me have the missive. I promise, I will guard it with care from the messenger so welcome as yourself. For you would never find her. The land, as you say, is lonely. Besides, for to-day, you shall be my guest: it is our wont: never would June be kind to us if we forgot her festival, which, being alone, I was like to do." He answers quickly, "On such an errand, you must needs be a sure messenger. And, as to your asking, Lady! I am glad to stay on my march. When others are thus arranging their pleasures through us, surely their ministers may rejoice together. And may I see you at Camelot for the bridal!" She looks again to the Gwili. "As to that last, who knows what our Princess will grant? Besides, I love my home: there I was born, there I ply my sweet toil: my mother, too, sleeps there in the sun even now; and with her my baby sister, who cries now – hark! Let me go. I will haste. Now also I will hide the scrolls safely; for a day they shall stay closed; we will not risk chance under such heavens. See! The lark is weary with over-sweet. He does but flit singing from tuft to tuft: yet I think the voice sweeter thus than in soaring. Let me guard, also, that fresh bough in your hand, lest the sun looks on withered green before it is midsummer." So Sir Agravaine gives her the bough. "You shall take the larch sprig," he cries, "but at my gift. Keep it. I wait."

She runs: and when she is lost to his eyes, he rapidly lightens himself of the great steel and stalls his horse on the dry brown beneath the beech. A while he stays beside the crystal beginnings of a stream, his soul swayed and mazed by the motion of the waters, when, swift as a great liking, she returns to him. The green larch twig is at her girdle. Let the June sun be tender to it!

Together they seek the alders of Gwili, the hazel of its raised banks, and the windy gorse beyond. Talking sweetly, and sweetly making silence, they go. At one time she points him the gathered children plucking flowers in the field. "How they hasten, leaving half the host of flowers, in their gay strife! They cross the field, passing and repassing one another, and again overtaken, carelessly and hastily, like a flock of starlings." And one of the sweet small voices from the south sings hidden in the green leaves overhanging Gwili. They reach the moneywort gold of the banks, and her first care is to bury his armour in flowers. "There! You shall not go from me until they fade." So she cries. "I have had a care; be sure; the alders of the Gwili are close, and the sun will be tender to these, ay! and to me." White wild rose, therefore, heavy purple crane's-bill, gold & green gorse picked easily by fine fingers, yellow flag, honeysuckle, and all the heaped sweets of summer, dim the great steel which blood only has dimmed before this.

They try together the forgotten path of the ancients, or pass where only the children of future time will again make a way. Now they stop to look on the sparkling fords, or where girls dip pitchers in the fast water; and the water shines as it drops from the mouth of the pitcher; and the girls laugh as they wait. Now they see a lonely child in robes of white sailing flat reeds for boats in the reaches of calm. And far off, at intervals so long that each is forgotten before one succeeds, great seas fall heavily on the shore. Masts cross and interlace on the shining sea. at times they see a white cloud scale the immense sky, hover thinned almost to nothing by the sun, and dip to hills and sea, leaving the sky bare for hours. Once, as she threads a thicket of fern, she cries aloud with a cry of pain. He is with her. "Is it a snake?" she has crushed a flower. And so they pass: and the dew is dry almost in the coolest hollows of the wood.

Sweetly they talk of the sweets of silence, they brood sweetly in silence over the sweets of past speech. They are happy. She shows him the lonely footprints of her childish walks, or fears for her baby sister, or laughs at to-day. As they pause together on the green steeps, he names to her knight after knight travelling the pass with song. Here, men are charging beneath them, but as in dream: they see only the flash of armour. Here white maidens dance, but as in dream. Masts, clouds, hosts, all move like stars.

Dusk mellows into evening, and the lily over the steel smells once more of the earth from which it came, pleasant in death. The moon rounds the forest slowly from tree to tree. The lonely night passes, while the home of Bronwen paves the rising white footsteps of the moon. And the knight rides quietly into the blue west: and Bronwen is lost awhile to the south wind: and the bee swoons in the meadowsweet beside the brook Gwili. But, as they tell, Bronwen the Princess, on Midsummer Day, married Sir Agravaine at Camelot, before the larch spray had lost scent in her girdle.

***

Beautiful Wales, 1905

This was Thomas's second book in the popular Black's Colour Book series. He had provided the text for the volume on Oxford in 1903, and would later write smaller books on Windsor Castle and the Isle of Wight for the same publishers. These books were offered primarily as a writer's response to the reproductions of topographical watercolour paintings by eminent and popular painters. For Beautiful Wales Thomas had to deal with the illustrations that the artist, Robert Fowler, had provided. However Fowler's paint-

ings were mostly depictions of the more picturesque North Wales, a region of Wales Thomas was not familiar with. Part of his solution was to offer few actual place names, but to fill the text with material on Welsh legend, myth and literature, together with a healthy dose of his observations on natural history. The book also included 'She is dead, Eluned', Thomas's first published poem. R. George Thomas, concludes in his biography of Edward Thomas that,

> Beautiful Wales still remains – like the district of Dolau Cothi – a neglected goldmine for any Welshman who wishes to understand his own heritage.

Preliminary Remarks On Men, Authors, And Things In Wales

Among friends and acquaintances and authors, I have met many men who have seen and read more of Wales than I can ever do. But I am somewhat less fearful in writing about the country, inasmuch as few of them seem to know the things which I know, and fewer still in the same way. When I read their books or hear them speak, I am interested, pleased, amazed, but seldom am I quite sure that we mean the same thing by Wales; sometimes I am sure that we do not. One man writes of the country as the home of legends, whose irresponsibility puzzles him, whose naïveté shocks him. Another, and his name his legion, regards it as littered with dead men's bones, among which a few shepherds and miners pick their way without caring for the lover of bones. Another, of the same venerable and numerous family as the last, has admired the silver lake of Llanberis or blue Plynlimmon; has been pestered by the pronunciation of Machynlleth, and has carried away a low opinion of the whole language because his own attempts at uttering it are unmelodious and even disgusting; has fallen entirely in love with the fragrant Welsh ham, preferring it, in fact, to the curer and the cook. Others, who have not, as a rule, gone the length of visiting the persons they condemn, call the Welshmen thieving, lying, religious, and rebellious knaves. Others would repeat with fervour the verse which Evan sings in Ben Jonson's masque, *For the Honour of Wales:*

> *And once but taste o' the Welsh mutton,*
> *Your English seep's not worth a button:*

and so they would conclude, admitting that the trout are good when caught, some think, and are not afraid of saying, that Wales will be quite a good place(in the season) when it has been chastened a little by English enterprise: and I should not be surprised were they to begin by introducing English sheep, though I hardly see what would be done with them, should they be cut up and exposed for sale. The great disadvantage of Wales seems to be that it is not England, and the only solution is for the malcontents to divide their bodies, and, leaving one part in their native land, to have the rest sent to Wales, as they used to send Welsh princes to enjoy the air of two, three, and even four English towns, at the same time and in an elevated position.

Then also there are the benevolent writers of books, who have for a century repeated, sometimes not unmusically, the words of a fellow who wrote in 1798, that the beauty of Llangollen "has been universally allowed by gentlemen of distinguished taste," and that, in short, many parts of Wales "have excited the applause of tourists and poets." Would that many of them had been provided with pens like those at the catalogue desks of the British Museum! Admirable pens! that may be put to so many uses and should be put into so many hands to-day and to-morrow. Admirable pens! and yet no one has praised them before. Admirable pens that will not write; and, by the way, how unlike those which wrote this:

"Caldecot Castle, a grand and spacious edifice of high antiquity, occurs to arrest the observation of the passing stranger about two miles beyond the new passage; appearing at no great distance across the meadows that lie to the left of the Newport road. The shattered remnants of this curious example of early military architecture are still so far considerable as to be much more interesting than we could possibly have been at first aware, and amply repaid the trouble of a visit we bestowed upon it, in our return through Monmouthshire by the way of Caldecot village. In the distance truly it does not fail to impress the mind with some idea of its ancient splendour, for it assumes an aspect of no common dignity: a friendly mantling of luxuriant ivy improves, in an eminent degree, the picturesque effect of its venerable mouldering turrets; and, upon the whole, the ruin altogether would appear unquestionably to great advantage, were it, fortunately for the admirers of artless beauty, stationed in a more conspicuous situation, like the greater number of edifices of a similar nature in other parts of the country."

The decency, the dignity, the gentlemanliness (*circa 1778*), the fatuity of it, whether they tickle or affront, are more fascinating than many better but less portentous things. There was, too, a Fellow of the Royal Society who said in the last century that, in the Middle Ages, St. Winifred's Well and Chapel, and the river, and the Basingwerk, must have been "worthy of a photograph."

Yet there are two others who might make any crowd respectable – the lively, the keen-eyed, the versatile Mr. A. G. Bradley, and George Borrow, whose very name has by this time absorbed and come to imply more epithets than I have room to give. From the former, a contemporary, it would be effrontery to quote. From the latter I allow myself the pleasure of quoting at least this, and with the more readiness because hereafter it cannot justly be said that this book does not contain a fine thing about Wales. Borrow had just been sitting (bareheaded) in the outdoor chair of Huw Morus, whose songs he had read "in the most distant part of Lloegr, when he was a brown-haired boy"; and on his way to Llangollen, he had gone into a little inn, where the Tarw joins the Ceiriog brook. "'We had been to Pont-y-Meibion,' said Jones, 'to see the chair of Huw Morus,' adding that the Gwr Boneddig was a great admirer of the songs of the Eos Ceiriog. He had no sooner said these words than the intoxicated militiaman started up, and, striking the table with his fist, said: 'I am a poor stone-cutter – this is a rainy day and I have come here to pass it in the best way I can. I am somewhat drunk, but though I am a poor stonemason, a private in the militia, and not so sober as I should be, I can repeat more of the songs of the Eos than any man alive, however great a gentleman, however sober – more than Sir Watkin, more than Colonel Biddulph himself.'

"He then began to repeat what appeared to be poetry, for I could distinguish the rhymes occasionally, though owing to his broken utterance it was impossible for me to make out the sense of the words. Feeling a great desire to know what verses of Huw Morus the intoxicated youth would repeat, I took out my pocket-book and requested Jones, who was much better acquainted with Welsh pronunciation, under any circumstances, than myself, to endeavour to write down from the mouth of the young fellow any verses uppermost in his mind. Jones took the pocket-book and pencil and went to the window, followed by the young man, scarcely able to support himself. Here a curious scene took place, the drinker hiccupping up verses, and Jones dotting them down, in the best manner he could, though he had evidently great difficulty to distinguish what was said to him. At last methought the young man said, 'There they are, the verses of the Nightingale (Eos), on his deathbed...'

"... A scene in a public-house, yes! but in a Welsh public-house. Only think of a Suffolk toper repeating the deathbed verses of a poet; surely there is a considerable difference between the Celt and the Saxon?"

But the number is so great of sensible, educated men who have written on Wales, or would have written on Wales, or would have written if business or pleasure or indolence or dislike of fame had not prevented them, that either I find it impossible to visit the famous places (and if I visit them, my predecessors fetter my capacity and actually put in abeyance the powers of the places), or, very rarely, I see that they were imperfect tellers of the truth, and yet feel myself unwilling to say an unpleasant new thing of village or mountain because it will not be believed, and a pleasant one because it puts so many excellent people in the wrong. Of Wales, therefore, as a place consisting of Llandudno, Llangammarch, Llanwrtyd, Builth, Barmouth, Penmaenmawr, Llanberis, Tenby,... and the adjacent streams and mountains, I cannot speak. At____, indeed, I ate poached salmon and found it better than any preserver of rivers would admit; it was dressed and served by an Eluned (Lynette), with a complexion so like a rose that I missed the fragrance, and movements like those of a fountain when the south wind blows; and all the evening they sang, or when they did not sing, their delicate voices made "llech" and "llawr" lovely words: but I remember nothing else. At _____ I heard someone playing *Là ci darem la mano:* and I remember nothing else. Then, too, there was _____, with its castle and cross and the memory of the anger of a king: and I remember that the rain outside my door was the only real thing in the world except the book in my hand; for the trees were as the dreams of one who does not care for dreams; the mountains were as things on a map; and the men and women passing were but as words unspoken and without melody. All I remember of ____ is that, as I drew near to it on a glorious wet Sunday in winter, on the stony roads, the soles began to leave my boots. I knew no one there; I was to reach a place twelve miles ahead among the mountains; I was assured that nobody in the town would cobble on Sunday: and I began to doubt whether, after all, I had been wise in steadily preferring football boots to good-looking things at four times the price; when, finally, I had the honour of meeting a Baptist – a Christian – a man –

who, for threepence, fixed my soles so firmly that he assured me they would last until I reached the fiery place to which he believed I was travelling, and serve me well there. I distrusted his theology, and have yet to try them on "burning marl," but they have taken me some hundreds of miles on earth since then.

It would be an impertinence to tell the reader what Llangollen is like, especially as he probably knows and I do not. Also, I confess that its very notoriety stupefies me, and I see it through a cloud of newspapers and books, and amid a din of applausive voices, above which towers a tremendous female form "like Teneriffe or Atlas unremoved," which I suppose to be Lady Eleanor Butler.

Nevertheless, I will please myself and the discerning reader by repeating the names of a few of the places to which I have never been, or of which I will not speak, namely, Llangollen, Aberglaslyn, Bettws-y-Coed, the Fairy Glen, Capel Curig, Colwyn, Tintern, Bethesda, Llanfairfechan, Llanrhaiadr, Llanynys, Tenby (a beautiful flower with a beetle in it), Mostyn, Glyder Fach and Glyder Fawr, Penmaenmawr, Pen-y-Gader, Pen-y-Gwryd, Prestatyn, Tremadoc, the Swallow Falls, the Devil's Bridge, the Mumbles, Harlech, Portmadoc, Towyn, and Aberdovey (with its song and still a poet there). I have read many lyrics worse than that inventory.

***

Cwellyn

Near the river which falls from Cwellyn Lake, they say that the fairies used to dance in a meadow on fair moonlit nights. One evening the heir to the farm of Ystrad, to which the meadow belonged, hid himself in a thicket near the meadow. And while the fairies were dancing, he ran out and carried off one of the fairy women. The others at once disappeared. she resisted and cried, but he led her to his home, where he was tender to her, so that she was willing to remain as his maid-servant. But she would not tell him her name. Some time afterward he again saw the fairies in the meadow and overheard one of them saying, "The last time we met here, our sister Penelope was snatched away from us by one of the mortals." So he returned and offered to marry her, because she was hard-working and beautiful. For a long time she would not consent; but at last she gave way, on the condition "that if ever he should strike her with iron, she would leave him and never return to him again." They were happy together for many years; and she bore him a son and a daughter; and so wise and active was she, that he became one of the richest men of that country, and besides the farm of Ystrad, he farmed all the lands on the north side of Nant-y-Bettws to the top of Snowdon, and all Cwm Brwynog in Llanberis, or about five thousand acres. But one day Penelope went with him into a field to catch a horse; and as the horse ran away from him, he was angry and threw the bridle at him, but struck Penelope instead. She disappeared. He never saw her again, but one night afterward he heard her voice at his window, asking him to take care of the children, in these words:

Oh, lest my son should suffer cold,
Him in his father's coat enfold:
Lest cold should seize my darling fair,
For her, her mother's robe prepare.

These children and their descendants were called the Pellings, says the teller of the tale; and "there are," he adds, "still living several opulent and respectable persons who are known to have sprung from the *Pellings*. The best blood in my own veins is this fairy's."

And of the lakes, I have known Llyn-y-Fan Fach, the lonely, deep, gentle lake on the Caermarthen Fan, two thousand feet high, where, if the dawn would but last a few moments longer, or could one swim but just once more across, or sink but a little lower in its loving icy depths, one would have such dreams that the legend of the shepherd and the lady whom he loved and gained and lost upon the edge of it would fade away: and Llyn Llech Owen, and have wondered that only one legend should be remembered of those that had been born of all the gloom and the golden lilies and the plover that glories in its loneliness; for I stand in need of a legend when I come down to it through rolling heathery land, through bogs, among blanched and lichened crags, and the deep sea of heather, with a few flowers and many withered ones, of red and purple whin, of gorse and gorse-flower, and (amongst the gorse) a grey curling dead grass, which all together make the desolate colour of a "black mountain"; and when I see the water for ever waved except among the weeds in the centre, and see the water-lily leaves lifted & resembling a flock of wild-fowl, I cannot always be content to see it so remote, so entirely inhuman, and like a thing a poet might make to show a fool what solitude was, and as it remains with its one poor legend of a man who watered his horse at a well, and forgot to cover it with the stone, and riding away, saw the water swelling over the land from the well, and galloped back to stop it, and saw the lake thus created & bounded by the track of his horse's hooves; and thus it is a thing from the beginning of the world that has never exchanged a word with men, and now never will, since we have forgotten the language, though on some days the lake seems not to have forgotten it. And I have known the sombre Cenfig water among the sands, where I found the wild goose feather with which I write.

And I have seen other waters; but least of them all can I forget the little unnecessary pool that waited alongside a quiet road & near a grim, black village. Reed and rush and moss guarded one side of it, near the road; a few hazels overhung the other side; and in their discontented writhing roots there was always an empty moorhen's nest, and sometimes I heard the bird hoot unseen (a sound by which the pool complained, as clearly as the uprooted trees over the grave of Polydorus complained), and sometimes in the unkind grey haze of winter dawns, I saw her swimming as if vainly she would disentangle herself from the two golden chains of ripples behind her. In the summer, the surface was a lawn of duckweed on which the gloom from the hazels found something to please itself with, in a slow meditative way, by showing how green could grow from a pure emerald, at the edge of the shadow, into a brooding vapourish hue in the last recess of the hazels. The smell of it made one shudder at it, as at poison. An artist would hardly dare to sit near enough to mark all the greens, like a family of snaky essences, from the ancient and mysterious one within to the happy one in the sun. When the duckweed had dissolved in December, the pool did but whisper that of all things in that season, when

Blue is the mist and hollow the corn parsnep,

it alone rejoiced. It was in sight of the smoke and the toy-like chimney-stacks of the village, of new houses all around, and of the mountains. It had no possible use – nothing would drink of it. It did not serve as a sink, like the blithe stream below. It produced neither a legend nor a brook. It was a whole half-acre given up to a moorhen and innumerable frogs. It was not even beautiful. And yet, there was the divinity of the place, embodied, though there was no need for that, in the few broken brown reeds that stood all the winter, each like a capital Greek *lambda,* out of the water. When the pool harboured the image of the moon for an hour in a winter night, it seemed to be comforted. But when the image had gone, the loss of that lovely captive was more eloquent than the little romantic hour. And I think that, after all, the pool means the beauty of a pure negation, the sweetness of utter and resolved despair, the greatness of Death itself.

***

Llewelyn The Bard

Of Llewelyn, the bard, I cannot decide whether he most loves man or men. He is forever building castles in the air and filling them with splendid creatures, whom he calls men. Then he laments that he cannot find any like them on hill or in valley: when, straightway, he will meet some human being, old friend or passing stranger, on the road or in a shop, and away go the phantoms of his castles, and he is wild in adoration of the new thing he has found. His grandmother, by the way, was called a fairy's child, though the truth seems to have been that her mother was a gipsy girl. Perhaps that is why he has no creed but many creeds, and was looked upon with great favour by the Calvinists until they found that he liked the Church as well. Yet I think that he likes men truly because they remind him of something he has read or dreamed, or because they make him dream; herein somewhat resembling the fellow who paid much court to another because he reminded him of the late Duke of _____, and he was a lover of dukes. Or he is like some that have seen processions of phantoms and say that sometimes the phantoms are simply fairies speaking an unknown tongue, but that sometimes several have the faces and voices of some among the dead whom they used to know. Why he is so glad to be among us at the farmhouse I have not discovered, but I suppose we remind him of Hebrew prophets or Greekish kings, for of our established merits he takes no thought.

I think he wastes so much pity for Annie of Lochroyan that other maids find him passionless, and he grows tender over Burd Ellen and Cynisca as their lovers never did. Arthur and Gwalchmai and Gwenhwyvar, the most unreal and unloving of all the persons of literature, please him most. In a world where all things are passing, he loves best those things which, having past and having left a ghost of fame behind, can live for ever in minds like his. In London he saw but a place where marsh and river and woods had been and might again; or where

Sometimes a lily petal floated down
From dear, remote pools to the dreary town;

where the gulls flew over in the mournful January light; where a few friends had fires and lamps and books – their light faintly flickering in tremendous gloom and making one faint reality in the place; where wind and rain sometimes brought the past again; for the very touch of rain and wind beckoned to him, as it is fabled that the foam driven from waters that cover old towns will draw the unwary whom it touches into the deeps.

He himself professes to care only for his own childhood and youth; only he is aware, as not every one is, that the childhood began in Eden, and is ages old, so that, after all, the few years that make middle age do not count for much. His life and his way of looking at it remind me of a story of a young Eastern prince. Every day, from his early childhood, a story-teller had told him a tale. But, soon after he was sixteen, the story-teller came to him, and, falling on his knees, told him that he had no more stories to tell. The young prince fell into a range and swore that he would kill the man if, in a week, he had no new story ready. And the story-teller, who was very old and unwilling to die, went into the desert and neither ate nor drank, and made a plan by which to save his life. So he returned to the young prince, who asked if he had a new story, and he said that he had. And the prince bade him tell the story; and he began to speak, and told the prince the story which he had told him first, when he was a small child; and the prince was pleased. And until the old man died, he never told a story which he had not told before; and the prince was always pleased.

His poetry, if it could be understood, might be counted great, and perhaps it is so in a world where trees and animals are reverenced in a way which is hardly dawning here. He is a kind of mad Blake. He sees the world from among the stars, and those who see it from an elevation of five or six feet, and think that they see it as it really is, are not satisfied. He would make human the stars and seasons; he would make starry the flowers and the grass. He would have it that the world is but a shadow of Blake's "Real and Eternal world": that we who are shadows cling to the superstition that we are not, and have but prejudiced and fearful ears for his prophecies. He sees the world as a commonwealth of angels and men and beasts and herbs; and in it, horrible discords that we others scarcely hear seem to him to strike the stars.

Each outcry of the hunted hare
A fibre from the brain doth tear;
A skylark wounded on the wing
Doth make a cherub cease to sing.

After all, in matters of the spirit, men are all engaged in colloquies with themselves. Some of them are overheard, and they are the poets. It is his fortune that he is not overheard, at least by men.

Yet how much would he sacrifice could he but write a few verses in the old Welsh manner, – but a few verses like those he repeats as lovingly as others would their own. First, there is the elegy on Gwenhwyvar by Griffith ap Meredith ap Davydd:

The wearer of white and green, of red and blue,
Is now in the painful fold of death.
The Church conceals her – she whom velvet so adorned.
Wearer of velvet,
We mourn with tears now that the flush of her beauty
*   has faded,*
Now that the wearer of velvet and red is no more.

That he praises for its clear-eyed simplicity, its mournfulness direct as the cry of a child, as the bravery of this is as direct as the laughter of a child (it is by a poet who was also a prince):

I love the time of summer, when the charger
Of the exulting chief prances in the presence of a gallant
*   lord,*
When the nimbly moving wave is covered with foam,
When the apple tree is in flower,
And the white shield is borne on my shoulder to battle.

This, also, for its simple pride:

The men who went to Cattraeth were men of name:
Wine and mead out of gold was their drink:
Three men, and threescore, and three hundred, with
golden torques.

How often will he repeat "with golden torques"!

But (and here some will reconsider their opinion that he is a fool, or one "not wise" as the pleasant Welsh phrase goes) there is no one that can laugh more loudly than he; or sing a song more happily; or join more lustily than he in hunting on foot, over the craggy hills, some fox which the farmer can never shoot when he comes for the turkeys in November; and in the heat of the run he will curse the hounds for gaining on the fox, and the fox for running no faster, saying that the worst of fox-hunting is that it is so one-sided, since the fox is not allowed to rejoice at the end with hounds and men.

And here is one of his imitative songs, reduced to its lowest terms by a translator:

She is dead, Eluned,
Whom the young men and the old men
And the old women and even the young women
Came to the gates in the village
To see, because she walked as beautifully as a heifer.
She is dead, Eluned,
Who sang the new songs
And the old; and made the new
Seem old, and the old
As if they were just born and she had christened them.
She is dead, Eluned,

Whom I admired and loved,
When she was gathering red apples,
When she was making bread and cakes,
When she was smiling to herself alone and not thinking
of me.
She is dead, Eluned,
Who was part of Spring,
And of blue Summer and red Autumn,
And made the Winter beloved;
She is dead, and these things come not again.

***

March

I

Just before dawn, I came to a cleft high in the hills, so that I could only see a little copse of oak and hazel, and in the dying moonlight a thousand white islands of cloud and mountain

Totus conlucens veste atque insignibus albis.

The night had gone, and the day had not come; and the little copse had the serious, brooding air which all things have at that hour, and especially when the land is tender with the first hope of spring and in that reverie-

Cette rêverie
Que ne pense à rien.

For what I saw seemed but the fragments of something which night had built for its own delight, and as they became clearer and clearer they had more and more the appearance of being unbuilt and dissolved. But, gradually, the birds were let out and they sang. Their songs, on the wintry hill, which I had last visited in summer, broke upon the silence as in summer they never do, like the opening of the door of a room that is empty but has once been gay with fire and books and men; and sweet though the blackbird was, and shrill the missal-thrush, their songs were awful, and said that "a large part of the earth is still in the urn unto us." The grass, which had truly been of no colour, though my urgent memory persuaded me that it was green, began to awake to colour, and, while in the shadow of the copse the dusk was impenetrable, the light reached a knoll where there was dead bracken still. "Colour," said Novalis, "is an effort of matter to become light," and for one moment the grass upon that knoll ceased to strive and was light. A plover that wheeled close by disappeared and was but a glow.

I went on, and on a lower slope the ploughman was beginning to plough in the shadow. Grim and worthless looked the work, until I looked round and saw the dawn that was being prepared. But I watched too carefully, for I saw it all. Ever, as it grew, statelier and richer, I said to myself, that in a little while it would be perfected: yet still I watched and I began to think of those who saw it, as I had seen it before, from windows of towns, as they rose for work, or as they doubted the candles and put away cards or books, and paused perhaps for a minute, and gazed as they never gazed at human beauty, because, though they revered it, they feared it also, and though they feared it they were fascinated. I thought of those that leapt up at it; those that mourned because they had seen it pass so often before into a common day; those that, on inhospitable roads, saw it and neglected it, or cursed it after a night in which they had drunk their last poor earnings altogether. If it would but last... I had been looking at it and had not seen it, and when I dropped these thoughts I knew that it was gone, the slowly prepared and solemn dawn which made the splendid spring of that year._

II

Then I took a path which led out of sight of the white crested mountain and down among larches and oaks.

The wind was changing the grass from green to silver, and back again, rhythmically. In the pallid herbage at the edge of the wood it produced many little sounds, the combination of them barely louder than the sound which fancy makes among tombs; and yet that little concert passed into the ear and heart, giving a sympathy with the thousand minute sorrows of the inanimate world and a feeling that is part of the melancholy so importunately intruding on a spring day. But there, too, was trefoil, delicatest herbage of the early year, with its trick of globing and preserving rain upon its foliage, so that it is more delicate still in the grey dawn. One stalk with all its leaf singularly fine and small had grown out of a scar in a teasel stem.

So I came into a valley, and there was one white house it in, with a green, glowing, and humming garden, and at the door a woman who might have been the Old Year. It was one of those white houses so fair that in the old time a poet compared a girl's complexion with them, as with lilies and foam. It held all the sun, so that suddenly I knew that in another valley, farther south and farther east, the rooks were making the lanes sleepy with their busy talk; the kingfishers were in pairs on the brooks, whose gentle water was waving and combing the hair of the river moss; the gold of the willow catkin was darkened by bees; over an old root of dock was a heaving colony of gleaming ants; perhaps the chiffchaff had come to the larches and the little green moschatel was in flower with large primroses among the ash stoles in wet woods; and in the splendid moments of the day the poplars seemed to come into the world, suddenly, all purple...

Yet here there was no rich high-hedged lane, no poplar, no noise of rooks, but only a desolate brown moorland crossed by deep swift brooks through which the one foot-path ran, and this white house, like a flower on a grave, recalling these memories of other valleys; so that I forgot that near by the birches stood each in a basin of foam from the dripping mist and rain, and that I had not yet seen a thrush's nest in any hawthorn on those hills. Therefore, I counted that house as lucky for me as the Welshman's hazel-stick in the tale that is told in Iolo Morganwg's life.

This is the tale.

A Welshman, with a fine hazel-stick in his hand, was once stopped on London Bridge by an Englishman, who asked whence he came. "From my own country," said the Welshman churlishly. "Do not take it amiss," said the

Englishman; "and if you will tell me what I ask, and take my advice, it will be much for your good. Under the roots of the tree from which came your stick, there are great treasures of gold and silver; if you can remember the place, and will take me to it, I will make the treasure yours."

Now knowing that the fellow was a magician, the Welshman, though at first unwilling to be a party in this strange thing, at length agreed, and went with him to Craig-y-Dinas and showed him the hazel-tree. They dug out the root and found a broad flat stone underneath, which covered the entrance to a cave. They went in, the magician warning the Welshman lest he should touch a bell that hung in the middle of their path. At the spacious further end of the cave, they saw many warriors lying asleep in a circle, with bright armour on, and weapons ready at hand. One of the warriors, refulgent above all the rest, had a jewelled and golden crown along with the shield and battle-axe at his side.

At the feet of the warriors, in the middle of the circle, they saw two immense heaps, the one of gold, the other of silver, and the magician told the Welshman that he might take away as much as he could carry from either of the heaps. So he took much gold. The magician took nothing. On their way out of the cave he again warned the Welshman lest he should touch the bell. But should he touch it, said the magician, some of the warriors would surely wake and ask "if it was yet day": to which he must at once answer: "No, sleep thou on," whereupon the warriors would sleep again. And this the Welshman found to be true when he staggered under his gold and grazed the bell; but remembering the other's words, he said: "Sleep thou on" when the warriors asked if it were day; and they slept.

When they had left the cave, and closed the entrance, the magician told the Welshman that he might return to the cave whenever he wished; that the warriors were the knights of King Arthur, and the warrior with the jewelled and golden crown was King Arthur; that they were awaiting the day when the Black Eagle and the Golden Eagle should go to war; for on that day the trembling earth would toll the bell, and at that sound the king and the knights of the king would awake, take their weapons, overthrow the Saxon, recover the island of Britain, and again establish their king at Caerlleon, in justice and in peace and for ever. But the Welshman spent his gold. He went again to the cave; he overloaded his back with gold; he stumbled and the bell rang; he forgot the password. And the knights rose and leaned upon their elbows, and one of them stood up and took away his gold and beat him and thrust him out and closed the mouth of the cave; and though he and many others made all the hill sore with their digging, the cave was not found again.

***

August

I

On a fine, very hot day I had to wait three hours for a train, and should have left the bald junction for that time, if I had not seen there a poet of my acquaintance, contentedly reading Spenser on the central platform. I sat down with him, but he preferred reading to talking, and I looked over his shoulder to read:

Begin then, O my dearest sacred Dame!
Daughter of Phœbus and of Memorye...

And I could not sufficiently admire his fortitude, until, on the arrival of a train, he left the book on the seat, and walked down alongside the train. It stopped ten minutes, and he talked with persons in three different carriages before it left. He came back unperturbed, and told me briefly that _____ from Patagonia was in the train, with _____ the bard from North Wales, and a friend from London. Seeing me surprised, he explained that every Saturday in the summer he spent entirely on the platform, waiting for surprises of this kind. Four trains stopped there before I left, and each seemed to be laden with friends and acquaintances, – some who lived in distant parts and even overseas, and some whom he had not seen for years. And some of the persons whom he greeted he had never seen before, which was a good reason for greeting them; he had perhaps heard of them, or they of him; and so they talked.

The liking of Welshmen for Welshmen is very strong, and that not only when they meet on foreign soil, as in London, but in their own land. They do not, I suppose, love their neighbours more than other men do, but when they meet a fellow-countryman for the first time they seem to have a kind of surprise and joy, in spite of the commonness of such meetings. They do not acquiesce in the fact that the man they shake hands with is of their race, as English people do. They converse readily in trains: they are all of one family, and indeed if you are Welsh, not only can you not avoid meeting relatives, but you do not wish to. Small news about the coming and going of people travels among them rapidly, and I have never got out of a train in Wales without feeling that I shall meet some one whom I should like to meet, on the platform or in the first street. They like their own land in the same way. I do not easily believe in patriotism, in times of peace or war, except as a party cry, or the result of intoxication or an article in a newspaper, unless I am in Wales.

I did not know before that any save sellers of newspapers were happy in railway stations, and as my train went out, I passed the poet at his Spenser again and recalled the poem called "Howell's Delight," which was written by a young, unfortunate prince of North Wales in the twelfth century:

> *A white foam-crowned wave flows o'er the grave*
> *Of Rhuvawn Bevyr, chief of Rulers.*
> *I this day hate England, a flat and inactive land,*
> *With a people involved in every wile;*
> *I love the land where I had the much-desired gift of mead,*
> *Where the shores extend in tedious conflict;*
> *I love the society and the numerous inhabitants*
> *Therein, who, obedient to their Lord,*
> *Direct their views of peace;*
> *I love its sea-coast and its mountains,*
> *Its cities bordering on its forests, its fair landscapes,*
> *Its dales, its waters, and its vales,*
> *Its white seamews, and its beauteous women;*

I love its warriors, and its well-trained steeds,
Its woods, its strongholds, and its social domicile;
I love its fields clothed with tender trefoil,
Where I had the glory of a lasting triumph;
I love its cultivated regions, the prerogative of heroism,
Its far extended wilds, and its sports of the chase,
Which, Son of God ! are great and wonderful.
How sleek the majestic deer, and in what plenty found;
I achieved with a push of a spear the task of honour
Between the Chief of Powys and fair Gwynedd;
And if I am pale in the rush of conflict,
'Tis that I know I shall be compelled to leave my country,
For it is certain that I cannot hold out till my party comes,
A dream has revealed it, and God says 'tis true.
A white foam-crowned wave flows o'er the grave,
A white bright-foaming wave boldly raves against the
   towns,
Tinted the time it swells like glittering hoar.
I love the marches of Merioneth,
Where my head was pillowed on a snow-white arm;
I love the nightingale on the privet wood
In the famous vale of Cymmer Deuddwfr,
Lord of heaven and earth, the glory of Gwyneddians.
Though it is so far from Keri to Caerliwelydd,
I mounted the yellow steed, and from Maelienydd
Reached the land of Reged between night and day.
Before I am in the grave, may I enjoy a new blessing
From the land of Tegyngyl of fairest aspect!

II

The flowers by the road, wood-betony, sage, mallow, ragwort... were dry; the larches, that were fitted to the hillside like scales or breast feathers, were dry; but a mountain stream, which many stones tore to ribbons, was with me for miles, and to the left and to the right many paths over the hills ran with alluring courses for half a mile, like happy thoughts or lively fancies, and ended suddenly. The mountains increased in height as the sun sank, and their sides began to give a home to enormous, still shadows and to rich, inaccessible groves among the clefts. And in the end of the afternoon I came to a village I knew, which grew round an irregular town.

From the inn, I could see the whole village. The limes before me were full of light; the green grass beyond was tending to be grey. There were not far fewer people than usual in the neighbourhood, yet the calm was great. It seemed to have something to announce and to call solemnly for silence; the voice of a child crying, a man with shining cuffs, was an extraordinary impertinence.

But two reclining cows were calm enough, and in the middle distance an oak was stately enough. A tramp, his wife, and five children spoke with quiet, husky voices that were sad enough. A passage from *Hyperion* which I recalled was noble enough. Six bells that rang three miles off and some white downs of cloud on the horizon were in harmony. It was a time when the whole universe strove to speak a universal speech, the speech of the stars in their courses, of the flower that is beautiful, of the soul that aspires, of the mind that thinks. But, as it seemed, owing to my fault, the effort was unsuccessful, and I rose hurriedly and left the village behind.

III

And while the hedgerows on one side of the road were in places rich with the heavy, horizontal sunshine that came through gateways on the other side, I saw the star-like shining of the windows of an old house on a hill. A difficult winding lane led up to it, and so long was the lane that between the road and the house a badger and a raven had their homes. When I came near the house one pallid angle of it glowed, and only where it glowed was it visible.

The house was perhaps two hundred years old – stately, grey as the old blackthorns in the hedge, and it was, perhaps because I knew of the fading race that had lived within it, the oldest thing among those old hills. It was more unchangeable than the most grim crag on the hills which had its milkwhite harebell on that day. It was a survival from winter, from hundreds of winters, and therefore, though young in years, it spoke a language which time, knowing that the unchangeable is dead, had forgotten:

A spirit calling in an old old tongue
Forgotten in lost graves in lonesome places;
A spirit huddled in an old old heart
Like a blind crone crouched o'er a long-dead fire. ...

Nothing ever happened among the Powells at _____. The lawn was mowed; the fern from the hill was carted down;

the little red apples ripened; the Powell hair turned from gold to grey. A stranger, indeed, heard much of them, but when he asked where they lived, he was told that there were thirty of them in the church and one at ＿＿＿ on the hill. Five generations of them had lived there, since the only conspicuous one of the family had died in the first war with Napoleon. Of those five, the last could only say that theirs had been the most desperate of quests, for they knew not what they sought. They had lived in dignity and simplicity, neither sporting nor cultured, yet loving foxhounds and books. Generation after generation of the children had learned "L'Allegro" and "Il Penseroso" from their fathers, and with all their happiness in that dim house, they learned to love "Il Penseroso" best.

The Pocket Book of Poems & Songs for the Open Air, 1907

Robert P. Eckert comments that this anthology, 'is a convincing illustration of Thomas's wide knowledge of English Literature and of the splendid catholicity of his taste'. Thomas selected two Welsh poems for this anthology; one by Taliesin, 'The Poet's Birth', and the other, 'The Prince and Spring', translated from Howel ab Owain. No indication is given as to who made the translations but Jonathan Barker in his essay on this book, Edward Thomas and the Folk Tradition (in The Art of Edward Thomas. Poetry Wales 1987) writes;

> *...with songs in French and Latin and translations from the Gaelic and Welsh, presumably by the compiler.*

The Poet's Birth

Primary chief bard am I to Elphin,
And my original country is the region of the
summer stars;
Idno and Heinin called me Merddin,
At length every king will call me Taliesin.
I was with my Lord in the highest sphere,
On the fall of Lucifer into the depth of hell;
I have borne a banner before Alexander;
I know the names of the stars from north to south;
I have been on the galaxy at the throne of the
    Distributor...
I have been with my Lord in the manger of the ass;
I strengthened Moses through the water of Jordan;
I have been in the firmament with Mary Magdalen;
I have obtained the muse from the cauldron of Ceridwen;
I have been bard of the harp to Lleon of Lochlin;
I have been on the White Hill, in the court of Cynvelyn;
For a day and a year in stocks and fetters,
I have suffered for the Son of the Virgin.
I have been fostered in the land of the Deity,
I have been teacher to all intelligences,
I am able to instruct the whole universe,
I shall be until the day of doom on the face of the earth;
And it is not known whether my body is flesh or fish.

Taliesin

The Prince and Spring

I love the time of summer, when the steed
Of the exulting chief prances before a gallant lord,
When the nimbly moving wave is covered with foam,
When the apple tree is transfigured with blossom,
And when the white shield is borne on my shoulder
to the conflict.

Howel ab Owain

***

Rest And Unrest, 1910

This collection of essays earned a positive review from The Times Literary Supplement; 'not a thought is expressed, nor a single view of the world described in it, but has come from his own consciousness... it is a real delight to read pure delicate prose, undulled and undiluted'.

Like most of his uncommissioned writings Thomas was encouraged to write these essays by Edward Garnett. The two stories selected here, 'Mothers and Sons' and 'From a Cottage Door', are singled out by Eckert for special praise:

> *Two brilliant pictures of old and new Wales... slight in story, possibly too long, are obviously written from a deep and understanding experience. They are strong and convincing and... unforgettable.*

The location for the first extract, 'Mothers and Sons', when taken from internal evidence, is likely to be Swansea, being similar to some of the prose in Thomas's later essay

'Swansea Village'. The second piece, At a Cottage Door, was first published in 1909 in the Cardiff-based magazine The Nationalist, edited by Thomas Marchant Williams. Andrew Webb, writing in his book, Edward Thomas and World Literary Studies, points out that 'no previous writers' have mentioned that Thomas had made two contributions to this important journal.

Mothers And Sons

Years ago, continued my bald fellow-passenger, lifting his fez, I used to think that I had discovered youth. I went about repeating such phrases as: "The respect due to age is a ceremony carried out to weariness. The respect due to youth is as great and is never paid." I used to pretend to show that the respect paid to old men arose from the eloquence of the dying "old John of Gaunt, time-honoured Lancaster," and I collected the dying speeches of old men to confute my many enemies. Along with this, and by some mysterious process harmonised with it, was a great sentiment for the old things, for almost everything old in the ways of life. The new things around did not please me: I was in my own opinion born long after or before my time. For some years I conducted my attack with that cruel scorn of which ardent youth, bearing no flowers without thorns, is particularly capable. But gradually, in the wilderness I created about me, I lost sight of those sublime truths, except that I continued to consider blasphemous the world's way of not accepting the young until they show that they are as harmless as the old.

It was when I was still young, not yet thirty I should

say, that I stumbled from my lofty position, in a village or small town in Wales. I had been there many times before, but never shall I forget that one visit. In order to spend a long day there with my friend the poet I had started on foot some hours before sunrise. It was the beginning of winter. The night was cold and clear and blue, lit by a few stars and a moon so bright that it appeared to throb in the sky. My road climbed to the top of many a hill simply because some farmer who, I suppose, sometimes stooped to the valleys, chose to live there with his cows and sheep. In those days they still used to kill a cow once a year and the tallow made candles to light them to the milking in the winter mornings, the lambing at midnight, the reading of the Bible and "The Sleeping Bard" in the evenings; and every two years the farmer had a few yards of grey fleecy cloth for a suit made at the mill below from the wool of his own sheep. Probably there had been a dwelling of some kind on those hill-tops ever since the earth rose out of the waters.

The night was still and I was going to say silent, in spite of the fact that little rivers never cease to roar and foam below me in the ravines of the forest through which I passed. This unchanging sound comforted the ear more than silence ever can.

They had been felling much timber, and it lay about on the steep slopes under the moon, more like the crude shapes of chaos out of which trees and men might some day be made. But for the most part I saw nothing and thought of nothing. I was well and warm and pleased by the ring of my shoes upon the rocks of the wild roadways. I was living that deep, beneficent, unconscious life which is what after all we remember with most satisfaction and learn, often too late, to label happiness when the pleasures have all fallen away.

It was the dawn that recalled me to myself. I was making for the east, and in the south-east the sky, as quiet as my mind, had brought forth a scene of clouds so harmonious with my unconscious life that at first I looked upon it rather as it had been some noble dream blessedly given to me than something which all men might see; and I was astonished as perhaps a poet is when he was wrought something lovelier than he knew out of a long silent strife.

The sky before me, almost up to the zenith and almost down to the rigid but tumultuous line of hills, dark and far off, was lightly covered with a cold marbling of bossy white clouds slightly stained by the blue behind them. Just below this and just above the hills in the south-east the clouds ceased, and there the blue had given way to a luminous silver, very soft and cold. Slowly this silver changed to a green of a saintly paleness, majestic and innocent, and the lower surfaces of the clouds above were more and more tawnily fired, while the snow of those nearest the zenith hardly flushed.

In the little white farms there were lights stirring and a clink of pans and clatter of hoofs, and many of the loops of the river beneath had begun to gleam among the still gloomy woods, but the farms and the river were infinitely small compared with the great spaces of the valleys and the dark mountains beyond and the lightening sky, and their sounds reached the ear but not the spirit, and for some time it had seemed that the brooks were hushed.

And now the green of the lower sky was crossed by long flat clouds of the colour of dark sand newly wetted by the tide, but warm, and in a little while these clouds had arranged themselves by imperceptible craft into the likeness of an immense tract of unpeopled country into which a green sea ran far, in many a bay and estuary without a sail. The clouds above had become more closely packed, so that their prominences made almost uninterrupted mountain ranges of fire.

I know not how to explain it, but I felt I was seeing this immense country and sea before me inverted by some imperfection of sight, that I was seeing only a reflection in calm water, that it was a perhaps not unalterable weakness that prevented me from seeing the thing itself. Thinking of a remedy, by a sudden impulse I threw myself down in the bracken and heather by the road the better to enter into that kingdom of the dawn. I thus shut out from my sight everything but the open sea of pale and now gleaming green, and its long inlets into the land of tawny coast and fiery hills, and the mountain ridges of the earth which were dissolved to a thin vapour under the increasing light. At first I had no doubt that I was right. That kingdom became mine in oblivious ecstasy, just as the hills and the fallen trees and the rivers in the woods under the moon had been mine before the dawn. I was wafted upon that sea to the untrodden shore and among the hills where not even wings might travel, and there I heard the symphony which the stars and the mountains of earth and the hearts of men and the songs of rivers and birds make together in immortal ears, but make, alas! only once or twice for mortals. I closed my eyes and the scene remained.

And then, whether in an actual dream of sleep I do not know, I found myself thinking that I would take away with me the music I heard and would be happy always and show other men the way that looked so clear. But I began to struggle against falling through an abyss at some supreme command. I was aware of anger and dismay. I believed myself accused of being a spy and a contrabandist in that land which now veils of smoke were concealing from my eyes. I awoke, crying aloud that I would not have at all what I could not possess for ever, but no answer came. When I sat up I saw that the earth was below me and the sky above, as on an ordinary day. Half of the sun was crimson above a peak which his fire appeared to burn right through, and from horizon to horizon the grey clouds were consuming themselves in crimson and gold, except where a valley opened wide apart in the east and showed a giant company of chimneys, black and sinister, plumed with smoke as black. The earth itself was pleasant to see, especially where the moss was golden in the soft light of the old oak woods, but to my eyes it looked invalid, pathetic, and bereaved, as if that glory in the sky had been taken away from it or were indeed the reflection of something now withdrawn into the hollows of the hills. I therefore walked rapidly on towards the village dominated by those chimneys, my destination.

It stands at the meeting of three rivers, and the streets look up the crooked valleys where those rivers leap down among oaks and birches and alders, now deep enough for the otter and now only a cascade and salmon leap. Just outside the village the combined waters form an estuary; a broad and steady flood, sliding with solemnity between the level marshes at the feet of lesser hills. At my first visit fifteen years before I swam gently down the ebbing tide and saw on one side a belt of marsh divided by a road and a thin chain of cottages from higher ground, here ploughland, there craggy pasture, or a scramble of oaks over a precipice, or the gorse-grown refuse of a deserted mine whose chimneys the ivy had bewitched: on the other side, the ancient church of the parish, standing alone, four white walls and a grey roof amidst a graveyard encircled by white stones; then a high round barrow covered with little old oak trees; more marsh, and a mile farther on a white farm called after the name of the castle ruins at its gate; and, where the marshland narrowed, a hill of grey crags and purple bracken almost at the water's edge; more hills and coombes contributing rivulets, until the estuary wound out of sight between round brown hills to the rocks and the sea. Then I got out and ran back, as anyone could then, three miles over the close green turf, scattering the sheep and the cattle from my nakedness.

A few years earlier still the parish had consisted of three or four farms, three mills (one among the oaks of each valley), the church, a venerable chapel in a wood, and a few cottages buried away – all but their smoke and their linen shining on the gorse – in brambly chasms reached by lanes that were streams for half the year. Now only one mill was left, the cottages were empty and dislocated and long lost among the brambles.

As I entered the village I began to lose my way. In the old days the village was clustered about the streams and every road led down and across them. Their sound and glitter could not be avoided. Salmon big enough to make legends were taken from under the bridges at night, almost in the streets, and their heads, as likely as not, impaled upon the railings before the policeman's house. Nor had the huge boulders been moved from the banks. But now the streets went this way and that, according to the whim or craft of those who had land to sell, and when I came to running water it was confined between straight banks and lined with houses on both sides, in order that the inhabitants might more easily throw their filth in as well as draw out their drink. The water looked colder and blacker, the corpse of its old self, all savour of the mountains departed. The boulders were gone; so, too, the stepping-stones. The children could no longer walk half the way to school in water. One of the rivers was now increased by waste from the chemical works, and the water was of mingled yellow and red that suggested the fat and the lean of carcasses in a butcher's shop when "the time draws near the birth of Christ." No salmon would face such a flood, but one girl, I was informed, had lately chosen the deep pool where the poison entered to drown herself. She was alone in this choice. Other suicides preferred more luxurious deaths. A young farmer had hanged himself in his barn and was not found until days later when his hair and beard had grown all over his face. Nobody had anything against him – save debts – but he was morose and discontented with everything. And so he died. It was considered an unlucky death because coal was shortly afterwards found under his land. Not long before, an inn keeper had killed himself with fox poison because he had committed the sin against the Holy Ghost.

The streets were oily black and deeply rutted. Houses built twenty years before looked old, so dark were they and so simple compared with the new fashion which loved painted woodwork, stained glass, large balls of stone on the pillars of the gateways. Some roads led only to the railway and you crossed as you pleased. Others ended in factory yards among rusty strips of tin-like scimitars and creases, in heaps, among yellow pools, where bright, pale work-girls were going to and fro with black-faced men among engines, truckloads of the rusty tin, wreckage of machinery thrown down carelessly. Another passed alongside an ever-steaming pool where gold-fish swam among pallid reeds in the water that never froze.

In the centre of the village stood its principal public house that far outshone the church, the chapels and the new school, with its cut glass and its many lights in the windows of three storeys; opposite stood two others, close together, small and homely, no longer rural though they belonged to the rural days of the village, but squalid from urban usage.

Luckily I met a youth who could show me the way and explain the changes. He told me that my friend, the poet, would not be in until midday, and I decided to look round and see the old church, the fulling mill, the otter's holt as well as the new things.

My companion knew the price of the houses that were built. He marvelled at "the amount of money in the place." In half the roads trenches were being dug for the drainage, which ran at present wherever it found a slope: tired and dirty men just released from their work stood outside their gates and ate bacon and pickles while they watched the digging. The new drains, "the pride of the village," were to run into the estuary just past the meeting of the waters. At a corner there was an Italian ice-cream vendor, hands in pockets, by his yellow hand-cart. Over all whirled the smoke of the seven chimneys in tawny or white or black clouds. Engines panted and roared, and in black caves at the roadside half-naked men moved in front of white-hot fires and their boots squelched with sweat as they walked. Backwards and forwards went the workers to and from their work, swift, thin men, gossiping young women, children saluting those who were lately their schoolfellows. Cattle passed through and sometimes lost their way among the planks and bricks of half-built houses or the refuse of the factories.

The streets ran in all directions, and new gardens bordered on the moss and whinberry of the bounding hills. And as there were straggling lines of houses running far out and up into the pasture and plough-land and waste, so there were still open spaces among the streets where cows or horses or pigs fed until the land was taken up, while some pieces were unfenced and trodden into mire or used for nothing or for the deposit of rubbish. One such little place was where "the murder" took place. In the darkness, but close to the flare of a fried-fish stall, two young married men had battered the head of an older man against a stone until he was dead. When they were standing on the platform for the train that was to take them to the gaol, they smoked cigarettes and joked with the crowd. "When I was in the coalpit," said the lad, "I knew one of them. He used to make three or four of us get into an old truck with him, and he stood up while we

69

ran at him, heads down like bulls. He liked it. We couldn't hurt him. It's lucky he's gone so soon, for he might have done more harm. But you should see his whippets, regular beauties. He was fond of them, too, yes."

Thence a footpath led us out through the fields towards the old church, a beautiful sloping walk that followed for some way the windings of the chief river and its rustling drab reeds. "There's nice the old church looks," said my companion; for it was bright white amidst the green marsh turf, and the grey estuary flowed close under the church-yard walls to the bracken-coloured hills and the white clouds over the sea. Just there the sewage was to go out, and the lad laughed at the discomfiture of the cocklers down there on the coast whose trade would now be gone. In the churchyard a few new graves had been made under the sycamores, and all the occupants were over eighty, at which the lad observed: "'Twas time for them to die, yes," and smiled because it seemed absurd in this brand-new hurrying world to live so long. The old grave-stones leaned all ways, and some were prone; few kept their legends readable. We peeped inside the church: it was white and cool as a dairy, undisturbed by the violation of the river nymphs yonder.

We ascended the gentle hill beyond the church, once a favourite walk on summer evenings, to see the sun set over the mountains. A large field had been recently en-closed as a cemetery on the brow, and already it was sprinkled with white stones and plumy sable trees. "It will come nice in a year or two," said my companion. We looked down at the estuary, and he showed me with delight where the new railway bridge was to be carried across it in order to save London passengers three minutes in a five hours' journey. I like to see a train going swift and low above a broad water against a background of hills, but I thought it would spoil the old view. He on the contrary was so lost in awe at the cost of the short cut that he had no thought of lesser things.

We returned by the fulling mill. There the stream was as bright as ever and full of dash and foam. The little house was cleanly thatched and whitewashed, the wall round it also was white, and the apple-tree beside it was bushy with mistletoe. Brass and steel and lustre ware shone in the firelight within. There were wall-flowers as ever at the gate, a handful only, but perpetual. Picture postcards of the house were to be bought in the village, I was told: everyone bought them to send away to friends as *Souvenirs of D.*

As we walked a stuck pig began to scream, and continued to do so while we travelled half a mile: "It takes a long time dying," remarked the lad who was careless of the marriage bells that accompanied the unwavering scream.

Before entering among the streets again I turned to see once more in the moist sunshine the church and the sycamores and wall, the tumulus and its oaks on one side, the river winding bright and bowing its reeds, the estuary, the mountains beyond, the white cloud mountains in the blue that spoke clearly of the invisible sea below.

As I walked past the shops, neither urban nor rustic, entirely new and as glaring as possible, but awkward, without traditions and without originality, I was full of magnificent regrets. I ought to have had a mantle of tragic hue to swathe myself in mysterious and haughty woe and to flutter ineffable things in the wind, as I trod the streets that were desolate for me.

It was now time to make for the poet's house. This was one of the oldest houses, about thirty years old, – his age. It was a stone building of displeasing proportions, meant to be one of a row but standing alone, – unlike the native style, – with iron railings in front on the precipitous road. The vegetable garden behind fell down to the least of the three rivers, which as yet was almost undefiled because it flowed for the greater part of its course through a deep and narrow and very steep-sided coombe whose rocks and spindly but dense oaks and underwood of bramble and hazel were impassable.

Inside, the house was divided strictly into two, the poet's half and the other half.

The poet's half consisted above all of the largest room in the house. The walls were hidden by books and portraits of poets and bards. Its floors were almost as densely overgrown as the coombe, with oak armchairs whose richness of decorative carving equalled their discomfort. These were prizes won at Eisteddfodau by the successful poem on some religious subject or subject which could be treated religiously. The poet had written more poems than there were chairs; for he was well-read in English and classical literatures and had a boldness of imagery which the judges, ministers of various sects, sometimes declared in marginal notes to be affected. In spite of anti-macassars on the chairs, in spite of thousands of books which generations of critics had approved (for the most part complete sets in uniform and unworn bindings), in spite of the poet's ever boyish face, his rough black hair and clothes that had just scrambled up the river bed from stone to stone and root to root of alder and oak, and the deep melodious voice that turned prose into epic poetry as he read it, in spite of ferns in the fireplace, the room was cold with a moral and spiritual chill.

I was glad of the voice which summoned us into the next room, the long flagged kitchen, a little dark, but lit as by lightning from the great fire whose flames were repeated by lustre-ware and brass candlesticks on the mantelpiece, a hundred brightly coloured jugs upon the black dresser, a long polished gun hanging from the rafters, and the glass which protected the pictures of many celebrities and the sheets of memorial verses for dead members of the family. There, I remember, I had read the *Mabinogion* long before … Mrs Morgan, the bard's mother, greeted me as usual in Welsh and then laughed in broken English at the fact that I seemed to know less Welsh than ever, though I still knew the Welsh names for King Arthur's sword, spear and shield. "But I am glad to see you, dear Mr Philips."

She was a tall yellow-haired woman with a family of children ranging from forty to ten years of age. Her decided stoop seemed the product rather of her humility of mind than of decay, for her activity was endless and never overtaxed. She had large bony restless hands contrasting humorously with the decent black of her dress. She talked caressingly in Welsh to the silent beautiful daughter who helped her in the work of the house.

The table was set for two: such was the inevitable custom. The poet and I sat down, and as we did so, his mother set a steaming joint at a side table and carved it rapidly while she stood and talked, the daughter at the same time bringing two blue dishes of leeks and baked potatoes to the white cloth and returning, without an interval, for two plates from the oven; these her mother covered with meat, and they were immediately laid before us. Then mother and daughter stood, both silent now, at either side of the fire while we ate and languidly talked.

The girl was black-haired, straight, and well-proportioned, her cheeks rosy, her full-dark lips eloquently curved, her eyes large and brown like a child's, and her whole face beaming with profound brightness, simplicity, holiness. She might have been twenty-five years old, and was one of those infinitely tender, self-sacrificing girls in whom children at once salute the spiritual motherhood, who are learned in all mother's ways, can play and nurse and manage, and yet, unconsciously detecting some weakness in the awful opposite sex, are destined never to be mothers in the flesh. Love and fear melt their eyes to a softness that is very wonderful and govern their silent ways; love is the stronger, but the fear though it is often forgotten is never destroyed.

When these two women saw that our plates were nearly empty they came forward, one to each of us, and helped us to more or took away our plates; and so long as I am ignorant of what it is to be waited on by angels I cannot forget this meal. They uttered no word while we talked of Virgil and Alexander Smith and the taxation of land-values, but tut! I was sick of such talk as I was of my host's apple-green tie. As I got up from the table I felt something between shame and the pride of the convalescent in his tyrant bed. We returned to the study.

Well, we talked, I know, but I have forgotten what. The poet recited some of his own verses, and we complained together in raptures of regret about the growth of the village, and as we were doing so his mother entered, but would not sit.

"I hear," said I, anxious to speak to her, "that they are going to open a new coal mine up by the Great Crag and the otter's holt. It used to be a favourite place of yours, Mrs Morgan, and mine too; there was not a nicer place in the country when the nuts were ripe and the harvest ending."

"'Tis beautiful, truly," she said gravely; "I hope the mine will give many men work; there are many needing it, Mr Phillips."

"But they will spoil the beautiful angle of the river there. Think of it – *your* river, *your* crag – no more nuts, all the royal fern buried in coal dust."

"Mother isn't a poet, are you, mother?" said my host.

"No, Willy," said she, "and if I were I couldn't tell you the things I have seen and thought about by the Great Crag. I am sorry the fern will have to go, but, dear me, the poor of us must have shoes and bread and a pasty now and then, Mr Phillips, and the rich must have their carriages and money to buy the poetry books, Willy."

"You've a hard spot in your heart, mother."

"Yes, and I daresay I need it, my son. When a woman begins to work at six years old like me and a man at five like your father, they must get a bit hard if they are to keep on, and there's many are all hard and small blame to them. Yes, sure, I think the world of these soft ladies, but I can't set myself up against them; I haven't had their privileges.

Oh, I look for wonderful things from you young ones that have had your way made easy. It will be a kind good world I am sure, though I'm not grumbling at what we're living in. we old ones didn't exactly look to be happy in this world except on New Year's Eve and the like, and yet it came about that we were happy, too, beyond our deserts, I daresay. I have seen changes in my time, and wages have gone up and food gone down, and glad I was when the loaf came cheap and we could afford to fat three pigs and sell one, but, bless you, it isn't by wages and food that we are made happy. They were good things, and I hope they will stay and wages be higher and food as good as it is cheap, but there's something else, though what it is I'm not going to try to say; that's for the poets, Willy."

She went out to get tea ready and to leave us to our loftiness.

After tea – apple pasties, you know, homemade bread, little flat currant cakes, all Mrs Morgan's baking – I had to choose between staying indoors and talking about books and going to see the Owens, Mrs Morgan's cousins. She liked to show round a visitor from London, and she could wear her best bonnet with violets in it and gossip freely. It was the beginning of the cooling of my friendship with Morgan when I chose to go with his mother: he saw that my love of poetry was only skin-deep. But what was the good? The mother was worth twenty of him though she had only one high-backed chair without arms were she never so tired. I never saw a sweeter and nobler accep-tance of life. She welcomed the new without forgetting the old and gave both their due because she felt – she would never have *said* it, for she would have considered such high thinking arrogant – that the new and the old, the institutions, the reforms, the shops, the drainage system, were the froth made by the deep tides of men's inexpressible perverse desires. On Sunday she was a Methodist, but hers was a real Catholicism. She saw good even in the new drains, and as we crossed the bridge over their little river she said:

"When the drain pipes are laid, I shan't have to let the slops run into Willy's river. He, good lad, doesn't know – how should he? he doesn't see such things – he doesn't know they run in now. I told him he mustn't drink the water there, that is all. But soon he will be able to. He is fond of the little river, he calls it Castaly or something, and says it is a poet's river. It runs from the little lake by where I was born – the pretty lake! have you been there in your long walks? Willy never went so far and he declares it runs from Mount Hel – Helicon. He is a true poet, I think, Mr Phillips. But the new poets are different. There was old Mr Jenkins, now, when he was a young preacher and poet his sweetheart died, and when they had let the coffin down into the grave he jumped in after it – lay down upon it and never said a word, and when they took him out, it was thought he would not be long for this world...."

The Owens' house stood opposite a waste field where the neighbours threw broken crockery, and a donkey grazed round the broken shell of a factory lately deserted. In ruins these mean buildings took on some venerableness in my sight.

Mrs Owen knew less English than Mrs Morgan. She greeted me so warmly that I was abashed to think I brought nothing but myself.

"How are you, Mr Phillips? No more Welsh, I see, and I've forgotten my English."

Here the children who spoke both languages laughed with good-humoured contempt.

"How are the children and Mrs Phillips?... How many children is it now?"

"Still two," I said.

"Two!" she replied with a smile, and wiped the dough from her fingers in her apron: she spoke in genial irony.

"You forget that Mr Phillips is a very wise young man, Sarah," said Mrs Morgan, chidingly.

"He will be wiser," snapped Mrs Owen, "when he has had ten children and seen five of them go away, and some not come back. As for two, two is toys."

I wish I could paint that tin-plater's house – not the outside which was horrible, and designed by Mr Owen himself, though I noticed that two pairs of martins had blessed its stucco with their nests in the past summer. Inside there were two large rooms, cold and stark and full of the best furniture, huge chests of drawers for Sunday clothes, family Bibles, photographs on gaudy frames, linoleum like painted ice. They were the chapels sacred to the family's respectability, and I could not understand the rites and ceremonies and sacrifices thereof. The third room had a perennial broad fire, summer and winter, for baking, cooking, and drying clothes. Everything shone with use, and aloft in Mr Owen's tobacco smoke piped the canary who seemed to wish for nothing better. The door opened into a little wash-house, where they kept the flour and the enormous sides of the last-killed pig lay white in saltpetre and brine. Bacon hung from the rafters of the kitchen itself, a whole side, a whole ham, and a long thin strip that had just supplied the frying pan which Mrs Owen was holding.

"This frying pan has fried forty pigs," she remarked, holding back her head from the hissing rashers while she turned them.

When she was not at the fire she was opening the oven to take out an apple pasty, or getting on with the spreading of the table for the meal, or sorting the clothes that overflowed two baskets of the largest size, or buttering a slice of bread to silence the youngest girl, or telling Tommy not to play football in the room while visitors were there, or preparing the supper of bread and bacon and soup which Tommy was to take for his eldest brother to eat at his night's work, or wiping her grandchildren's noses as they flocked in to get some bread and bacon fat and stare at the stranger who knew no Welsh: or she was sighing with a smile at her weakness and lack of two pairs of hands while she rested those she had upon her hips for a moment only, and talking all the time, asking questions, giving orders, describing her visit to London which she detests ("dear me, Mr Phillips, however can you live in it? There isn't a loaf of bread fit to eat to be bought there and scarcely a woman with sense to make her own, and you daren't keep a pig, nor yet breathe for fear of swallowing what doesn't belong to you and you don't want") or singing in a wild contralto the most melancholy and most splendid of the Welsh hymns. She weighed nearly twenty stone, but she never sat down.

Her husband, a pale man whose work you might think (if you hadn't seen him gardening, or taking his children ten miles away into the mountains with a present of seed potatoes for a cousin) had worn out everything in him but his good nature and love of a pipe of shag. The words of his conversation came from a daily paper, but he had the peace which passes understanding, and for wisdom he could depend on his wife. Neither she in her strength nor he in his sensibility had ever struck one of their children. He was whittling an oak stick, but he stopped to take me up the garden where he showed me by lantern light his tomato plants in a green-house of his own making, and then stirred out the vast pig for me to admire. He seemed to regard the pig as a kind of brother who sacrificed himself for the good of others almost willingly out of consideration for the expensive food which had fattened him; and until the day of the knife he was treated as a brother seldom is.

On the wall of the kitchen there were a few pictures, of Spurgeon, of Gladstone, of the Crucifixion, and a portrait of the eldest child, born out of wedlock and dead long ago, a pretty maid, Olwen Angharad. Six of the children were in the room, two of them married sons, pale, overworked but handsome, cheerful men who had dropped in to ask questions about London, to tell their father the weight of the pigs they were fattening and ask after his, and to exchange banter with their inexhaustible mother – their wives were not like that, but just pretty slips of women beginning to bear children and not baking their own bread, either.

After their mother, they admired most their eldest sister, aged eighteen. She worked at the tin-works all day and had done so for four years and was now as busy as her mother by the fire and at the table, talking little except with her eyes which flashed a variety of speeches between the look of command to her youngest brother and sister and the look of comprehension or expectancy to her mother. She had reached the perfect height of woman, which height I had never been sure of until I saw her. Her hair was of the nearest yellow to gold that is compatible with great physical energy and strength. I cannot explain how it was bound up in such a way as to boast of its luxuriance and yet leave the delicate even shape of her head unspoiled. Her face was rather long than short, her nose of good size and straight, her lips inclining to be full, kind and strong also, her grey eyes burning with splendour, her eyebrows darker than her hair and curved like two wings of a falcon, her ears – but such an inventory is absurd. Her face, whether in repose or radiant, expressed health, courage, kindliness, intelligence, with superb unconscious pride. She could bandy words with any man, and there were not wanting men to tell her – with a calculating eye for the effect of their words – that she had reached physical perfection; yet she was not wanton, not bashful nor vain. No Roman woman could have excelled her in power and dignity, no barbarian in exuberant strength. She had grace but no graces, beauty but no beauties. She ruled – even her mother; but she did not know it. So much loved was she that her youngest sister was heard praying that her lover would die, lest he should take her away from home.

Her three younger sisters showed what she had been: the one of seventeen was still too hesitating and slender in her grace; the next, of fifteen, was too impudent, though for the moment she was quiet and sleeping away her weariness on the horse-hair sofa under the canary's cage; the youngest, aged thirteen, was still too much of a powerful animal.

Her youngest brother was fourteen, almost his eldest sister's equal in height, brawnily made, unwieldy, fierce except at home where at most he was lazily, laughingly truculent, more often grumbling amiably over some task. They were all but pure Welsh, one grandmother being from Cornwall. The girls were fair, the boys black-haired.

Admirable as they were apart they made an indescribable harmony together. Sometimes all talked at once, they youngest boy's deep brawl almost overpowering the rest. Sometimes one told a tale and all attended. Sometimes the talk travelled mysteriously from one to another, and to and fro and crosswise, as if some outside power had descended invisibly in their midst and were making a melody out of their lips and eyes, a melody which, I think, never ceased in their hearts. Nearly always they smiled and if the gravity of the talk seemed about to extinguish this smile there was one pair of eyes or lips at least sparkling or rippling with the profound joy which no plummet of sorrow sounded. Nor was this talk mild gossip undertaken unconsciously to meet the fact that they were all of one family and in the presence of the father and the mother. For it was fearless. The father spoke his thoughts and the boy his, and there was nothing which anyone of them would have said or secretly laughed at with companions which they would not say before all.

There was noise and stir unceasing, but no haste, no care.

"What a flower bed it is, to be sure," whispered Mrs Morgan to Mrs Owen as we concluded the skirmish of a crowded meal of new loaves, seaweed "bread," bacon, apple pasty, and plentiful thin tea.

"Ah, you are a poet's mother, Mrs Morgan," she replied. They gossiped in low tones.

"How is poor Mrs Howell's son that lost his arm in the works by you?"

"Getting on well. He has two nurses in the hospital and they are very kind. But you know these women: he wants his mother."

"Poor boy. He was playing when it happened, wasn't he?"

"Yes. They say it was his own fault, as if that made it any better for him or the manager who will prove negligence, of course. It won't stop the boys playing, and my husband wasn't playing when he met his death. Never mind. They are going to set him up in a fried fish shop, a good idea."

While these two gossiped the eldest boy sang "Morfa Rhuddlan" and "Hob y deri dando" the most mournful and the merriest of the old Welsh songs.

I was a little sad at times. I was disturbed, as Mrs Morgan could not be, at all this gaiety in the heart of the village darkness, partly because I was unable to see why it should exist, and as foolishly sure that there would never be an end to the darkness unless it eclipsed this gaiety in a revolution of some kind – impious thought and unpardonable if it had not been in vain. That gaiety cannot be quenched.

I stayed that night with the pet, begging to be allowed to sit in the kitchen, where his mother left us with a parting look of reverence for those who would be talking about books while she lay awake thinking of her daughter in a London shop where she had never been, her son in the far west, her husband dead.

Next morning she took me by a long way round to the station. I remember I was wearing a coat which I had had made for me five years before with three pockets in it especially to hold copies of the poems of Shelley, of Sophocles, of Catullus; even then I bulged with the books, but carried them out of superstition, not for use.

We passed the estuary, and she pointed out the long barrow on one side and the tumulus on the other. The men in the old time had a bridge from one to the other, she had heard. We emerged from the last clustered cottages of the village on to a road high above Castaly. There were the goldfinches! – as many as ever in the rough pasture above the copse: she knew them. Didn't I think the copse the same, and the foaming river in the heart of it? One by one she named the bright farms on the side of the Great Crag opposite. White cloud rack was decamping from the red bracken and yellow larch on its flanks, and from the gaunt grey humps and cairns of its summit. The bracken was redder, the larch yellower, than ever, as if all had been the work of the spirits of the mist. The curlew's cry and chuckle were more wildly sweet. Our feet deep in the red mud of the road, we saw, fresher than ever, the gleaming wavering last hazel leaves and the stems of the oaks and hazels.

"And that is pretty too, isn't it?" asked Mrs Morgan, pointing to the seven black chimneys grouped just as I had seen them in the dawn of the day before. "I can't walk farther than this nowadays, but I like to come here and look first at Great Crag and then at the village, then at Great Crag and then at the village again, and I don't turn any more but go straight down hill and home. You must go that way, too, to catch your train. Leave me, I will go slow and you must hurry. Good-bye, Mr Phillips. Come again and bring your books and stay a long time, and you shan't be disturbed."

If I go again, I shall not trouble to take my books. But I shan't go. She has left the village. Her son tore himself away with infinite tears of rhyme for the river, and she silently. He got work elsewhere, and she of course must follow with her daughter, to bake the bread by which poets live.

***

At a Cottage Door

The cottage was built upon the rock which just there protruded from the earth; and which was the rock and which was the rough stone of the walls could not easily be told, so rude was the structure and so neatly was it whitened from the low eaves down to the soil. The threshold was whitened, so also were the stones of the path, the low wall in front, and several huge fragments here and there both within and without the gate. These white stones served instead of flowers. Other ornaments outside there were not, except stonecrop on the garden wall and at the sides of the threshold flagstone, a tall solitary spire of yellow mullein growing out of the top of the garden wall, and on the thatch itself a young elder tree against the white chimney stump, and an archipelago of darkest green moss which was about to become a solid continent and to obliterate the straw. Thatch and moss beetled over the walls which were pierced by two small windows of diamond panes. The chief light, when the door between these windows was shut, came from the fire-place which, with its iron and brasswork and the door of the brick oven adjacent, nearly filled one side of the living room. But the door was nearly always open, revealing most of the dark cave within, its red flameless fire, its bright knobs and bars of iron and brass, and the polished odds and ends of copper and brass on the mantelpiece or hanging on the wall – candlesticks, snuffers, horse-trappings, a gill measure, part of an old pair of scales, a small shell from a Boer battlefield.

The cottage must have been built before the road was made, or the roadmakers had omitted to notice it; for it lay back a hundred yards from the high hedge on top of a wall, through which a stile led over a rough meadow, between almost solid hillocks of brambles and clusters of royal fern under alder trees, to the white wall, the white stones, the cabbage plot and the white house itself. To a passing child it appeared that the cottage had originally been built in the heart of the stony wood; gradually the larger number of trees had been cut down, thus exposing the cottage to someone on the road who had then been inspired to cut through the hedge and its wall, to cross the field, to drive out the savage or fairy inhabitants, and to take possession of it. In the field there were still great butts of oak visible, and on the further side of the house, showing above the chimney, were three dead trees close together raising a few shortened stripped, and rigid pale arms to the sky and to the deities who had long ago deserted them, the house and the surrounding land of small fields as rough as a windy sea, stone walls, hedges of aspen, oak and ash, rocky rises clothed lightly in oaks of snaky and slender growth, and beyond and above, on all sides but one, hills so covered with loose silvern crags among their bracken and birch that they resembled enormous cairns – where perhaps those deities had been buried under loads sufficient to keep them dungeoned away from any chance of meddling with a changed world.

In the cottage lived a mother and son. She was very little and very old. Her hair was still dark brown, her eyes almost as dark, her skin not quite so dark as her eyes, a nut-brown woman, lean, sweet, and wholesome-looking as a nut. She might often be seen sitting and looking to the south-west when a gap in the fields framed a vision of mountain peaks twenty miles beyond; and always she smiled a little. A passer-by might have thought that she never did anything but sit inside or outside the open door unless he had noticed the whiteness of the stones and the polish on the metal in the room where she had for fifty years collected things that could be polished. Few ever saw Catherine Anne at work save her son, and he not often, for he was away early and home late. He left her entirely alone, visited of none unless on days when the smart tradesmen strode up the path, deposited her weekly packages on the table while he commented on the weather, and then replacing his pencil behind his ear bade her "Good Afternoon" in English. It was one of the few English remarks to which she could reply in English. Her only other English words were "beautiful" and "excursion train." For though some of the brown in her face was a gift of tropic suns in the days when she sailed with her husband on his ship, she had learned nothing but Welsh. The old man, so she called him though dead these forty years, had been against her learning English. A God-knowing and God-fearing Methodist, he had seen in that tongue the avenue through which his beautiful young wife might receive the knowledge of good and evil. After his death at sea she had of her own accord refused all contact with the thing, and now when it was all around her she never moved from the house. Her son knew it, but at home he spoke the native idiom, and when she heard him she seemed to be once more in her father's house, or in the orchard where little red apples overhung the rocky brook at the mountain foot. There it was that she gained, no one knows how, the nourishment from mother earth that gave her the deep contentment expressed in her health and her smile, in the shining metal, and in her patience – which was not endurance or torpor – patience of an order that seemed to be all but extinct in the world. Memory and hope were at balance in the brain that looked out of her brown eyes, and the present moment, often dull-seeming or even unkind, did not exist for her. Those eyes never closed while she sat by her door, and it might be conjectured that as she gazed east and north and west she saw more than the white stones and yellow stonecrop, the alders and royal fern, the hedge following the road, the lean oak trees among the rocks, the farther hills and their curlews and cairns, the sky, and now and then the uttermost mountains, which were all that an observer could see. If the casual observer waited more than a few moments in summer he might see that she was never quite alone. The air between her and the hills was the playground of several pairs of black swifts, wheeling and leaping round and up and down and straight forward, so that the bluest sky was never blank or the brightest grass without a shadow. Out of these birds two often screamed down precipitously to the white cottage and disappeared in their nests under the thatch above her head. Catherine Anne smiled a little more at these sudden stormy visits, and there were times when it seemed certain that she received others, though neither visible nor audible.

Some thought that she believed the swifts to be some kind of spirits, and one who was very wise said that if Catherine Anne Jones had been cleverer she might have been a wicked woman.

All the other swifts lived in the church. These had singled out her roof. They always returned to her; they had been there, ever since she came, every summer, singling that little place out of the whole earth and sky. She saw them high and swift and wild in the blue, and then she felt the flutter of their wings as they arrived at the eaves, and heard their soft talk together in the darkness. On summer evenings she saw them ascend into the heavens and not return, as blessed spirits might do; only on the morrow they were back again. They were always young, always equally dashing and joyous. It was whispered that she believed them to be the souls of her two children that died as babes, and they had come to her soon after the loss. "They were too young to know what to do in Heaven," she was reported to have said, "and so they were allowed to play about in Wales all the summer. But at night they have to return to see if they are wanted. Blessed birds. I daresay all birds are good if we only knew. I suppose I am too old to be one, but if it were lawful I should like nothing better than to live like them, passing the time until Judgement Day. What a lot of people there will be there to be sure – there were over three hundred in my native place when I was a girl, and I don't think there is one alive but me. I think some ought to be birds. Birds take up so little room, and they could not do any mischief if they wanted to. Now, if only the town people were all to be turned into birds. Lord, such a fright I had two years ago last February. I was sitting here, it being fine, to see the sun rise, and up from the town came a swarm of wings as many as there are leaves in yonder wood, small dark birds all close together and making a whistling noise, and I thought to myself, It has happened after all; they have changed all the people into blessed birds. No, I was not afraid about my son, for, thought I, now he will not be able to drink anything but cold water, and perhaps he will come to live in the church. I was glad. I thought of taking a walk down there just to see how the place looked, when along came the Insurance man – He isn't a bird, I thought to myself – and says: 'Are you looking at the starlings, mam?' 'No,' says I, and I was vexed. Dear me, all those birds was a beautiful sight, and such a nice noise they made between them as if they were glad to be going away from the place. It is a funny thing about birds, how different they are. Mrs Williams said to me once when she was courting, 'Why, Mrs Jones there are several kinds of birds.' Several! There are as many different kinds as there are men, and that is saying a lot, and remember I have sailed over the ocean five years and went ashore in all the ports of this mortal world. They are like people, only they don't seem to do any harm. Nice things! I used to think they must be very good no to be jealous of us having all the houses and food and things, but if people only knew they would be jealous of the birds. They are all different, or else how could He know when any one of the sparrows falls to the ground. They don't know what it is to be idle or too busy, nor the difference between work and play. There are not any rich and poor, and they respect one another. They are not all tangled up and darkened with a number of things. Then look how few of them die – did you ever see a dead bird? – except men shoot them. The reason is, they are good enough for Heaven as they are, so up they go like the dew when we are not looking."

It was not entirely due to the position of her front door that she always looked north or east or west, and chiefly west. From the back door her son's feet had worn a path which could be seen winding south over several fields until it was lost, by the next cottage, in another road, also going south, towards "that place."

She considered herself on the edge of the town, but still distinctly out of it. The next cottage, where the footpath joined the road, was in the town, so she thought; yet there was no outward sign of it unless that its low walls were not as clean, nor its brass so plentiful and so bright, and that its door, facing south, was often shut, and always when the wind was from that quarter.

From Catherine Anne's back door could be seen the roof and part of the wall of this cottage, another like it a little beyond, then a cluster, including one not of whitened native stone, but of red brick and black mortar. All these were on the road. On either side of it, southward, there was a farm or two, white, but with sheds of corrugated iron that rattled under the mist drops from the ash trees embracing the group. From these farmyards the geese strutted across wet meadows in a line as if setting out on a long voyage. Beyond, the rough land sank, hiding all but the smoke of yet more houses in a hollow, and rose again to an unbroken line of slate roofs and dirty white walls, cutting into the bases of snowy cloud mountains whose look told that underneath them was the sea. Similar houses in irregular lines and groups, were dotted on the treeless fields to the east and west of this main line. These were the first houses of the town and they were not a mile from the cottage. Beyond them the land fell away but rose again after several lesser rises and falls into great hills whose tops commanded the sea to the south and east and, on the clearer Sundays of the year, the same mountains as Catherine Anne's front door. These concealed rises and falls, and the slopes of the great hills, were the town.

From the brink, where that unbroken line of roofs notched the white clouds with its chimneys, the whole town could be seen. Over this brink fell the southward road and with its lesser roads which soon branched and multiplied into the mass of the town which choked the valleys as if it had slid down the hills in avalanches. The hills formed almost a circle, broken only by a gap on either side letting in the river from the mountains and out to the sea. Thus the town sprawled over the edges of a rudely carven bowl with deeply scalloped edges and with a bottom flat nowhere save at the narrow strip around the stream. The summit of these hills were clear of houses, and great expanses of their sides, though obviously conquered by the town, were still virgin and green and strewn with great stones.

Two of the hills on one side, that farthest from the stream, were not marked by a single street. Of these one, the highest of all, was clothed in grass from foot to ridge except on a broad lap which it made halfway up, and on that there was a house standing at the edge of a field sometimes golden with corn, and divided from it by a clump of black firs. The house was huge, both tall and wide, grey and square, with many windows towards the sea lighted only at sunset and that by the last beams in which a score of them blazed together. No road was seen climbing the steep slope to the house or leaving it for the ridge above. Some poet or haughty extravagant prince must have built it there inaccessibly with windows for the great town, the sea, the mountains. It was sombre and menacing. It was empty. It scorned the town. In its turn the town had left it up there to perish like an eagle upon a mountain ledge, shot by the hunter, but out of his reach. The neighbour hill was not so high, but it was bare not only of houses but of grass and corn and every green thing, and its only trees stood near the summit, leafless and birdless, stark and pale as if newly disinterred from an ancient grave. They were being slowly buried by the brown and fatal refuse – scarred deeply by rains and by ever new cataracts of the same substance – which covered and largely composed this hill. Out of its summit stuck a chimney and round it the black figures of men came and went against the sky. At the foot were other chimneys, gigantic and black, and below them black buildings whose windows glowed night and day with fire such as the old house had for a few moments at sunset. The smoke mingled with white rain, and mist wreathed wildly about the brown and the green hill.

***

Light And Twilight, 1911

Eckert writes of Light and Twilight that 'unquestionably, Thomas's finest prose is to be found in this book; it is the work of the poet in essence and outlook'. John Moore writes, 'those exquisite, almost-perfect essays in Light and Twilight... had given him a taste of the agony and the delight of writing as a poet writes, because he must'. In her recent biography Jean Moorcroft Wilson writes:

> *Other stories like Home and Olwen... express Thomas's love of Wales. (He had been re-reading the Mabinogion and would take Mervyn on a ten-day visit to Wales in April 1909.)*

'Olwen' was first published in The Nation in May, 1910, and the story echoes the Mabinogion legend Culhwch and Olwen. Edward Garnett writes of this story in his 1926 introduction to the Gregynog edition of Chosen Essays:

If Thomas' fancy runs here or there over exuberantly it is in his youthful pieces... His mature style as in "Olwen" is more restrained and firmer in contour.

'Home' is an adaptation of 'The Patriot', a story which had previously been published in The Nationalist in 1909. In his note on 'Home', Guy Cuthbertson writes:

In the relationship between Johnny and his father, Thomas offers a fictionalised account of his own ties to Welsh Nationality and culture... 'Home' is a very important word and place for Thomas – three of his poems use the word in their title._

Olwen

Olwen was eighteen, a Welsh girl, with light brown hair so loosely coiled and so abundant that no fancy was needed to see it down to her knees; an oval face, not plump enough to conceal the bones of cheeks and bold chin; a clear, wild-rose complexion, lit up from within as by moonlight; dark eyebrows that had wild, clear curves like the wings of some bird of free waste lands, and curved lips that never hid the perfect teeth when at rest. She wore the clothes of a slattern. She walked and stood still and sat down with the pride of an animal in the first year when it has a mate. The curlew, the hare, the sheep upon the mountain, were not wilder, or swifter, or more gentle than she. Her face and stature were those of a queen in the old time, whose father was a shepherd on the solitary mountains. Being as strong as a man, she had finished her work early in the factory and come straight home, and tucking up her skirts, had scrubbed and polished her mother's home. There was no pleasant way of being idle in the daytime, for, except with her lover, she did not care to walk to the mountain or to the black village streets. She laid tea, served it, and washed up. She was the only one who was not going out for the evening, for she had to bake the week's bread. Before the lamp had to be lit, her brother's wife came in with her baby. The first batch of cakes was already out of the oven. Their perfume streamed out through the open door, which let in the song of the blackbird, the wind from the mountains, and the majesty of evening. Olwen could rest now; she took the baby, and they sat down and began to gossip.

The married girl was a little older, slender and dark-haired, with small, sharp features and full lips, pleasure-loving, gay, and sharp-tempered, rapid in her speech. This was her first child, and she kept, as yet, all her maiden attractiveness and irresponsibility, and added to it the different power of one who is captive but unconquered. She sighed lightly now and then, as if she relished and remembered over-much the youth she retained. She seemed to feel the advantages she had over the unmarried Olwen, without being able to overcome a phantom of admiration for her that might at any moment turn to envy.

Olwen, being the eldest of ten, held the baby like a mother. Her face bent down to it, her shoulders and arms walled it, in an experienced way. She knew all that she would ever know about the care of infants – even their death. The young mother, watching her, would now and then cull the baby from her lap and press it to herself, and cover it with kisses. If there were cries, it was Olwen who silenced them in her deep breast; but the mother had the craftiness to let the maid seem to be their cause, and when the child was with the other she would tease it, in the hope of being the comforter. It would have been hard for a stranger to say whose was the child, since Olwen's attention to this one baby out of many was as perfect as the mother's to the only one. The mother was lively and effusive, yet careless; the maid was calm and tender, and never forgetful. The mother could have been a model for Aphrodite, the maid for Demeter. The mother was a lover first; the maid was born maternal, and her heart could be stormed by a sweetheart, but ruled only by a child.

The mother was destined for a man or for several men; there was somewhere a man destined for the maid, to open for her a kingdom which she would enter alone. The mother pressed the child to her with a luxurious smile, as if the lover were there, too; the maid resembled some noble animal, calm, but with a half-hid ferocity that would have talons if need were, even for the father of its brood. The mother was an elf, a not purely human creature, a haunting, disquieting form of life, a marshlight out of the wilds of time, and to be blown away with time again; the maid was the beginning and the end of human life, necessity itself made beauty, mere humanity raised to a divine height, the very topmost plume on the crest of life's pride. And yet behind the physical glory of Olwen, her bold, easy gait, her deep vice, full of nobility and sweetness, behind all her courage and robustness and independence, there was something like the timidity of the stag who stands on the rock in the moment of his greatest power and joy, without fear, and yet with an ear and a nostril for every breath of the summer gale.

The baby was with its mother when Olwen's lover entered the room. It was still half-lit by the great fire and the pale sky after sunset. Seeing the two girls and the child, he sat in the darkest of the chairs and kept his cap in his fingers. The mother gave the child to Olwen, and the young man became silent. The maid hardly looked at him, while the young mother, glad to see a man, bantered her visitor in vain even when she said laughing:

"Olwen has a baby now, John, and you see she can do without its father."

The young man fingered his cap, but looked musingly at Olwen out of the shadow. She had no eyes or ears but for the little thing that was now fully awake and standing on her lap and putting its hands into her mouth and eyes. Now she caught it quickly under the armpits and, throwing back her head, lifted it at arm's length and let it plant its feet upon her throat, then between her breasts, and so down to her lap; it crowed and waved its limbs. The mother looked into the fire. Again Olwen stood the baby upon her head where its curled feet were entangled in her hair; her eyes were towards the young man but not looking at him, though her thoughts might have been of him. still turned towards him, she lowered the child to her knees and jutted her bright face forward, pouting her mouth for kisses while the child tried to take away one of her glistening teeth; then she let it down flat on her knees and buried her head in the laughing and quaking form. The young man's dark eyes fixed upon her grew more and more dark and sullen, with admiration of her, jealousy of the child, and indignation that she was so careless. She had not given him a glance. She sang, she talked, she laughed, she feigned to cry, she cooed, for the child. She allowed it to do as it liked and as nobody else had done except in thought. Her cheeks glowed with pleasure and exercise and thoughts unexpressed; the white skin of her brows and throat gleamed moist and whiter than ever; her grey eyes flamed softly. Never had she been happier, and the happiness was at one with her beauty, so that a stranger watching might have thought that her happiness made her beautiful, or even that it was the consciousness of her beauty. She looked taller and her shoulders more massive than before, her back more powerful in the gentleness of its maternal stoop, her breast more deep, her dark voice more than ever the music of her noble body and blissful nature. Fit to be the bride of a hero and the mother of beautiful women and heroes and poets, she gave herself to the child.

Presently the child grew more silent, playing with a lock of her hair which now fell half over one shoulder down to her lap. She smiled musingly and caught the eye of her lover and began to tell him what she had been doing that day – how the manager had told her not to work so fast, and then asked her when she was to be married – but he remained silent. The child reared itself up by her hair and pulled at her chin and ears. She took no notice save to smile good-humouredly and shake her head, and continued to talk. Her two arms imprisoned the child; her head was raised in a pretence of keeping her chin from the enemy. Cheated of the smooth chin and soft ears the child was still a little while, and remained so still and so silent that it had been forgotten, when suddenly the mother broke into a laugh and cried:

"Well, I never, Olwen, the impudence of the child, you will be suckling her next!"

Olwen rose up undisturbed, smiling to herself, and then glancing over at John as she fastened two buttons below her neck.

"Now, Caroline," she said, "you take a turn with baby and let me talk to John."

John stood up and came forward very slowly and very stiffly, and took the child from her arms. It began at once to cry and the mother, rising in a temper, carried it swiftly away, leaving the lovers silent:

John was the first to speak, saying:

"And what did you say to the manager Olwen? Shall we get married this summer?"

"Yes, she said; waiting is not much fun for you, John."

And she gave him a kiss that he was too slow to return, so that she broke away, saying:

"And now I must take out these cakes. You light the lamp, John. Yes, come along, no nonsense. Bless me," she added, opening the oven door and letting out a smell as sweet as the first heat of May. "It's lucky I wasn't a minute later. There! Take one while it's hot and don't burn yourself. Hot cakes and maids' lips, John." And John split the cake in two and buttered it, and they ate the halves together.

***

Home

A little square sitting room, not very high, and hardly wider than it was high, yellow-lit by a brass lamp in the centre, and shutting out the visible world by three walls of a pleasant dull gold and indistinguishable pattern, and by three narrow curtains of a ruddiness that was dreamily heavy and sombre. On the walls, five pictures at the same height above the tops of the dark chairs, the mantelpiece and the sideboard; and on one, three shelves of books. A very still, silent room; and in it, motionless as in amber, a man standing before the books, and a woman with raised eyebrows and stiff but unquiet hands, dove-tailed together, staring into the black-crusted fire. The man, chin on one hand, elbow on the other, tall and upright and dark like a pinnacle of black rock, looking sternly out of kind eyes at the books as at children. The woman, trying to drowse herself through her eyes by the fire and through every pore of her body by the silentness, yet aware all the time of the husband between her and the windows, as though his shadow blackened her instead of half the books. These two, separate and careful not to look at one another. Had they been utterly alone they would hardly have looked thus. They were not alone. In the stillness and silence, despite the walls and curtains, there was another presence, and a greater than they. It was London, a presence mighty as winter, though as invisible. Its face was pressed up against the window; its spirit was within. And there was yet another, almost invisible, and as frail as the other was mighty – the spirit of the one who saw the room and felt the enchantment of

London upon it. Neither the man nor the woman knew what was this second spirit in their room, yet the room was its home. It was the spirit of a young soldier dying in a far land. He was calm and easy now, without pain and without motion. Only his dark eyes told that he lived. As still was he, with bright fixed eyes, as a bird sitting on its nest. One had just left him who had spoken a few words intended to comfort him; but all the words had faded as soon as spoken, just as wavelets on a burning sand which they do not even stain, all except 'for your country.' He had heard these before without considering them, though he would have struck the man who mocked at them. this time they remained because they instantly recalled the first time he had heard them used, eighteen years before. His father had said to him one morning, 'Johnny, I am going to take you to see your country, tomorrow.' His pale mother had smiled her patient, weary smile – with some gentle ridicule added – at these words. Then she looked admiringly at her husband, the big, gaunt wry-faced man, whose eyes laughed so under his black brows. She had no country. She was born in the great city where they lived, where Johnny was born, and she had never left it. Nearly everything outside her home inspired her with wonder, awe, or fear, and she held her husband in awe because he had a country of which he frequently talked, where they spoke a different language, had queer names, different food, different ways and, as she dimly conjectured, a kind of common life as of one big family. Her husband had told her often that he had only to take a train to his country and get out at any station over the border, and somebody, most likely a cousin, would step up as if he had been waiting, and say, with his face all cut up by a smile, 'And how are you, David John, this long time?' but somehow he never went until this April. He had had to be content with talking, with taking the boy on his lap and singing the songs of his country, grand wailing songs that would often make him happy for the rest of the evening, merry, quick songs that made him tap the ground with his toes and yet brought tears into his eyes, so that he set the child down and went out into the street and came home, bitterly, hours afterwards to the dark house and the meek waiting wife.

But now he was really going to his country. 'To-morrow,' he said, 'we will take the train at midnight, and before noon we will be finding a curlew's nest on the moor just by where the old battle was.'

'What battle, father?' said the boy.

'Why, one of the old battles when we beat the English, I suppose,' said he.

'But what was the name of it, and when was it fought?'

'Ah, I cannot tell you that now: it is not in the history books. But the river there is called the River with the Red Voice, and there is a battle mound. The air is so clean there that a collar lasts you a fortnight.'

'Dear me,' said his mother, waking with a start from her musing.

Then the boy fell a-dreaming about his father picking up mottled eggs among dead men's bones by a river that ran red with blood.

Those bright eyes in the hospital tent saw now the railway station like a huge palace, sprinkled with lights and paved with multitudes of men and women, and good silent trains stretched out among them which the people had caught by a hundred handles and were mounting, to persuade them to carry them far off into the black night beyond, the unmapped black night with its timorous lines of small lights. He and his father entered the multitude and crept in and out alongside the train; and it was very wonderful, but many of the groups who talked were talking in the tongue in which his father used to sing, and he looked up at their pallid faces and black hair and agitated smiles and boldly moving lips, and was inclined to be afraid, but remembering that they were his father's people he was not afraid, but filled with wonder and admiration. Even some very little children, smaller than himself, were chattering in that same tongue quite easily; it seemed to Johnny that they were very clever little children. How kind everybody looked now! He had never seen so many people smiling and talking friendly before.

'Where is our country now?' said Johnny, and as soon as he had sat down with his face towards the land of his desire, the train was gliding out past a hedge of white faces and white lifted hands into the darkness.

The carriage was full, and the boy liked pressing up against his countrymen on both sides and touching their boots with his toes, and watching the thoughts on their faces and the books and the papers they were reading, and how they would sometimes let their books and their papers fall on their laps, and look out at the wild-starred night seriously as if, perhaps, 'it had come... their country.' In a corner opposite sat a young woman, and next to her a young man. He was reading. She was doing nothing but thinking, with her eyes turned towards Johnny. Soon the man closed his eyes; his head sank upon the woman's shoulder, but she did not move, only took away the book lest it should fall, and she offered Johnny a sweet, but he was too busy looking at her, and would not take it. The young woman's brown eyes fixed on him softly, and, his father's arm round him, he began to dream; and he awoke, surprised that he had been asleep, at a cold glittering station with a few faces staring in from the platform, looking for seats. 'Is this-?' He was going to ask his father if they had arrived, but he saw the name of a well-known town on the seats and lamps and again closed his eyes; the others also had looked and immediately closed their eyes. Then nothing – tiny lamps in the darkness – nothing again – then over a hill a large moon began to light a watery sky, black cloud and blacker earth, and looked afraid of the huge world over which she reigned. Another stop, a well-known name on the lamps, and then sleep to the sound of the train expressing steadiness, determination, and content in its rhythm and hope in its speed. If he opened his sleepy lids he saw the young woman's soft eyes, and the earth now grey and not black, and the moon high, without a cloud around or below, with groups of houses lost – as it seemed – in the night and cowering under the trees, here and there a light burning where someone, perhaps, was enviously watching the train on its march of discovery and conquest; or, still later, a pale sky lit from below and behind, as well as from the now invisible moon above, a river gleaming, a horse knee-deep in white mist looking up at the train, a church upon a hill that seemed awake but alone, small contemptible stations where they did not stop.

The fixed bright eyes in the bed saw these stations

again in their dreariness, and saddened with the dream that he now was upon such a station, and the lighted train was rushing by and forgetting him, with its proud freight of living men looking ahead towards their country.

Nodding awake again, he saw the girl eating an orange, a wide water like a sea and the pale moon shrivelled beyond it, a farm and its cattle streaming out under a hill covered with crooked oaks, and the cattle were bowed under the weight of their long horns. 'It is near,' whispered his father: he slept.

When he awoke he was upon his father's knee, and both with cheeks together were looking, over frosty meadows and blown trees, at sand hills and sea beyond, and on the other side at hills crimsoned with bracken, their summits invisible, so steep were they. 'This is it,' said the father. 'Yes,' whispered the son, and both looked through and beyond the mountains and the sea to their country, the country of their souls, so that the child's first thought – that this was not what he had expected – never appeared again, until now in the tent. When a gap in the near hill showed them greater giants beyond that appeared to have descended out of the sky, and only half descended as yet, for their crests were in the clouds, the two were not more moved; they could see, far beyond these distances, greater hills, a land even more free.

They stopped, and there were wizard faces waiting, and the strange tongue that was the boy's own was spoken, and they seemed to welcome him. he began to step down from his father's knee to get out – but no, not yet.

They stopped again where there was only a black-bearded, tall man and a sheep-dog waiting. They could hear the thrushes sing, under the clear blue and the light-less moon, from out of dark thickets in a hollow rushy, land, backed by the sea and the orange sails of vessels that caught the dawn. 'Over there,' said his father, point-ing beyond the ships, 'is the land we have come from.' It was as faint and grey and incredible in the distance as his own land was clear and true; and he sighed with happiness and security, and also with anticipation of the further deeps that were to be revealed, the battlefield, the curlew's eggs, the castles, the harps, the harpers harping all the songs of his father. He had got so used to the faces of the men, which were like his father's, that when his father asked him whether they were not different from the English, he said 'No,' and was scolded for it.

The sun and the bright world dazzled his eyes. He slept. Then, a black barren land, a host of tall black chimneys between hills and sea, fountains of black smoke, sheaves of scarlet flame, red-hot caves... Young men crowded into the carriage and burst out into a song. It was in the lan-guage that Johnny spoke, but the beauty of their voices in harmony made it different from anything he had heard before that day.

A marsh and a thousand sheep, gaunt hills on one side, sea on the other, and the young men singing a war march in their own tongue at his father's request. It made him afraid at first. Then he fancied that the battlefield was not far off, and they were going to it, and the song was sung to hearten a host of which he was one. He felt grim, but glad and bold as he looked at the dark young men and thought of 'his country.'

'My country,' muttered the dreamer lying still, and blinked his eyes as the tent flapped and he saw outside the sun of another country blazing and terrible as a lion above the tawny hills. The country that he had been fighting for was not this solitude of the marsh, the mountains beyond, the farms nestling in the bears of the mountains, the brooks and the great water, the land of his father and of his father's fathers, of those who sang the same songs, the young men and the old, and the women who had looked kindly on him. where were those young men scattered? Where had their war march on that April morning led them?

A grim, black-bearded face was bending over him, with smiles deeply entrenched all over it. He was lifted straight into a cart behind a chestnut pony with his father and the man.

The sun was hot. They climbed up high among the hedgeless and pathless mountain, always up. The larks sang. The mountain lambs skipped before the cart.

They alighted by a solitary cottage under the road, whence a maid brought ale for the men and milk for the boy. They sat down among gorse bushes and ate apple tart and cheese, wafers of oat and currant cakes. The men talked. Johnny wandered up from the road with a girl of the cottage. And there with the rough strange mountain boys they set fire to the gorse and dead bracken. The flames leapt up like the genii out of the imprisoning jar in the Arabian tales, and he drew back. The earth was crowded with little flickering plants of fire spreading this way and that. Huge whirls and rounds of the yellow-white smoke soared up against the milky sky. The smell of smoke heated by fire and sun was delicious. when the earth was black they moved on, while some sent the grey boulders galloping downward till they bounded over the road with a hero leap, and struck sparks out of other boulders or plunged into the gorse. They boys roared, the girls shrieked. All disappeared. But all day they could see the smoke of one conflagration pouring upwards before the wind in a great river, lost awhile in the hollows, seen again continually surging towards the high crests mile after mile, like a gigantic engine smoking wildly over the wilds.

Outside one cottage there stood a little old man, naked to the waist, washing himself and talking to three foxes chained up to a shed. The foxes seemed to understand his tongue and he theirs, and neither heeded the cart as it drove on. And now, careless of waterfalls thundering among low woods beneath the road, of flames and smoke clouds hunting upwards over the moor, and of mountains such as he had dreamed lying across their course a day ahead, Johnny fell asleep, content, not even rousing himself to make sure whether that was the cuckoo he heard upon the hillside.

The dream of the fixed open eyes wreathed and wavered. Was it the same day – it was morning and about noon – when he stood by the door of a long white inn fronting the sun? The wide courtyard, bounded on one side by the road and on the other by a green hedge, was dotted with fowls pecking idly or lying down. In the midst rose a brown oak, very thick and stiff and well stricken in years, and at its side a very tall gentleman with a fishing-rod was mounting a trap; and the boy watching him and thinking of his wealth and happiness was happier than he. On the hot white pavement by the door all the dogs were lazy in the sun. Each one, except the big, smooth pointer, had a bone, and each snarled as the pointer strolled past. There was a greyhound, a spaniel, a sheepdog with one eye almost white, a mongrel, resembling both the spaniel and the pointer, and a fox-hound. From time to time the spaniel's puppies – pure spaniels – broke in among the fowls, and the mother raised her head and left the bone under her paws until the pointer re-appeared. It seemed to Johnny that the sun was always full upon that white inn, that the dogs were always lying down there in the sun, and that it had been so and would be so for all time. He longed to have an inn with a white wall facing the sun, and many dogs to take the sun upon the pavement in the front. The fisherman drove away.

The father and son walked into a solitary wood upon the side of a steep hill, and at the foot of it was a green vale that wound with the windings of a broad stream running fast, and at the top of the hill, where it was a precipice, hung a castle with trees growing in its crevices, and its windows looked out through ivy thicker than its vast walls down at several miles of the green vale on either hand, at the sun-bathed gloom of the oakwoods of the opposite slope, at the other castles, bleached crags which could be recognized as the work of men only because they were even bolder and more gaunt than the natural crags round about. Sometimes it rained, sometimes the sun shone, and the father and son were glad of both as they gathered blue violets and white sorrel in the dripping and glistening woods. Under the castle wall they sat down, and the father brought out a book and read: 'King Arthur was at Caerlleon upon Usk...' and Johnny began to think of bowmen shooting through the ivy about the windows, of king and queen walking in the grassy courts within the walls, whose roof was the sky. His father told him that the book was written by his countrymen about the heroes of his country, and the child made over to those heroes the glories that had once been Aladdin's, and the Marsh King's, and King Solomon's....

The dark eyes gleamed like a thrush's upon her nest when she is watched.

They saw more mountains, and the cart creeping over them and among them, small as a stone upon the road. And by and by they got down to a brook and began to travel upward towards the source. There were clear and dark pools in the brook where the trout darted and the man with them said: 'The fish runs away, who knows that man has sinned.' They were among steep woods of oak trees as dense almost as grass, all twisted and grey as if made of stone and very old, but based in greenest leaves and flowers of white, of gold, of golden green. The blackbird sang, and the brook gushed, but they did not speak, except that as they left, the strange man said: 'This is the Castle of Leaves.' Now, there was no longer a path, and the way was over whistling dead grass and grey stones, like ruins of a palace that must have been lofty as the heavens, and when they had gone further still the man said it was 'The Castle of the Wind.' And now the mist washed over all and hid everything but silvered stones and dead grass blades underfoot, and the rain that was like bent grass blades of crystal, through which for a moment a sheep crept up and crept away again, or a hare, grey as the grass, but blackened as if by fire, leaped up and dived into the wind, the mist, and the rain. Stumbling still among the ruins of the wind's castle, they continued to climb, until the rocks, now tall as a man and so dense that some had to be scaled, came to an end at the shore of a lake which they surrounded – 'The Shepherd's Lake.' The cry of a raven repeated at intervals from the same spot high up above told them that the mountains rose higher yet and in a precipice. The boy sat upon a rock while the two men went out of sight to the other side; his father to bathe, as he had dome twenty years before when a young man. The wind hissed as through closed lips and jagged teeth. The mist wavered over the polished ripples of the lake that resembled a broad and level courtyard of glass among the rough hills. The men were silent, and the sounds of their footsteps were caught up and carried away in the wind. The boy was thoughtless and motionless, with a pleasure that was astonished at itself. He could not have told how long he had been staring at nothing over the lake when, at his feet, his father's head was thrust up laughing out of the water, turned with a swirl, and disappeared again into the mist. He had not ceased to try and disentangle that head from the mist when once more he heard that wailing song that used to make his father so glad, and he himself sang back such words as, without knowing their meaning, he remembered; his brain full of the mists, the mountains, the rivers, the fire in the fern, the castles, the knights, the kings and queens, the mountain boys at cricket, the old man with the foxes, the inn dogs lying in the sun...

the sun... the mist... his country... not the country he had fought for... the country he was going to, up and up and over the mountains, now that he was dying... now that he was dead.

***

Celtic Stories, 1911

This was one of Thomas's few commercially successful publications – due largely to the Australian Government ordering 2000 copies for use in their schools. Thomas's surprised response to this success being, "I didn't think Colonials had any virtues!" It is in this book, more than any other, that Thomas tackles Welsh culture head-on. The book retells four Welsh, and seven Irish tales. Thomas's opening assertion in his 'Note on Sources' makes his position on Welsh culture quite clear.

Note On Sources

These tales are founded upon ancient ones, the work of Welshmen and Irishmen when Wales and Ireland were entirely independent of England. The Welsh tales come from a book now known as the *Mabinogion*. They were written down at the end of the Middle Ages, and translated from Welsh into English by Lady Guest in the nineteenth century. The original Welsh manuscript (called 'The Red Book of Hergest', because it was once at Hergest in Radnor) belongs to the fourteenth and fifteenth centuries, but the stories had been told over and over again, and probably written down many times, before they were copied into 'The Red Book'. They were being told in the years between the Norman conquest of England and Edward I's conquest of Wales. But the subjects of them were much earlier. Even those who told the tales would, perhaps, have been unable to say when a man as huge as Bran was ruling at Harlech, nor did they consider the matter any more than children to-day consider the tale of 'Jack the Giant-killer' in its relation to scientific fact. But in 'Kilhugh and Olwen' and 'The Dream of Rhonabwy' King Arthur appears. The men who told these two stories were probably thinking of a glorious heroic age, when Arthur was a supreme king, resisting the Roman and Saxon invader. They gave a strange reality to some of the wonders by connecting them with actual places in Wales, so that a man to-day could walk in the steps of Kilhugh and Rhonabwy. Even 'The Dream of Maxen', which is about a Roman emperor, comes to its height and to its end in Wales, and in places which are still to be seen. Very little was known to the mediaeval writers about the age of the Saxon invaders and the seventh-century King Arthur, except that it was one of greater men than any that were living; and therefore they described their heroes as if they were Welsh and Norman warriors in dress and manners, but of greater stature and prowess. They were certain that Arthur had once been king in Britain, and they were ready to come to blows with men who denied it. In one story, 'The Dream of Rhonabwy,' they put along with the King two young princes, Madoc and Iorwerth, who actually belonged to the twelfth century.

The name 'Mabinogion' means something like 'twice-told tales': it means precisely the old tales on which a young writer practised.

***

Note On Charlotte Guest And Spelling
[added to the second edition]

My debt to Lady Charlotte Guest's *Mabinogion* is as plain as it is huge. But those who read this book will not have read hers, while many if not all who have read mine will very soon afterward read hers: so that if I am an insolvent debtor at least I am no thief.

The spelling of some of the chief names in these stories has been changed so that English children may at once be able to pronounce them, as Uspathadden Penkower for Yspaddaden Pencawr. I hope this will give no trouble to bilingual Welsh children.

***

The Dream Of Rhonabwy

Iorwerth, younger son of Meredith, refused to live at ease in the palace of his brother, King Madoc. He rode therefore into Logres to steal a kingdom. He and his men plundered, and none could withstand them. But one day he vanished. Madoc sent men on all sides to seek him. But in vain they sought, and the searchers were foiled again and again, and found themselves often in strange countries.

Now Rhonabwy and two others made one search-party
and they could come upon no traces and hear no news of
Iorwerth. One night of rain they arrived at an old dark
house. Heavy smoke billowed out of the hall over the
mire and the dead thistle as they entered. The floor was
all mounds and puddles, foul and slippery as a cattlefold,
but carpeted in places with boughs of holly. At one side
was a range of dark chambers full of dust; at the other a
hag, too old to be quite human, bent shivering to feed a
bad fire with lapfuls of damp chaff. Rhonabwy and his
companions could hardly endure the cold smoke that
poured from the chaff. Nevertheless, they did not go out
again into the tempest of rain and wind, but lay down to
rest on a couch that had given its choicest portions to the
cattle for provender. The other two fell asleep in spite of
the knotty bed and the vermin, but only when he had
lain down on a yellow calfskin before the fire could
Rhonabwy sleep.

While Rhonabwy slept on this calfskin he dreamed.
With his two companions he was traversing a plain in
North Wales towards the Ford of the Cross. As he rode he
heard a noise such as he had never heard before, and
turning round he saw a fierce youth of gigantic stature
with curled yellow hair, riding on a chestnut horse. He
was carrying a golden-hilted sword; his coat and scarf
were of yellow satin sewn with green silk. The horse was
caparisoned in the same colours; the green like that of
the larch tree in April, the yellow like broom-flower. Fear
overcame their admiration of this horse and horseman
and the three began to fly, but in vain; for though the
horse's breath drove them far away on its current it drew

them back again right to his chest. They asked for mercy and the youth gave it, and they continued their journey in his company. Rhonabwy asked his name. He told them that he was Iddawc, who had stirred up strife between Arthur and his nephew Mordred, in mere youthful love of battles; and for that reason he was called Iddawc the Hammer of Britain. So Rhonabwy and his companions and Iddawc reached the ford together.

There Rhonabwy saw a city of tents and heard the cries of an innumerable army. On a flat islet in the Severn below the ford, Arthur the emperor was sitting between Bedwini the bishop and Gwarthegyd; and a tall youth with auburn hair and jet-black eyebrows stood before him, bearing a sheathed sword and wearing a coat and cap of jet-black satin. Riding a little into the shadows Iddawc and Rhonabwy and the other saluted those four upon the islet, and Arthur spoke:

'Iddawc,' he asked, 'where didst thou find these little men?'

'Yonder, lord, upon the road,' replied Iddawc, and Arthur smiled.

'Why dost thou laugh?' said Iddawc.

'I do not laugh,' was the reply; 'but pity it is that men so little should be guardians of this island after the men who used to guard it.'

Then they stretched themselves out to rest on the grass under an alder, and Iddawc pointed out to Rhonabwy a stone in the ring of Arthur, telling him that it had the power to make him remember all that he would see this day.

As they rested, Rhonabwy saw troop after troop of armed men riding down and encamping about the ford, and Iddawc told him who were the men and horses all in crimson; who were those riding upon black-legged white horses; and those who were all white except for the jet-black borders of their white scarves, the black shoulders of the white horses, and the black points to their snowy banners; and those who were jet-black with white points and borders. All were haughty riders and one of the knights on the black-legged white horses spurred so furiously into the river that he drenched Arthur and his counsellors. The youth standing before Arthur turned, therefore, and struck the knight's horse over the nostrils with the sheathed sword. Instantly the man reined in his horse with a scattering of foam like a mill-wheel, and drew his sword half out of the scabbard, asking loudly:

'Didst thou strike for insult or for counsel?'

'Thou dost lack counsel,' said the youth, 'thus to drench the Emperor.'

'For counsel then will I take the blow,' answered the knight, and mounted the bank.

'That', said Iddawc, 'was Adaon the son of Taliesin, wisest and most eloquent youth in this island. The quick-tempered youth standing before Arthur is Elphin the son of Gwyddno.'

In a little while Rhonabwy saw a tall man rise up and speak to Arthur:

'By noon, lord, we are to be at the battle of Badon, fighting Osla. I at least will set out at once, either with or without thee.'

'Thou sayest well,' said Arthur, 'we will go together.'

'Rhonabwy,' said Iddawc, 'that man of daring and

mighty speech was Caradoc, cousin and chief counsellor to Arthur, a man who may speak as he pleases to any man.'

Then the army crossed the Severn and the river swelled over its banks with the multitude of men and horses. Iddawc and Rhonabwy and his companions rode with them, not dismounting until they looked up at Badon Castle and heard the wind roar in ten thousand beeches on Badon hill; whether this were Bath, or Baydon in Wiltshire, few care and no man knows. When they had halted, one knight in white mail with rivets of blood-red set the host in tumult by his wondrous and fierce riding. 'That,' said Iddawc to Rhonabwy, 'is Kay.' The tumult was stilled only by a prince lifting up the sword of Arthur in its scabbard that was like two serpents. When he drew forth the blade it resembled the gushing of flames out of the mouths of the serpents, and it was hard to look, and hard not to look, upon this marvel. 'That man', said Iddawc, 'is Cador Earl of Cornwall, who arms the Emperor.'

When all was quiet a huge red man rod up on a huge red horse, rough and hideous like his master, and dismounted before Arthur. He brought a chair large enough to seat three armed warriors, and a satin carpet which had an apple of ruddy gold at each corner and made any one upon it invisible. In the chair Arthur sat down, and Owen the son of Urien stood before him. 'Owen,' said Arthur, 'wilt thou play chess?'

'I will, lord' replied Owen.

So the red man brought a chessboard of silver and golden chess-men, and Arthur began to play with Owen.

While they were deep in their game, Rhonabwy sitting among the beeches saw a white tent having a red canopy and on top a jet-black serpent painted, with red eyes and a red tongue in his open gorge. Out of the tent strode a yellow-haired page in coat and surcoat of yellow satin, greenish-yellow hose, and parti-coloured shoes fastened with golden clasps. His three-edged sword had a golden hilt and a gold-pointed black scabbard. He advanced to Owen and saluted him.

'Lord,' he said, 'is it by thy permission that the young pages and attendants of the Emperor torment thy Ravens? If not, beseech the Emperor to forbid them.'

'Lord,' said Owen, 'thou hearest the youth; if it seems good to thee, forbid thy pages and attendants.'

'Owen,' said Arthur, 'it is thy turn to play.'

So the youth returned to the tent, and Arthur and Owen finished the game of chess and began another. In the midst of this game Rhonabwy saw a goodly youth emerging from a yellow tent that had a bright red lion painted on top of it. He was ruddy, with auburn curled hair. His coat was of yellow satin and red silk embroidery, his hose were white, his buskins black and their clasps of gold. He carried a huge three-edged sword in a gold-tipped scabbard of red deer-hide. He also strode up to Owen and saluted him, saying:

'Lord, is it by thy permission that the young pages and attendants of the Emperor torment thy Ravens? If not, beseech the Emperor to forbid them.'

'Lord,' said Owen, 'thou hearest the youth; if it seem good to thee, forbid thy pages and attendants.'

'Owen,' said Arthur, 'it is thy turn to play.'

So the youth returned to the tent, and Arthur and Owen finished the game and began another. At the beginning of this game Rhonabwy saw a goodly youth striding out of a great tent speckled yellow and adorned with an eagle of gold, having a precious stone on its head. His hair was thick and yellow, his cheeks ruddy, and his eyes large and like a hawk's, and he wore a scarf of blue satin fastened on his right shoulder by a golden brooch. His shoes of parti-coloured leather were clasped with gold. In his right hand he bore a mighty lance, speckled yellow and displaying a banner. Anger was in his speed as he came up to the chess-players and saluted Owen.

'Lord,' he said, 'most of thy Ravens are dead. Those that live are so wounded they cannot raise their wings a fathom above the earth.'

'Lord,' said Owen, 'forbid thy men.'

'Play,' said Arthur, his eyes on the board.

Till he had spoken to the youth, Owen did not regard the chess-men.

'Go back,' he said, 'and in the thickest of the strife lift up the banner and let come what pleases Heaven.'

So the youth returned, and where the Ravens most suffered, Rhonabwy saw him lift up the banner on his yellow-speckled lance. Immediately the Ravens clapped their wings in the wind with a noise that drowned the roaring of the trees. They were shaking off their hurts and their weariness and even death. They rose up into the air boldly and very angrily, and swept down together in a frenzy on Arthur's men. They caught the men by their heads, by their eyes, by their ears, by their arms, and soared with them on high. The air was full of the flapping and croaking of the triumphant Ravens and the groans of their victims struggling and wounded.

Arthur and Owen, still playing their game, marvelled at this conflict, and Rhonabwy noticed that Owen looked rather at Arthur than at the board. Then there galloped towards them a knight upon a dun horse, his right shoulder bright red, his legs yellow to the hoof. Both were in heavy foreign armour, and the caparison of the horse was bright red above and bright yellow below. Golden-hilted was the knight's sword and the scabbard light blue. His helmet was of gold set with precious stones, the crest a flame-coloured leopard with eyes of rubies. His blue-shafted lance was crimson red from haft to point with the blood of the Ravens. The face of the knight, even more than the leopard, astounded the heart of stoutest warriors.

Enraged but weary he saluted Arthur and said: 'Lord, the Ravens of Owen are slaying thy young men and attendants.'

'Forbid thy Ravens,' said Arthur, looking at Owen.

'Lord,' answered Owen, staring at the board, 'it is thy turn to play.'

So they played on and the knight returned to the tumult of men and Ravens, and the chess-players could not but hear the wails of men and the croaking of Ravens as they sailed with the men through the air and tore them and let them fall piecemeal to the earth. A second knight galloped towards them on a light-grey horse whose left foreleg was jet-black to the hoof. Both were in heavy blue armour. The knight's robe of honour was of yellow-diapered satin, blue-bordered; the horse was caparisoned in jet-black with yellow border. Three-edged and heavy was the knight's sword, and the scabbard on his thigh was of red leather;

his helmet was gold, set with sapphires of great virtue and crested with a lion of flame-colour, having a fiery red tongue and crimson eyes; the ashen lance headed with silver in his right hand was steeped in blood. He saluted the Emperor and said:

'Lord, dost thou not heed this slaughter? Thy pages and thy young men and the sons of the nobles of Britain are being killed, and who is to defend this island?'

'Owen,' said Arthur, 'forbid thy Ravens,' and it seemed to Rhonabwy that as the Emperor spoke there was no other sound in the world. But Owen answered only:

'Lord, play the game.'

Owen lost, and they began another game. As they were finishing, Rhonabwy heard a great clamour of armed men and a yet greater croaking and flapping of Ravens flinging down armour and shreddings of men and horses. A third knight was riding up on a lofty-headed piebald horse, its left shoulder bright red and its right foreleg pure white. Horse and man were in armour of speckled yellow, and both wore robes of honour, black and white and bordered with purple. The knight's sword was three-edged and golden-hilted; his yellow helmet was set with crystals, and its crest was a griffin with a stone of many virtues in its head; and his spear was ashen, the shaft azure, the head overlaid with silver and stained with new blood. He came in anger.

'Lord,' he said to Arthur, 'the Ravens have slain the men of your household and the chief men of the island. Command Owen to forbid his Ravens.'

'Owen,' said Arthur, 'forbid them'; and Arthur's hands crushed the golden chess-men like clay under Owen's eyes. Then Owen ordered the young man with the mighty lance speckled yellow to lower his banner. He lowered it and Rhonabwy saw peace and heard great silence. The Ravens gathered in ranks about the banner, and as their human fellows walked in and out amongst them not a beak or an eyelid stirred, and they looked wiser than any man that Rhonabwy had ever seen.

Rhonabwy now saw twenty-four knights come up to Arthur from Osla to crave a truce. The Emperor rose up and assembled his counsellors, Rhun the son of Maelgwn Gwynedd, Bedwini the bishop, Mark, Caradoc, Gwalchmai, Mabon, Peredur, Trystan, Morien, Cador, Adaon the son of Taliesin, and Cadyriaith, and men of Norway and Denmark and men of Greece and many others.

'Who is the tall auburn knight?' asked Rhonabwy.

'He,' said Iddawc, 'is Rhun son of Maelgwn Gwynedd.'

'And why,' again asked Rhonabwy, 'why is such a stripling as Cadyriaith admitted to this council?'

'Because,' answered Iddawc, 'there is no man through-out Britain more skilled in counsel.'

Then the bards came and recited verses before Arthur, but no man save Cadyriaith understood more of them than that they were in praise of the Emperor. Next arrived twenty-four wayworn men leading each an ass, bearing gold and silver as tribute to Arthur from the Islands of Greece, and Cadyriaith rose and spoke, proposing that the asses and the gold and silver should be given to the bards as a reward for their verses, and that the truce should be granted to Osla.

'Rhonabwy,' said Iddawc, 'would it not be wrong to exclude so liberal a youth as Cadyriaith from the councils of his Lord?'

As Cadyriaith proposed, so it was agreed, and Kay rose up and spoke to the host:

'Let whosoever will follow Arthur be with him tonight in Cornwall, and whosoever will not is Arthur's enemy.' Not a man, not a raven, remained still or silent at these words, and in the clamour of that host beginning to surge towards Cornwall, Rhonabwy awoke upon the yellow calf-skin. His sleep was three nights and three days long when he dreamed this dream.

***

The Dream Of Maxen

One day Maxen the Roman Emperor, handsomest of men and wisest of emperors, held a council of kings and said to them: 'To-morrow I will hunt.' With two and thirty crowned kings who were his vassals he hunted along the river until mid-day. Then he slept in the great heat and men stood round him and kept off the sun with their shields. In his sleep he had a dream.

Riding along the valley of the river, he came to the highest mountain in the world, and from the summit he saw mighty rivers descending to the sea. Towards the mouths of the rivers he travelled over the fairest of plains. At length his road followed one of these rivers, the broad-est he had ever seen, and at its mouth he came to a great city and a castle with many towers of different coloured stone. A fleet, the largest ever seen, was anchored in the river. To the largest and fairest of the ships led a bridge of whalebone, and he went over it into the ship. A sail of the ship was hoisted and he sailed over sea and ocean to the shore of the fairest island of the whole world. He landed and traversed the island to the furthest shore. He saw high mountains and deep valleys and terrible precipices, such as he had never seen before. From the top of one mountain he saw another island and a river flowing from the mountain into the sea. At the mouth of this river was a castle, the fairest that man ever saw, and the gate was open and he went in.

The hall was beautiful, having a roof of gold and walls of glittering gems, and doors also of gold. The tables were silver, the seats of gold. At one of the tables two youths with auburn hair were playing at chess, and they had a silver board and golden pieces. Their garments were of jet-black satin; their buskins of new Cordovan leather buckled with gold; and their hair was bound with chaplets of ruddy gold and jewels.

Beside one of the pillars of the hall Maxen saw a hoary-headed and mighty-looking man in a chair of ivory with two eagles of ruddy gold upon it. Gold bracelets were upon his arms, and many rings on his hands, and a collar of gold about his neck, and on his head a golden diadem. He had before him a golden chess-board and a rod of gold, and a steel file in his hand; and he was carving chess-men.

Facing the old man sat a maiden in a chair of ruddy gold. It was not more easy to gaze upon her than upon the sun at its brightest, she was so beautiful. She wore a vest of white silk clasped with red gold at her breast, a surcoat of gold tissue and a golden girdle; and a circlet of red gold, rubies and pearls upon her head.

The maiden rose from her chair and Maxen threw his

arms about her neck and kissed her, but even while his arms were round her and his cheek against her cheek, the clashing of shields and the neighing of horses awoke the Emperor.

His attendants said to him: 'Lord, is it not past the time for thee to eat?' But he had no life or spirit left in him for the love of that maiden. He mounted his horse, the saddest man that ever a man saw, and rode to Rome.

For a week it was vain to offer the Emperor meat or drink. He would hear no songs or tales; he would do nothing but sleep and strive by all possible means to sleep again, because in his dreams he could see that maiden. One day a page came into his room and told him that the people were discontented and speaking ill of him because he took no notice of anything that was said or done. 'Young man,' said Maxen, 'bring to me the wise men of Rome and I will tell them why I am sorrowful.'

The wise men sat round, and Maxen said:

'Wise men of Rome, I have had a dream. In the dream I saw a maiden, and for thinking of her I have no life or spirit left in me, and I can think of nothing but her.'

'Lord,' answered the wise men, 'since thou judgest us worthy to advise thee, this is our advice: that thou shalt send messengers into the three parts of the world to seek for the maiden of the dream. As thou knowest not what day or night may bring good news of her, the hope will give thee life.'

Messengers travelled for a year, wandering over the earth, seeking news of the island, the castle, and the maiden of Maxen's dream. But at the end of the year, though they had seen many islands, many castles, many maidens, they had discovered nothing about the dream. The Emperor was now more sorrowful than ever; he thought that he should never see the maiden again, and all his hours of sleep were busy with visions as if he had been awake, and his waking hours were all one dream.

Then the King of the Romans advised the Emperor to go forth to hunt as he had done on the day of the dream, and he did so and came to the bank of the river where he had slept. 'This,' said he, 'is where I was lying when I had the dream, and from here I seemed to go westward. 'Thirteen messengers, who had been taught about his dream, set out in search towards the west. They came to the highest mountain in the world, and from the summit they saw mighty rivers descending to the sea. they travelled over the fairest of plains, and came to a great city at the mouth of one of the rivers of the plain. They knew that this was the land of Maxen's dream, and they saw the fleet anchored in the river-mouth under the many-coloured high towers of the castle. As the Emperor had done, they went on board the fairest of the ships and sailed over sea and ocean till they came to an island. This island was Britain. They traversed it until they came to Snowdon. 'This,' they said, 'is the land of high mountains, deep valleys and terrible precipices that the Emperor saw.' From one of the crests they saw the island of Anglesey, and they knew that that was the other island of Maxen's dream. They saw also Aber Sain and a castle at the river's mouth. The gate was open and they went in. They knew the hall. The two youths with auburn hair were playing chess; the mighty old man was carving chess-men in the chair with the eagles of gold; the maiden was sitting opposite. The messengers fell down upon their knees before her, saying, 'Empress of Rome, all hail!'

'You seem honourable men, wearing the badge of envoys,' said the maiden, 'why then do ye mock me in this manner?'

'We mock thee not, lady. The Emperor of Rome has seen thee in his sleep, and since then he has no life or spirit left in him because of thee. Wilt thou come with us to Rome to be made empress, or wouldest thou rather that the Emperor should come hither to wed thee?'

'Lords,' she answered, 'I cannot deny what ye have said, neither can I believe it. If the Emperor love me, let him come hither.'

The messengers hastened day and night back to Rome, and saluted the Emperor saying: 'We have seen her; Helen is her name; and willingly shall we guide thee to her castle.'

Immediately the Emperor set forth with his army, and as he galloped over the mountains or walked up and down the ship he knew what was the difference between a dream and what is not a dream. He recognized the island far off. He landed, and galloped forward until he saw again the castle at the river's mouth. The gate was open and he entered. There sat Helen, the maiden whom he had seen in his sleep, and he bowed before her, saying, 'Empress of Rome, all hail!' She became his bride, and he gave her as a gift the island of Britain and three lesser islands, and three castles to be built where she commanded. The highest she had made at Arvon, and the others at Caerlleon and Caermarthen. From one castle to another she made roads over the mountains right across Wales, and these are called to this day the roads of Helen; nor would the men of

Britain have made these great roads except for her. To the castle at Arvon men brought Roman earth, so that the Emperor might sleep and sit and walk on native soil. He stayed there seven years, and the men of Rome were tired of waiting and made a new emperor. This man wrote a letter to Maxen containing only these words: 'If thou comest, and if thou ever comest to Rome.' And Maxen sent a letter back containing these words: 'If I come to Rome, and if I come.' Following the letter he led an army to the gates of Rome, and the brothers of Helen, the young men with auburn hair, took possession of the city for Maxen. There he ruled with Helen. As to the brothers they set forth again with a host. They conquered lands and castles and cities, and when their heads were grey they returned to Britain, taking with them some of the beautiful women of the conquered, whose tongues they had cut out lest they should spoil the speech of Britain.

***

Two Letters, 1911

Sent from Laugharne in to Edward Garnett, an influential critic, editor, dramatist and publishers reader. He was a loyal and important friend to Thomas.

1911 was a bad year for Thomas's mental health and only a generous gift solicited by Helen from E. S. P Haynes allowed him to spend six weeks in Laugharne where he rested and worked on a draft of his biography of George Borrow.

Letter One

5. xi.11

c/o Mrs Wilkins
Victoria St
Llaugharne
Caermarthenshire

Dear Garnett

There was hardly any choice of lodgings but I took the rooms at the bend of the road from the ferry & they have turned out well so far. Mrs Wilkins is a cheerful & not too inquisitive woman & cooks well, & the house is quiet although right on the street. There is rather little to do at this time of year except work as I am not up to very much walking, so I may take a change before the end of the year, perhaps at Tregaron. By the way if you do hear of any work that I cd do I wish you wd let me know. Things go from bad to worse & I am being paid for here. I hope it is nothing more than bad luck – I don't make friends but neither do I make enemies as a rule. Is my work worse? I shd not be surprised if I were much more careless than I used to be, having to do so much against the grain. I told you I was doing a book on Borrow. What is there to say?

Yours

E. Thomas

Letter Two

2. xii. 11   *Llaugharne*

My Dear Garnett

I am glad to hear from you tho everybody is becoming rather remote by this time. With intervals I have been here all the time. I have been to Manorbier & Haverfordwest & St David's & Swansea but otherwise I have been immersed in Borrow & in my grievances. I tried to get Borrows' letters from Belloc but got no book or answer; I will try something else. As to my 'Maeterlinck' – & many thanks for the review – that '2nd edition in the press' is apparently only a dodge as it has been announced 6 weeks now. De la Mare did not write that review. I was glad to see him get that prize tho I much prefer the 'Mulla Mulgars' to 'The Return'. A little while ago I borrowed 'Gerald the Welshman'; but it is execrably written & colourless & at present I can't persuade myself to read anything – this is literally true; I read nothing except in the cause of my writing about Borrow. I wish you had put me up to something about Borrow. Mine will be a pure *ex nihilo* book without any foundation at all. It is 5/6 written & once it is done I shall hardly stay on here. After the New Year I may try Oxwich – if I can get on at all, but I have convinced myself that food &c & any physical régime is practically worthless. Something will have to take place which cannot be brought about by any deliberate method, I think. I get no books here to review: I suppose I have disgusted Evans as he never responds; same with the 'Saturday'; while Milne hypocritically regrets &c & employs new reviewers twice weekly.

I am very sorry about Hudson & Mrs Hudson. I have meant to write to him. Please give him a message if you see him on Tuesday.

Yours ever

E. Thomas

If you are the 'Irishman' who called here in the Spring Mrs Wilkins remembers you very pleasantly & well.

***

The Pilgrim, 1911

Set in Pembrokeshire on the way to St David's Cathedral, 'The Pilgrim' is included in The Last Sheaf, the collection of Thomas's essays that was published in 1928.

The place and publication date has not been given nor can I find it in any other mention of the piece. The National Library of Wales have digitised a notebook which contains a page with the last line of The Pilgrim ('I see no reason to doubt that he was writing a book') and their catalogue record states that the preceding 11 pages have been torn out, strongly suggesting this was the source of the original manuscript. The first page of the notebook is inscribed 1911. This corresponds with a letter Thomas sent to Garnett form Laugharne in October, 1911, in which he writes;

But with a fine morning I shall certainly get away from here for a day or two to St. David's.'

Which is doubtless where he encountered his 'pilgrim'.

R.George Thomas uses this piece as the title piece for his

1991 Everyman Library prose anthology 'A Pilgrim and Other Tales'.

The Pilgrim

The 'Dark Lane' is the final half-mile of a Pilgrim's Way to St David's. It may be seen turning out of the Cardiganshire coast road a little north of the city. Presently it crosses the 'Roman road' to Whitesand Bay, and then goes down into the little quiet valley that holds the cathedral and a farm and a mill or two. Travel has hollowed out this descent; bramble and furze bushes on the banks help to darken it. Yet the name of 'Dark Lane' is due rather to the sense of its ancientness than to an extremity of shade. Perhaps on account of the shadow it may cast on the spirits of men it is now little used, unless by the winter rains; and some days of storm had made it more a river than a road when I walked up it, away from St David's. I looked back once or twice at the valley, its rook – the Alan – its cathedral, and the geese on its rushy and stony pasture. I had no conscious thought of antiquity, or of anything older than the wet green money-wort leaves on the stone of the banks beside me, or the points of gorse blossom, or a jackdaw's laughter in the keen air. If the pilgrims never entered my mind, neither did living people. The lane itself, just for what it was, absorbed and quietened me.

I was therefore disturbed when suddenly, among the gorse bushes, I saw a young man kneeling on the ground, his back turned towards me. If he had not heard me approaching he knew, as soon as I stopped, that some one was there. He was more surprised and far more disturbed than I, for in a flash I had seen what he was kneeling for; and he knew it. He was cutting a cross on a piece of rock which had been left uncovered by money-wort. Obviously he felt that I must think it odd employment for him on that December day.

He was not a workman carving a sign or a boundary stone, or anything of that sort. He was nothing like a workman, but was clearly a young man on a walk. A knapsack and a thick stick lay at his side. He was dressed in clothes of a rough homespun, dark sandy in colour, good, and the better for wear, and with nothing remarkable about them except that the coat was not divided and buttoned down the front, but made to put on over his head. As he wore breeches he showed a sufficient pair of rather long legs. His head was bare, and his brown hair was untidy, and longer than is considered necessary for whatever purposes hair may be supposed to serve. He might have been twenty-five, and I put him down as perhaps a poet of a kind, who made a living out of prose.

He looked at me with his proud, helpless, blue eyes; his lips moving with unspoken words. He shut the knife he had been using as a chisel, and opened it again. I knew that he would have given anything for me to go on after saying 'Good morning,' but I did not go. I asked him how far it was to Llanrhian, and if the main road beyond here was the original continuation of the 'Dark Lane', or if part of it was missing, and so on. He answered, probably, by no means as best he could, for he was thinking hard about himself. In a few minutes he could no longer keep himself to himself, but began to talk.

'I suppose you wonder what I was doing, cutting that cross?' he said in a defensive tone.

'Was there an old pilgrim's cross there?' I asked inno-
cently. 'I have heard they carved crosses on some of the
stones along the road.'

'I have heard so, too,' said he; 'but I have been looking
out for them all the way from Cardigan and have not
found any.'

'Then you have carved this yourself?'

'Yes; and I suppose you wonder why. Well, I don't
know; I can't tell you; I don't suppose you would understand; I am not sure if I do myself; and at any rate it is no
good now.'

'I hope my interrupting you...'

'Oh no, I don't think so. But when I began I thought it
would be a good thing. I got as far as this at daybreak,
and I was feeling... what is it to you? Seeing this old
stone, which is perhaps the last before I reach the cathedral, and no cross on it any more than on the others, an
idea came to me. I had been thinking about those pilgrims,
some of them with torn feet, some hungry, or old, or
friendless, or with an incurable disease. And yet they
came here to St David's shrine. They must have thought
there was some good in doing so; they would be better,
even though their feet might still be torn, or they might
still be old, or hungry, or friendless, or have their incurable
disease. But the shrine is now empty. I did think that
perhaps the place where the relics used to be, when they
were not carried out to battle, would have some power.
All that faith would have given it some quality above
common stone. But I doubted. Then I thought. "But faith
is the thing. If those pilgrims had faith there was no
special good in St David's bones, except, again, that they

believed there was." I tried to think in what spirit one of them would have carved a cross. Perhaps just as a boy cuts his name or whatever it may be on a bridge, thinking about anything or nothing all the time, or sucking at a pebble to quench his thirst. At the sight of this stone – I may have been a fool – I thought – I had a feeling that while I was doing as the pilgrims did I might become like one of them. So I threw off my knapsack and chiselled away.... Please don't apologize. In any case it would have been no good. The knife was already too blunt, and I was cold an aching and also thinking of a wretched poem. Do you think a pilgrim ever had such thoughts? If there was such a one he would never have got far on his road.'

I tried hard to lure him into a Socratic dialogue to disclose what had brought him so far. He went on:

'The quickest city in the world is St Pierre, which was overwhelmed by the volcano on Mount Pelée. But one cannot easily become a citizen of St Pierre. Well, well, what is it to you that I want in some way to be better than I am? I must be born again: that is certain. So far as it is in my power, I have tried hard. For example, there is no ordinary food or drink or article of clothing I have not given up at some time, and no extraordinary one that I have not adopted. There remains only to wear a silk hat and to drink beer for breakfast.

'I have been to physicians, surgeons, and enchanters, but they all want to know what is the matter with me. I answer that I came to them to find out. Then they listen gravely while I tell them about a hundredth part of the outline of my life. They write out prescriptions; they order me to eat more or eat less, or to be very careful in every way, or not to worry about anything. They shake hands, saying: "I was just like you when I was your age. You will be all right before long. Good-bye."

'My family paid a specialist to come to see me at the house once. He and I had the usual conversation. Then he was given lunch, which he ate in complete silence, except for a complaint about the steak. After receiving his cheque my mother asked him rather tragically what to do. "Don't hurry him on, Mrs Jones," he said, "and don't keep him back, Mrs Jones."

'For forty days I visited an enchanter continually. He did not promise to cure me, though he also said that at my age he was just like me – which was untrue, for he had a Yorkshire accent. Day after day in his room I sat with closed eyes, repeating "Lycidas" silently with the object of not thinking about anything, especially the incantation. This consisted of a whispered, slightly hesitating assertion that I should get well, that I should be happy, that I should have faith, that I should have no more doubt, but confidence, concentration, self-control, and good sleep. After several minutes I always heard the enchanter take out his watch to see if he had given me enough. From that time until the end I was doing little but listening to the crackle of his shirt-front and cuffs. It was so funny that I was even more serious about it than he; but after forty days I had had enough. My rebirth did not take place in the house of the enchanter.'

'When I was your age...' I began; but luckily I was inaudible.

'I have tried many medicines,' he continued. 'I have been to a physician who offers to cure men who are suffering from many medicines. All in vain. I tried a medicine which all great writers take, and which presumably makes them greater or keeps them great; but it had no effect on me – my literary ambition died.'

Here he took out his watch.

'Zeus!' he said. 'I have been two hours at this thing,' and he rose up. 'I must photograph that cross and put it in my book. That will pay for the wasted time.'

He photographed the stone and cross, and departed with long strides down the 'Dark Lane' before I could ask him about his book, but I see no reason to doubt that he was writing a book.

***

Glamorgan, 1913

First published as 'Glamorgan: The Microcosm of Wales' in T. P.'s Weekly in May 1913, it was reprinted in The Last Sheaf in 1928. Thomas's father's family came from Glamorgan and Gwent and Thomas was a frequent visitor to these parts of Wales.

The man who knows Glamorgan knows Wales. It is a land of mountains much divided by rivers and rivulets, increasing in height and wilderness inland, but having between the mountains and the sea a fertile border which varies from a few hundred yards to several miles in breadth. This fertile land is decorated by the large number of castles which once protected the Normans against the mountain Welshmen.

The rivers supply large and numerous steel works, copper works, tinplate works, etc., and receive from them poison of many colours. The mountains are pierced by coal-mines and carved by quarries. Glamorgan possesses the great manufacturing towns and seaports of Cardiff and Swansea, the cathedral of Llandaff, the ancient townlet of Lantwit, and countless ruins, such as Neath Abbey, and the castles of Caerphilly, Coity, Kenfig, and Oystermouth. Some of its valleys, likes those of Rhondda and Maesteg, are of the blackest; others, like that of Neath, are among the greenest; those of the Twrch and Mellte are very wild. It includes Llanmaes, one of the quietest places under the sun, as well as Dowlais and Tonypandy; and the large peninsula of Gower is shared between visitors and agriculture, though at the very edge of it stands Landore, where men have toiled for centuries to show what a town is when it is nothing but a town, where earth and air and river are chiefly dirt. It has yellow rivers like the Tawe, and rivers like the Perddin, the Camffrd and the Thaw, which are as living crystal where they are not white as milk. The coast is one of precipices, as throughout half of Gower; of sandhills, as at Porthcawl. It is a land of mines, of furnaces, and slums, but also of the richest and gentlest fields, as in the Vale of Glamorgan, still gleaming with the white houses which were praised hundreds of years ago by poets. And, east and west, there is hardly a hill-top but commands the sea.

Other counties have a similar variety of characters, but Glamorgan shows them altogether in a hundred places. From the windmill tower above Swansea, for example, you see the ships and the chimneys of Swansea, Neath and Port Talbot; but you see also, on the one hand, corn, pasture, moorland, and white cottages, the rivers Neath and Tawe cleaving with their romantic valleys a great realm of mountains; on the other hand, the blue waters and yellow sands of a sea that extends thirty miles away southward to Exmoor. The same, or as much, can be commanded from the neighbourhood of Cardiff, Pontypridd, Neath, or Pontardulais. A composite portrait of the county would show green fields, black fields, a hundred chimneys pouring out fire and smoke, a white farm-house with its sheds and lodges shining like a negro's teeth, and a background of mountains with cataracts among their crags and fern. But composite portraits are without life. To combine, for example, the Vale of Glamorgan with Morriston, Landore, and Swansea, is like mixing an apple with a lump of coal, which would make neither food nor fuel. And yet you have often equally great contrasts side by side, especially during the first stages in the growth of a place like Pontardulais – when it is being transformed from a village with a fulling-mill and an inn to a Hell, fully equipped. Then the purest green fields border on the factory yard, and will be ready to encroach on it if deserted. The old white cottage of Glamorgan will stand side by side with the cheapest town type, in which the mortar is made with sand instead of coal. Where there used to be a live otter is now a dead dog or two. By the solitary farm under the four sycamores the miner greets the shepherd, and the mountain sheep and their lambs, which are prettier than deer, feed close to the smoke, provided that the west wind carries it off the pasture, not on to it. These things are to be found every year by anyone who walks twenty or thirty miles in Glamorgan.

In the course of such a walk you see every variety. In the morning you are in a green castle court which Owen Glendower visited; a horse grazes among the tall fragments of masonry, draped with ivy, felted with grass and daisy, tufted with little ash trees, and the blue of two peacocks nodding across burns in the sunshine. A robin sings, the rooks caw on their way to the stubble, the jackdaws chaff one another in the clear sky above their woods. In the south lies the sea, in the north the mountains; and the earth is as tranquil as the sky. You pass nothing worse all the morning than a quarry and golf-links. At midday you have on your left the sand-dunes, on your right the mountains, to which the trees, yellow and red and bare, are fitted like a bird's breast feathers. The curlews cry over the road as you approach factories and ships, and a town of mean streets and enormous 'pubs,' of bustle, prosperity, and pale faces. Before evening you are in a valley of chimneys, skirting a wide, barren marsh, where black streamlets run, and women search for something on the slopes of fuming slag-mountains. Gradually, the turns of the valley reveal, first, a hundred tall stacks and their attendant fleeces of smoke, white, black, or tawny, and then a hundred masts and funnels, a crescent of yellow sand, and the blue water of Swansea Bay, with the Mumbles lighthouse to the right, and to the left the horizontal white band of cottages on the red mountain above Port Talbot, three miles away. In many other directions a similar walk may be taken. The mountainous pit alone in which Swansea lies will furnish, on a lesser scale, the same contrasting and yet combining elements of grace, majesty, and horror, of blue sea and green hill, of coal-mine, copper works and slums. The town and its coast and hills make as accurately as possible a composite portrait of Glamorgan. But then it is also possible to spend a whole day within the county and never quit the fern, heather, and whinberry of the stony mountains; and another day in exuberant undulating country as sweet as Kent, but bounded by mountains; and yet another without any variety except in the smoke you breathe, the ashes you tread, the colour of the streams and the number of the pit-mouths or chimneys in sight. To see it all is to see Wales – I do not say to know it.

***

The Country, 1913

The Country was published by Batsford in their elegant, short-lived series of Fellowship Books. Edward Thomas's friends, James Guthrie, Clifford Bax and W.H. Davies also contributed volumes to the series. Although Thomas's book is largely a philosophical and general essay on the country-side, his choice for the book's opening is from a W.H. Davies poem about Wales;

> *Can I forget the sweet days that have been,*
> *The villages so green I have been in;*
> *Llantarnam, Magor, Malpas, and Llanwwern,*
> *Liswery, old Caerleon & Alteryn?*

This once gain shows Thomas's love of place-names in general and of Welsh place-names in particular. Both

Beautiful Wales and Thomas's biography of George Borrow have lists similar to the Davies' poem above but they comprise over twenty places-names.

For Nature includes Fleet Street as well as the Milky Way, Whitechapel as well as the valley of the Towy of the valley of the Wylye. There are eyes, and at least one pair of human eyes, that look with as much satisfaction on a lamp-post as on a poplar-tree, and see towns as beautiful birds' nests. For most of us this visionary or God-like view is impossible except in a few particular and irrecoverable moments. We cannot make harmony out of cities: often we think it a great triumph to become blind and deaf to them and without sense of smell; or we are proud that the rain on the windy 'bus-top has kissed us exactly as on Old Winchester Hill or St John's Hill at Laugharne and has brought them to mind. Roughly speaking, we still accept Cowper's hard-and-fast distinction between God-made country and man-made town. We may feel the painful splendour of our humanity in the town, but it is in the country more often that we become aware, in a sort of majestic quiet, of the destiny which binds us to infinity and eternity...

...As little will a man in this island to-day understand the Welsh poet's ode to David ap Jenkin, the outlawed Lancastrian, the tall Kay of the greenwood, huntsman and harper, good with his hands at all things, beloved of the stags and a very steward to the cuckoo: "eight woods and God shall keep thee safe" are the last words in the translation of Mr. H. Idris Bell. Not so few will yet echo that other Welsh poet's praise of the labourer: "When he pays his debt to God, a good soul and a righteous will he render up. It will be easy to the labourer of the smiling meads to put his trust in the Lord God; he passes no judgement save on the plough-beam, brawling goes not in his company, he wages no war nor follows it, he destroys no man for his goods, he does not lord it overweeningly over us, he cloaks no wrongful claim under a fair seeming. He is made but to suffer; there is no life, there is no world without him. Surely it is sweeter far to him, un-stained by guilt, to follow with patient long-suffering mien the plough and the ox-goad than to wear the shape of Arthur, waster of cities. Who speaks against him?..." Men will echo this without believing that the countryman is of necessity more virtuous, but only that his vices, like his virtues, are in the old style.

***

The Icknield Way, 1913

Although the book describes a very English landscape, the book's three-page dedication to Thomas's friend Harry Hooton is written from one of Thomas's favourite inns, the 'Dolau Cothi Arms' in Carmarthenshire, where George Borrow had also lodged. Harry Hooton was a very old and good friend, Hooton's wife Janet being Helen Thomas's best friend at school. Thomas met Hooton in 1898.

Dedication To Harry Hooton

When I sat down at the "Dolau Cothi Arms" this evening
I remembered my dedication to you. You said I could
dedicate this book to you if I would make a real dedication, not one of my shadowy salutes befitting shadows
rather than men and women. It seems odd you should
ask thus for a sovereign's worth of – shall I say? – English
prose from a writer by trade. But though I turn out a
large, if insufficient, number of sovereigns' worths, and
am becoming a writing animal, and could write something
or other about a broomstick, I do not write with ease: so
let that difficulty give the dedication its value.

It is right that I should remember you upon a walk, for
I have walked more miles with you than with anyone else
except myself. While I walked you very often danced, on
the roads of Kent, Sussex, Surrey, and Hampshire. This
evening when I went out on the Sarn Helen everybody
was in chapel, I think, unless it was the Lord, for he also
seemed to me to be walking in the cool. I was very much
alone, and glad to be. You were a ghost, and not a man of
fourteen stone, and I thought that perhaps after all that
shadowy salute would be fittest. But I have put my pen
to paper: I have set out and I will come to an end; for, as
I said, I am a writing animal. In the days of those old
walks I could have written a dedication in Norfolk-jacket
style, all about "the open road", and the search for something "over the hills and far away": I should have
reminded you at some length how Borrow stayed at this
inn, and that Dolau Cothi is the house where he could
have lived with satisfaction "if backed by a couple of

thousands a year." To-day I know there is nothing beyond the farthest of far ridges except a signpost to unknown places. The end is in the means – in the sight of that beautiful long straight line of the Downs in which a curve is latent – in the houses we shall never enter, with their dark secret windows and quiet hearth smoke, or their ruins friendly only to elders and nettles – in the people passing whom we shall never know though we may love them. Today I know that I walk because it is necessary to do so in order both to live and to make a living. Once those walks might have made a book; now they make a smile or a sigh, and I am glad they are in ghostland and not fettered in useless print. This book for you was to have been a country book, but I see that it has turned out to be another of those books made out of books founded on other books. Being but half mine it can only be half yours, and I owe you an apology as well as a dedication. It is, however, in some ways a fitting book for me to write. For it is about a road which begins many miles before I could come on its traces and ends miles beyond where I had to stop. I could find no excuse for supposing it to go to Wales and following it there into the Ceidrych Valley, along the Towy to Caermarthen, and so to St. David's which is now as holy as Rome, though once only a third as holy. Apparently no special mediaeval use revived it throughout its course, or gave it a new entity like that of the Pilgrims' Way from Winchester to Canterbury that you and I walked on many a time – by the "Cock" at Detling, the "Black Horse" at Thurnham, the "King's Head" (once, I believe, the "Pilgrims' Rest") at Hollingbourne, above Harrietsham, past Deodara Villas, above Lenham and Robert Philpot's "Woodman's Arms", and so on to Eastwell; always among beech and yew and Canterbury bells, and always over the silver of whitebeam leaves. I could not find a beginning or an end of the Icknield Way. It is thus a symbol of mortal things with their beginnings and ends always in immortal darkness. I wish the book had a little more of the mystery of the road about it. You at least will make allowances – and additions; and God send me many other readers like you. And as this is the bottom of the sheet, and ale is better than ink, though it is no substitute, I label this "Dedication", and wish you with me inside the "Dolau Cothi Arms" at Pumpsaint, in Caermarthenshire.

***

The Happy-Go-Lucky Morgans, 1913

The Happy-Go-Lucky Morgans was Thomas's only pub-lished novel. He would write of it as

> *a loose affair held together, if at all, by an oldish suburban home, half memory, half fancy, and a Welsh family (mostly memory) inhabiting it & collecting a number of men & boys including some I knew when I was from ten to fifteen.*

R. George Thomas considers it Thomas's 'most engaging and untypical work'. The novel, which is a sort of fiction-alised autobiography, is about a family living in Abercorran House in Balham, but we are quickly informed that the book is 'more Welsh than Balhamitish'. Abercorran is the

old Welsh name for the West Wales town of Laugharne,
where Thomas had visited and stayed. The contemporary
review in the Times Literary Supplement was largely
favourable and drew attention to the tales of folklore and
Welsh worthies. (see APPENDIX 3. for a review of The
Happy-Go-Lucky Morgans from The Welsh Outlook, Volume
1. November,1914).

This extract is the chapter that focuses on the wonderfully
eccentric, itinerant bookseller, stone mason, bibliophile and
Welsh scholar, Iolo Morganwg.

Chapter XIII – Ned Of Glamorgan

Long after his celebrated introduction to Abercorran
House, and soon after Philip and I had been asking old
Jack again about the blackthorn stick, Mr Stodham was
reminded of the story of the Welshman on London Bridge
who was carrying a hazel stick cut on Craig-y-Dinas. "Do
you remember it?" asked Mr Morgan.

"Certainly I do," replied Mr Stodham, "and some day
the stick you gave me from that same Craig-y-Dinas shall
carry me thither."

"I hope it will. It is a fine country for a man to walk in
with a light heart, or, the next best thing, with a heavy
heart. They will treat you well, because they will take
you for a red-haired Welshman and you like pastry. But
what I wanted to say was that the man who first told that
story of Craig-y-Dinas was one of the prime walkers of
the world. Look at this portrait of him..."

Here Mr Morgan opened a small book of our grandfather's time which had for a frontispiece a full-length

portrait of a short, old, spectacled man in knee breeches and buckled shoes, grasping a book in one hand, a very long staff in the other.

"Look at him. He was worthy to be immortalised in stained glass. He walked into London from Oxford one day and mentioned the fact to some acquaintances in a bookshop. They were rather hard of believing, but up spoke a stranger who had been observing the pedestrian, his way of walking, the shape of his legs, and the relative position of his knees and ankles whilst standing erect. This man declared that the Welshman could certainly have done the walk without fatigue; and he ought to have known, for he was the philosopher, Walking Stewart.

"It was as natural for this man in the picture to walk as for the sun to shine. You would like to know England, Mr Stodham, as he knew Wales, especially Glamorgan. Rightly was he entitled 'Iolo Morganwg,' or Edward of Glamorgan, or, rather, Ned of Glamorgan. The name will outlive most stained glass, for one of the finest collections of Welsh history, genealogies, fables, tales, poetry, etc., all in old manuscripts, was made by him, and was named after him in its published form – 'Iolo Manuscripts.' He was born in Glamorgan, namely at Penon, in 1746, and when he was eighty he died at Flimstone in the same county.

"As you may suppose, he was not a rich man, and nobody would trouble to call him a gentleman. But he was an Ancient Briton, and not the last one: he said once that he always possessed the freedom of his thoughts and the independence of his mind 'with an Ancient Briton's warm pride.'

"His father was a stonemason, working here, there, and everywhere, in England and Wales, in town and country.

When the boy first learnt his alphabet, it was from the letters cut by his father on tombstones. His mother – the daughter of a gentleman – undoubtedly a gentleman, for he had 'wasted a pretty fortune' – taught him to read from the songs in a 'Vocal Miscellany.' She read Milton, Pope, 'The Spectator,' 'The Whole duty of Man,' and 'Religio Medici,' and sang as well. But the boy had to begin working for his father at the age of nine. Having such a mother, he did not mix with other children, but returned nightly to read or talk with her, or, if he did not, he walked by himself in solitary places. Later on, he would always read by himself in the dinner-hour instead of going with his fellow-workmen to the inn. Once he was left, during the dinner-hour, in charge of a parsonage that was being repaired, and, having his own affairs to mind, he let all the fowls and pigs in. his father scolded him, and he went off, as the old man supposed, to put for a week or two with his mother's people at Aberpergwm, near Pont Neath Vaughan. It was, however, some months before he reappeared – from London, not Aberpergwm. Thus, in his own opinion, he became 'very pensive, melancholy, and very stupid,' but had fits of 'wild extravagance.' And thus, at the time of his mother's death, though he was twenty-three, he was 'as ignorant of the world as a new-born child.' Without his mother he could not stay in the house, so he set off on a long wandering. He went hither and thither over a large part of England and Wales, 'studying chiefly architecture and other sciences that his trade required.'"

"There was a mason," said Mr Stodham, "such as Ruskin wanted to set carving evangelists and kings."

"No. He knew too much, or half-knew too much.

Besides, he hated kings... Those travels confirmed him in the habit of walking. He was too busy and enthusiastic ever to have become an eater, and he found that walking saved him still more from eating. He could start early in the morning and walk the forty-three miles into Bristol without any food on the way; and then, after walking about the town on business, and breaking his fast with bread and butter and tea, and sleeping in a friend's chair, could walk back again with no more food; and, moreover, did so of choice, not from any beastly principle or necessity. He travelled thus with 'more alacrity and comfort,' than at other times when he had taken food more frequently. He always was indifferent to animal food and wine. Tea was his vice, tempered by sugar and plenty of milk and cream. Three or four distinct brews of an evening suited him. Once a lady assured him that she was handing him his sixteenth cup. He was not a teetotaller, though his verses for a society of journeymen masons 'that met weekly to spend a cheerful hour at the moderate and restricted expense of fourpence,' are no better than if he had been a teetotaller from his cradle:

"'Whilst Mirth and good ale our warm spirits recruit,

We'll drunk'ness avoid, that delight of a brute:
Of matters of State we'll have nothing to say,
Wise Reason shall rule and keep Discord away.
Whilst tuning our voices Jocundity sings,
Good fellows we toast, and know nothing of kings:
But to those who have brightened the gloom of our lives,
Give the song and full bumper – our sweethearts and
    wives.'"

At one time he made a fixed resolve not to *sit* in the public room of an ale-house, because he feared the conviviality to which his talent for song-writing conduced. But it is a fact that a man who lives out of doors can eat and drink anything, everything, or almost nothing, and thrive beyond the understanding of quacks.

"Iolo walked night and day, and would see a timid gentleman home at any hour if only he could have a chair by his fireside to sleep. He got to prefer sleeping in a chair partly because his asthma forbade him to lie down, partly because it was so convenient to be able to read and write up to the last moment and during any wakeful hours. With a table, and pen, ink, paper, and books beside him, he read, wrote, and slept, at intervals, and at dawn usually let himself out of the house for a walk. During a visit to the Bishop of St David's at Abergwili he was to be seen in the small hours pacing the hall of the episcopal palace, in his nightcap, a book in one hand, a candle in the other. Probably he read enormously, but too much alone, and with too little intercourse with other readers. Besides his native Welsh he taught himself English, French, Latin and Greek. His memory was wonderful, but he had no power of arrangement; when he came to write he could not find his papers without formidable searches, and when found could not put them in an available form. I imagine he did no treat what he read, like most of us, as if it were removed several degrees from what we choose to call reality. Everything that interested him at all he accepted eagerly unless it was one of the few things he was able to condemn outright as a lie. I suppose it was the example of Nebuchadnezzar that made him try one day 'in a thinly populated part of North Wales' eating nothing but grass, until the very end, when he gave way to bread and cheese.

"He had a passion for antiquities."

"What an extraordinary thing," ejaculated Mr Stodham.

"Not very," said Mr Morgan. "He was acquisitive and had little curiosity. He was a collector of every sort and quality of old manuscript. Being an imperfectly self-educated man he probably got an innocent conceit from his learned occupation…"

"But how could he be an old curiosity man, and such an out-door man as well?"

"His asthma and pulmonary trouble, whatever it was, probably drove him out of doors. Borrow, who was a similar man of a different class, was driven out in the same way as a lad. Iolo's passion for poetry was not destroyed, but heightened, by his travels. God knows what poetry meant to him. But when he was in London, thinking of Wales and the white cots of Glamorgan, he wrote several stanzas of English verse. Sometimes he wrote about nymphs and swains, called Celia, Damon, Colin, and the like. He wrote a poem to Laudanum:

"'O still exert thy soothing power,
Till Fate leads on the welcom'd hour,
To bear me hence away;
To where pursues no ruthless foe,
No feeling keen awakens woe,
No faithless friends betray.'"

"I could do no worse than that," murmured Mr Stodham confidently.

"He wrote a sonnet to a haycock, and another to Hope on an intention of emigrating to America:

> "'Th' American wilds, where Simplicity's reign
> Will cherish the Muse and her pupil defend...
> I'll dwell with Content in the desert alone.'

They were blessed days when Content still walked the earth with a capital C, and probably a female form in light classic drapery. There was Felicity also. Iolo wrote 'Felicity, a pastoral.' He composed a poem to the cuckoo, and translated the famous Latin couplet which says that two pilgrimages to St David's are equivalent to one to Rome itself:

> "Would haughty Popes your senses bubble,
> And once to Rome your steps entice;
> 'Tis quite as well, and saves some trouble,
> Go visit old Saint Taffy twice."

He wrote quantities of hymns. Once, to get some girls out of a scrape – one having played 'The Voice of Her I Love' on the organ after service – he wrote a hymn to the tune, 'The Voice of the Beloved,' and fathered it on an imaginary collection of Moravian hymns. One other virtue he had, as a bard: he never repeated his own verses. God rest his soul. He was a walker, not a writer. The best of him – in fact, the real man altogether – refused to go into verse at all.

"Yet he had peculiarities which might have adorned a poet. Once, when he was on a job in a churchyard at Dartford, his master told him to go next morning to take certain measurements. He went, and, having taken the measurements, *woke*. It was pitch dark, but soon afterwards a clock struck two. In spite of the darkness he had not only done what he had to do, but he said that on his way to the churchyard every object appeared to him as clear as by day. The measurements were correct.

"One night, asleep in his chair, three women appeared to him, one with a mantle over her head. There was a sound like a gun, and one of the others fell, covered in blood. Next day, chance took him – was it chance? – into a farm near Cowbridge where he was welcomed by three women, one hooded in a shawl. Presently a young man entered with a gun, and laid it on the table, pointing at one of the women. At Iolo's warning it was discovered that the gun was primed and at full cock.

"Another time, between Cowbridge and Flimstone, he hesitated thrice at a stile, and then, going over, was just not too late to save a drunken man from a farmer galloping down the path.

"In spite of his Love of Light and Liberty, he was not above turning necromancer with wand and magic circle to convert a sceptic inn-keeper. He undertook to call up the man's grandfather, and after some gesticulations and muttering unknown words, he whispered, 'I feel the approaching spirit. Shall it appear?' The man whom he was intending to benefit became alarmed, and begged to be allowed to hear the ghost speak, first of all. In a moment a deep, sepulchral voice pronounced the name of the grandfather. The man had had enough. He bolted from the place, leaving Iolo and his confederates triumphant.

"Iolo should have been content to leave it unproved

that he was no poet. But he had not an easy life, and I suppose he had to have frills of some sort.

"Well, he walked home to Glamorgan. There he took a Glamorgan wife, Margaret Roberts of Marychurch, and he had to read less and work more to provide for a family. By the nature of his handiwork he was able to make more out of his verses than he would have done by printing better poetry. The vile doggerel which he inscribed on tombstones gained him a living and a sort of an immortality. He was one of the masons employed on the monument to the Man of Ross.

"Though a bad poet he was a Welsh bard. It was not the first or the last occasion on which the two parts were combined. Bard, for him, was a noble name. He was a 'Christian Briton and Bard' – a 'Bard according to the rights and institutes of the Bards of the Island of Britain' – and he never forgot the bardic triad, 'Man, Liberty, and Light.' Once, at the prison levee of a dissenting minister, he signed himself, 'Bard of Liberty.' To Southey, whom he helped with much out-of-the-way bardic mythology for his 'Madoc,' he was 'Bard Williams.'

"Bardism brought him into strange company, which I dare say he did not think strange, and certainly not absurd. Anna Seward, who mistook herself for a poet, and was one of the worst poets ever denominated 'Swan,' was kind to him in London. He in return initiated her into the bardic order at a meeting of 'Ancient British Bards resident in London,' which convened on Primrose Hill at the Autumnal equinox, 1793. At an earlier meeting, also on Primrose Hill, he had recited an 'Ode on the Mythology of the British Bards in the manner of Taliesin,' and, since this poem was subsequently approved at the equinoctial, and ratified at the solstitial, convention, it was, according to ancient usage, fit for publication. It was not a reason. Nevertheless, a bard is a bard, whatever else he may or may not be.

"Iolo was proud to declare that the old Welsh bards had kept up a perpetual war with the church of Rome, and had suffered persecution. 'Man, Liberty, and Light.' You and I, Mr Stodham, perhaps don't know what he meant. But if Iolo did not know, he was too happy to allow the fact to emerge and trouble him.

"Of course, he connected the bards with Druidism, which he said they had kept alive. A good many sectarians would have said that he himself was as much a Druid as a Christian. He accepted the resurrection of the dead. He did not reject the Druid belief in transmigration of souls. He identified Druidism with the patriarchal religion of the Old Testament, but saw in it also a pacific and virtually Christian spirit. He affirmed that Ancient British Christianity was strongly tinctured by Druidism, and it was his opinion that the 'Dark Ages' were only dark through our lack of light. He hated the stories of Caesar and others about human sacrifices, and would say to opponents, 'You are talking of what you don't understand – of what none but a Welshman and a British bard *can possibly* understand.' He compared the British mythology favourably with the 'barbarous' Scandinavian mythology of Thor and Odin. He studied whatever he could come at concerning Druidism, with the 'peculiar bias and firm persuasion' that 'more wisdom and beneficence than is popularly attributed to them' would be revealed.

"In the French Revolution he recognised the spirit of 'Man, Liberty, and Light.' His friends deserted him. He in turn was willing to leave them for America, 'to fly from the numerous injuries he had received from the laws of this land.' He had, furthermore, the hope of discovering the colony settled in America, as some believed, by the mediaeval Welsh prince Madoc."

"That was like Borrow, too," suggested Mr Stodham.

"It was, and the likeness is even closer; for, like Borrow, Iolo did not go to America. Nevertheless, to prepare himself for the adventure, he lived out of doors for a time, sleeping in trees and on the ground, and incurring rheumatism.

"But though he did not go to America for love of Liberty, he had his papers seized, and is said to have been summoned by Pitt for disaffection to the State. Nothing worse was proved against him than the authorship of several songs in favour of Liberty, 'perhaps,' said his biographer, 'a little more extravagant than was quite commendable at that inflammatory period.' They expected him to remove his papers himself, but he refused, and had them formally restored by an official. When he was fifty he gave up his trade because the dust of the stone was injuring his lungs. He now earned a living by means of a shop at Cowbridge where books, stationery, and grocery were sold. His speciality was 'East India Sweets uncontaminated by human gore.' Brothers of his who had made money in Jamaica offered to allow him £50 a year, but in vain. 'It was a land of slaves,' he said. He would not even administer their property when it was left to him, though a small part was rescued later on by friends, for his son and daughter. The sound of the bells at Bristol celebrating the rejection of Wilberforce's Anti-Slavery Bill drove him straight out of the city. Believing that he was spied upon at Cowbridge he offered a book for sale in his window, labelled 'The Rights of Man.' He was successful. The spies descended on him, seized the book, and discovered that it was the Bible, not the work of Paine.

"He was personally acquainted with Paine and with a number of other celebrities, such as Benjamin Franklin, Bishop Percy, Horne Tooke, and Mrs Barbauld. Once in a bookshop he asked Dr Johnson to choose for him among three English grammars. Johnson was turning over the leaves of a book, 'rapidly and as the bard thought petulantly': 'Either of them will do for you, young man,' said he. 'Then, sir,' said Iolo, thinking Johnson was insulting his poverty, 'to make sure of having the best I will buy all'; and he used always to refer to them as 'Dr Johnson's Grammars.' It was once arranged that he should meet Cowper, but the poet sat, through the evening, silent, unable to encounter the introduction.

"The excesses of the Revolution, it is said, drove Iolo to abandon the idea of a Republic, except as a 'theoretical model for a free government.' He even composed an ode to the Cowbridge Volunteers. Above all, he wrote an epithalamium on the marriage of George the Fourth, which he himself presented, dressed in a new apron of white leather and carrying a bright trowel. His 'English Poems' were dedicated to the Prince of Wales."

"What a fearful fall," exclaimed Mr Strodham, who may himself have been a Bard of Liberty.

"But his business, apart from his trade, was antiquities, and especially the quest of them up and down Wales."

"I shouldn't be surprised," said Mr Stodham, "if the old man hoped for some grand result from meddling with those mysterious old books and papers – perhaps nothing definite, health, wealth, wisdom, beauty, everlasting life, or the philosopher's stone, – but some old secret of Bardism or Druidism, which would glorify Wales, or Cowbridge, or Old Iolo himself."

"Very likely. He was to a scientific antiquary what a witch is to an alchemist, and many a witch got a reputation with less to her credit than he had.

"As a boy he remembered hearing an old shoemaker of Llanmaes (near Lantwit) speak of the shaft of an ancient cross, in Lantwit churchyard, falling into a grave that had been dug too near it for Will the Giant of Lantwit. As a middle-aged man he dug up the stone. It was less love of antiquity than of mystery, buried treasure, and the like. He was unweariable in his search for the remains of Ancient British literature. At the age of seventy, when the Bishop of St David's had mislaid some of his manuscripts and they had thus been sold, Iolo walked over Caermarthenshire, Pembrokeshire, and Cardiganshire, and recovered the greater part. He took a pony with him as far as Caermarthen, but would not allow it to carry his wallets until at last it was arranged that his son should walk on one side and himself on the other, which made him remark that 'nothing was more fatiguing than a horse.' The horse appears in a triad of his own composition:

"There are three things I do not want. A Horse, for I have a good pair of legs:

A Cellar, for I drink no beer: a Purse, for I have no money.

"He would not ride in Lord Dunraven's carriage, but preferred to walk. That he did not dislike the animal personally is pretty clear. For at one time he kept a horse which followed him, of its own free will, upon his walks.

"Iolo was a sight worth seeing on the highways and byways of Glamorgan, and once had the honour of being taken for a conjuror. His biographer – a man named Elijah Waring, who was proud to have once carried his wallets – describes him 'wearing his long grey hair flowing over his high coat collar, which, by constant antagonism, had pushed up his hatbrim into a quaint angle of elevation behind. His countenance was marked by a combination of quiet intelligence and quick sensitiveness; the features regular, the lines deep, and the grey eye benevolent but highly excitable. He was clad, when he went to see a bishop, in a new coat fit for an admiral, with gilt buttons and buff waistcoat, but, as a rule, in rustic garb: the coat blue, with goodly brass buttons, and the nether integuments, good homely corduroy. He wore buckles in his shoes, and a pair of remarkably stout, well-set legs were vouchers for the great peripatetic powers he was well known to possess. A pair of canvas wallets were slung over his shoulders, one depending in front, the other behind. These contained a change of linen, and a few books and papers connected with his favourite pursuits. He generally read as he walked… .'"

"Tut, tut," remarked Mr Stodham, "that spoils all."

"He generally read as he walked, 'with spectacles on nose,' and a pencil in his hand, serving him to make notes as they suggested themselves. Yet he found time also, Mr Stodham, to sow the tea-plant on the hills of

Glamorgan. 'A tall staff which he grasped at about the level of his ear completed his equipment; and he was accustomed to assign as a reason for this mode of using it, that it tended to expand the pectoral muscles, and thus, in some degree, relieve a pulmonary malady inherent in his constitution.'

"He did not become a rich man. Late one evening he entered a Cardiganshire public-house and found the landlord refusing to let a pedlar pay for his lodging in kind, though he was penniless. Iolo paid the necessary shilling for a bed and rated the landlord, but had to walk on to a distant friend because it was his last shilling. Yet he wrote for the *Gentleman's Magazine* and corresponded with the *Monthly* and others, so that towards the end he was entitled to advances from the Literary Fund. An annual subscription was also raised for him in Neath and the neighbourhood. His last three years he spent at Flimstone, where he is buried. He was a cripple and confined to the house, until one day he rested his head on the side of his easy chair and told his daughter that he was free from pain and could sleep, and so he died."

"I will certainly go to Craig-y-Dinas," said Mr Stodham solemnly, "and to Penon, and to Cowbridge, and to Flimstone." "You will do well," said Mr Morgan, shutting up Elijah Waring's little book and getting out a map of Glamorgan.

****

Swansea Village, 1914

'Swansea Village' was first published in The English Review in June, 1914, and then reprinted in The Last Sheaf in 1928. Edward Thomas's fascination with Swansea grew throughout his life, at the start of this essay he says 'year after year I go there'. His first visits were to the picturesque areas of West Swansea – Mumbles and Gower, but later he discovered the docks and metalworks and working-class housing of the East, and he marvelled and wondered at those streets named after favourite Romantic poets. This profound dichotomy made a deep impression on him. He wrote to his friend Jesse Berridge after a visit to Swansea, describing it as a 'sublime and horrible town', continuing, 'it is very large... all furnaces, collieries, filth, stench, poverty and extravagant show, the country and the sea at the very edge of it'.

Edward Thomas's description of Swansea in this essay as 'not this or that, beautiful or hideous', seems to anticipate Dylan Thomas's famous description of the town as being an 'ugly, lovely town'. Certainly, in a letter Edward Thomas wrote to his friend from Oxford, A. D. Williams, in 1911, he seems to predict the arrival of Dylan Thomas into Swansea when he comments, 'if Wales could produce a poet he should be born in the hills and come here [to Swansea] at the age of 16. He would have no need of Heaven or Hell'.

In this context it's interesting to note what R.George Thomas had to say about Edward and Dylan Thomas:

When Dylan and I first met... and talked about poetry, we found we both admired Edward Thomas's personal yet mysteriously opaque poem The Other as much as we applauded his sharply critical essay on Swansea Village that had recently been reprinted in last Sheaf (1928).

George goes on to suggest that 'now for me the tone of this essay and many others in 'The Last Sheaf' is echoed in quite a few of Dylan's off-the-cuff radio commentaries on some towns where he happened to be.'

A great many people know that Swansea is a Welsh seaport and manufacturing town, the centre of a district where it has been said that 'nine-tenths of the entire make of copper in Great Britain' is smelted; that it has claims to be called the 'Metropolis of South Wales'; that its football team beat the South Africans; that Beau Nash was born there, and Landor dwelt there, making love to some one named Ione or Jones, and writing 'Gebir'; that it possesses a ruined castle and a new 'Empire'; that it lies across the visitor's road to Gower. Here and there more can be heard of it. One of its parks, says a lady, had for some time a clock with the hours (like Marvell's dial) marked in flowers. Another avers that the town smells, and that the inhabitants either do not know or do not care, some holding the opinion that one of the smells is beneficial. – It is a magnificent town, of which some, if not Landor, might say even to-day that for scenery and climate it excels the Gulf of Salerno or the Bay of Naples. – It is a sordid hag of a town, sitting shameless amid the ruins of its natural magnificence. – It is as good as Blackpool. –

There is 'nothing particular' in it, nothing old and picturesque, nothing new and grand or even expensive. – Many of its dark-haired and pale-skinned women are beautiful. – And so on.

But this I cannot understand: that some people should be – and some are – indifferent to Swansea. Year after year I go there (I do not mean to the Mumbles, but to the town, and nothing but the town), and walk up and down it and round about, inhaling sea air and mountain air, or the smells from copper works, cobalt works, manure works, and fried-fish shops; year after year I have felt that only friends could bring me again to Swansea. But the town is a dirty witch. You must hate or love her, and I both love her and hate her, and return to her as often as four times in a year. It is not this or that beautiful or hideous thing that draws me. I do not go to see a woman pitching broken crockery out of her front door into a street where children go barefooted; nor to smell the stale fat of the skin-yard, and see shaggy cattle driven into the slaughter-house, and a woman carrying a baby in a shawl after them; nor to hear midnight quarrelling in the Irish quarter – a woman at first having it her own way, shouting louder and louder and drowning the man's bass interjections, then wildly screaming 'Bastard, bastard,' until the cry is smothered in noises of scuffling and throttling, and the victor's voice rising for a moment as he strikes, and, after that, her sobbing and moaning, that ends in silence broken only by the child they have awakened. I do not go because they will tell me those brand-new edifices are on the site of the old block-cottages 'where the bad women lived' – as if the 'bad women' were used in the foundations or had been

scared out of their iniquity by the splendours of architecture. The pleasant accidents are many in Swansea. The
docks are always pleasant with the smell of tar, the weaving
whirl of sea-gulls, the still ships, the cold green water re-
flecting the gaudy figurehead of the *Kate,* the men unloading
potatoes, the painter slung under the bowsprit, with a fag
in his mouth, which he puts behind his ear to whistle
'Away to Rio.' For that minute the ship looks like a beautiful
great captive beast, beautiful in the same manner as the
neighbouring caged thrush's song of pure thickets, the sun,
the wind, and the rain. I like, too, the rag-and-bone man
blowing one deep note on his horn as he travels mean
streets; and the cockle-women (their white, scoured cockle-
tubs on their heads or under their arms) from Penclawdd,
dressed in half a dozen thicknesses of flannel, striped and
checked, all different and all showy – with broad hips, no
waists, stout legs slowly and powerfully moving, and the
clearest of complexions and brightest of lips and eyes under
their fine soft brown hair. Six days of the week I like the
whole Swansea crowd of factory men and girls, the shawled
mothers, the seamen, the country folk, though not one
element is exceptionally picturesque.

These pleasant and unpleasant things, however, have
little to do with the final effect, composite but very definite, of the whole town: they colour certain days, but no
more. What counts most is the careless, graceless nature
of Swansea, its lordly assemblage of chimney-stacks, its
position at a river mouth between mountains, and the
neighbourhood of the sea. Cheapness, *clapham-junction,*
squalor, or actual hideousness is everywhere in contrast
with grandeur, and even sublimity, and these qualities do

not alternate, but conflict, or in some way co-operate. In the central streets, broad and glassy, thronged to the point of tumult with men and beasts and every kind of vehicle; in the outward-going roads of monotonous, and dismal or unclean, cottages, threaded by electric trams and country carts, and in sunless courts where privacy and publicity are one, you have always in sight either sea or mountain.

For the greater part of the town is built on riverside and seaside ground, where the mountains open a little wider apart to make way for the River Tawe. Two steep and treeless mountains hang over it. One of them, called at different points Mount Pleasant (where the workhouse is), Gibbet Hill, and Town Hill, is more or less green, but carved by quarries, and now higher and higher up striped with horizontal lines of plainest cottages and of villas pretending to some form of prettiness, all set among wastes of poor grass, feverfew, and wormwood. The straight ascents are as steep as the street at Clovelly, the paving-stones in some being tilted out of the flush to give a foothold. Once the springs in this hillside fed several wells of some fame, such as the Baptist Well and St. Helen's Well, which are commemorated only in the names of streets. Kilvey, the other hill, is green to seaward, but where it falls most abruptly, and the valley between it and the Town Hill is narrowest, it has been stripped by poisonous smoke and covered with a deposit of slag, except on the perpendicular juts, which reveal the strata of blackish rock; a chimney pierces the summit and stands out against the sky. The lowest parts alone of this hill are littered with houses, but on a high green terrace seaward linger a white rustic cottage and a small farm-house or two, and above them, at the very ridge, an old windmill tower.

The town cannot forget these two hills, whether they rise clear in their green or their drabby black, or whether the flurries of mist reveal a momentary and fragmentary glimpse of Kilvey's hilltop chimney or windmill tower, a grisly baseless precipice and a gull passing it, a gleam of white wall. Between the hills bends the river, the yellow Tawe. The factories crowd to its right bank, opposite to Kilvey, in order to get rid of their gilded and other filth, and to receive the ships; in the mud and yellow stones rests the two-masted *Audacieuse,* of St. Valery-sur-Somme, discharging phosphates, while three men in blue stand below to caulk and paint her. In spite of the colour of the water, numbers of people have fallen into it, some by accident, some after deliberation. The one footbridge crosses at the docks, where the character of the river is lost. Only a ferry plies from among the factories to the few undesirable houses under the steepest and barest part of Kilvey. A man, therefore, might live in Swansea without knowing of the river. But the mountains which it cleaves are omnipresent, and from many places its course can be seen far away inland through heights green with grass, grey with bare rock, or violet with distance.

The low waterside crowd of copper, steel, tin, zinc, silver, cobalt, manure and other works is the real Swansea. The remainder, the miles of flat-faced cottages here or upon the hill, is but an inexpensive prison where the workers may feed, smoke, read the newspapers, breed, and sleep. Those works vomit the smokes which Swansea people either ignore or praise; for when the smell from the manure works pervades the town, they expect fine weather from a north or north-east wind. They take you up on the Town Hill at night to see the furnaces in the pit of the town blazing scarlet, and the parallel and crossing lines of lamps, which seem, like the stars, to be decoration. If it is always a city of dreadful day, it is for the moment and at that distance a city of wondrous night. I have seen the steel works – I think when the roof was uncovered for repairs – look like a range of burning organ-pies, while overhead hung, or imperceptibly flowed, a white spread of smoke, hiding the hills and half of the black, starry sky, but only half veiling the tall chimneys which silently increased it. At dawn it is worthwhile to see the furnaces paling, Kilvey very clear and dark, and the few stars white above it. Dawn climbs over Kilvey Hill into Swansea.

By day the scene is better, because the variety is greater, according to the wind and the lie of the sea mist, the river mist, and the smoke, both the accumulations and the individual tributaries of smoke; and because then can be seen the dim ridges of the greater mountains beyond the chimneys, and in the other direction a hundred moods of the sea and the coast hills. The furnaces, the vast, sooty sheds clanging and clattering, the fuming slag hills, where women crawl raking for something less than gold, and, above all, the grouped or single chimneys standing irregularly beside the river, are more worth looking at than a model town.

As for the chimneys, like gigantic tree-trunks or temple pillars that have survived some gigantic desolation, these and their plumes of smoke or of flame are among the most unforgettable things that men have made. The black hills and vales of Landore, its fire-palaces and hundred smoke-stacks, compose one of the sublimest of all absolutely human landscapes. The slag heaps are venerable even in age. One of them, still growing in the midst of the town, is about a century old, and with the two blackened cottages nestling at its foot it would seem a considerable hill were it not backed and dwarfed by Kilvey. It is one of the boundaries to a characteristic Swansea waste – several uneven acres, strewn with brickbats, trodden in all directions, without grass, and on the other sides bounded by houses, a big school, and a church about as high as the hill of slag. Evidently this land once served some purpose, is now disused, and is waiting for a day when time is no longer money. Similar spaces are sometimes occupied by the town refuse, which the east wind distributes and the 'Rising Sun' washes down. Out of one broad space, black and scarred by watercourses from the mountain, a small part has been railed in for a children's playground, with swings, parallel bars, and seats; but no grass grows there. Numerous lesser wastes mark where houses have been or are to be, and at present they are useful sites for a pile of tins, glass, earthenware, rags, sweepings, tea-leaves, and fish-bones; nettle and wormwood flourish. These are in the more domestic portions of the town. Among the factories can be seen many a disastrous black wilderness, a black, empty amphitheatre traversed by the yellow river. Another kind of waste is the marshland above the town proper, invaded on one side by tips of slag, but too marshy for the most cynical builder, and still left, therefore, to rush and thistle.

Everywhere decay and ruin make their boast side by

side with growth. Disused workshops are not supplanted, but are spared by some form of piety to stand and thin into skeletons, with gaping walls and roofs, to fall gradually in heaps among their successors. The sheds with rafters broken, tiles slipping, bricks dislodged, the derelict and tumbling cottages, the waste places of slag, old masonry, and dust, tufted with feverfew, the yards cumbered by rusty iron implements and rubbish, the red rivulet plunging in black gorges, speak rather of a bloodily conquered and deserted city than of a claimant to be the 'Metropolis of South Wales.' But round the corner a new block of buildings, including a chemist's and a sweet-shop, followed by cottages with painted wooden porches, and then a three-year-old chapel filled by a noble hymn wailing triumphantly, and next a view of twenty chimneys and of hills divided into squares of corn and grass and irregular woods, revive the claim. And yet this chapel is at the foot of a rough quarried slope sprinkled thinly and anyhow with white and whitish cottages among rushes and tufted grass, which is a scene of an almost moorland sweetness for those living in the new-old streets of eternal smoke under the mountain opposite, barren and black.

The same piety spares also the deserted dwelling. The old mountain farm-house, whose pastures entertain footballers instead of cattle, is left to gather moss and docks on its thatch, and stones (thrown at the windows) in all its rooms. The ferry-boat from the works over to Foxhole, a straggling settlement between the bare steep of Kilvey Hill and the river, lands you by a bunch of four old cottages of the colour of scorched paper, the walls of their tiny yards collapsing, and all windowless except the one which gives some reason for supposing it to be inhabited by human beings. Nearer the centre of the town other dwellings have attained a similar condition. Whole streets of houses, too old at fifty or sixty, have been condemned, but are still used because they are, at any rate, warmer than the outer air. When new cottages are built they often stand against the ruined ones instead of taking their places, just as the new church at Llansamlet stands against the partly ruinous old tower.

The houses are seldom of the material and make to be comely in their old age. The flat fronts shed their grimy plaster in flakes; the windows are like the eyes of the blind; the miniature gardens consist of fowl-houses, nasturtiums, and cats; and from the gramophone comes a frivolous London tune, or from the harmonium 'Yes, Jesus loves me,' while at the back door a woman washes in the sun. Until they are well advanced in decay, they are hardly interesting, save to the occupiers and to sanitary authorities and housing committees. Almost all of them have been erected in long, straight bars or blocks during the early or late nineteenth century. They peel or split and become dirty, but their two windows and a door, or three windows and a door, have to depend for variety of expression on a barber's pole or coloured advertisements; very few have front gardens. Old age and neatness seldom adorn the same house in Swansea. As it ages it falls into worse and worse hands; the garden is given over to wormwood, and a piece of semi-rustic slum is completed. Signs of ease, opulence and pleasure, mysteriously created by men and machinery, are to be seen in the high-placed villas towards the sea, but they have no individuality except what is given here and there by a piece of cliffy garden.

The best, as well as probably the oldest, building in Swansea is the castle. It is wedged in, and actually incorporated, among shops and dwellings, though it displays a beautiful range of arcading above their roofs; a telegraph-post sticks up in the middle; but it still protects a small, inaccessible patch of long green grass on one side between it and the street wall, where a building site is advertised. Its position low down near the river, obscured by the glories of the principal street, denies it the impressiveness of the so-called Trewyddfa Castle which crowns a steep isolated hill farther inland at the verge of the town. This is a spare, craggy ruin, like a few rotten old teeth, near Landore station, but high and distinct above the pale, scrambling cottages of the slopes. Not a hundred years ago, they say, the 'castle' was built by a public man as a residence, that he might refute with ostentation the charge of penury. But he was not a Norman baron, and, lacking power or courage or imagination to raid the neighbourhood with arms, he could not endure life on his eminence very long. The forsaken mansion was let out in tenements, failed as such, and was finally offered to rain and wind as the material for an apparently feudal ruin. They have performed their task to admiration: Trewyddfa Castle is the only thing in Swansea to satisfy a taste for the medi-aeval picturesque. At the foot of its hill, horses pasture among gipsy vans, slag heaps, cottages, and the remains of cottages.

Swansea is too busy to invent an Arthurian or feudal tale about this 'castle,' or in any way to coin money out of it. Of the vanity of picturesqueness the town altogether lacks traces. And yet some money has been spent on making the old round windmill tower, towards the seaward and green end of Kilvey Hill, impervious to weather, boys and the few dirty-faced cows of those pastures. Seats have been placed on two sides, because it is on the flat at the very top of the hill, and eastward, southward and northward the eye ranges without impediment. To the south are the lowest-lying parts of Swansea, the mathematical lines of the docks, a steamer hooting as she enters, many sailing vessels at rest and silent, and trains shunting with noises as of a drunken orchestra tuning up – the yellow-sanded bay curving under a wall of woods to the horned rocks and lighthouse of the Mumbles – the main sea and the aerial distant masses of Exmoor and the Mendips. A world of domed or abrupt mountains to the north is broken up by the valleys of the Neath and Tawe rivers. The waveless, effervescent blue sea to eastward is edged by dunes, and behind them by wooded or bracken-covered high hills with emerald clefts; and the white and the dirty smoke of Neath and Port Talbot rises between the sands and the hills.

The seats round the windmill tower are a little worn; but I never saw anyone there, nor met anyone who had been there. Why should people go up? Not to gain a view, certainly. Swansea has as many views as smells. Every street has a view at one end or the other; some have one at both. For example, Byron Crescent, and, better still, Shelley Crescent, new streets high up on the green hill and curving with it, command so much of sea and mountain that their names are not ridiculous.

Steepness forbids houses to be built on both sides of the horizontal street, and enables Shelley Crescent to look clear over the back of Byron Crescent. One end looks on Kilvey Hill, the riverside works at its foot, the lines of the multitudes of cottages, the dotted 'castle' mound, and beyond it the greater mountains. The scene from the other end includes first the docks, the slated, rectangular labyrinth of the town, hardly diversified by a few churches, a gasometer, and here and there a row of elms or poplars, or a single tree, projecting as it were out of fissures in that mass of brick and stone; and the silver, cold, rippled sea, with slashes of foam, stretching away to the hills of Glamorgan, hazy with smoke, and to the hills of Somerset, which are as clouds. In twenty years Shelley Crescent will be old, and they will have forgotten to paint the woodwork; but the sea and the far mountains will be the same, and Kilvey can hardly avoid being still half green, half black. By that time Swansea may have a quarter of a million inhabitants; I shall not guess whether the village will have become a town. At present it is probably more a village than when the borough counted about a thousand under Elizabeth. Its activity in spreading hither and thither has kept it from thinking about anything but factories, docks, and the necessities of life. That is the dark charm of Swansea to one who has not to live in it. It is careless of itself, of its majestic position, its lovely neighbourhood, its hundred and twenty thousand men, women, and children. Compared with Cardiff, it is a slattern. Yet, being a spectator, I am glad that I have known Swansea between these hills, and not a lesser Cardiff or Liverpool. Equally shameless and unpretentious, it swarms about the Tawe, climbs over the hill with inconsiderate vitality, always allowing the magnitude and precipitousness of its hills to have full effect, while they in their turn emphasize the rustic squalor and confused simplicity of the town, combining with it to make a character which at the same moment irritates and fascinates.

***

Penderyn, 1914

The holograph manuscript of this story is in the Berg Collection in New York Public Library. It is dated 6 November 1914. It was first published in Poetry Wales in 1978. R. George Thomas writes in his introduction to the 1981 edition:

Penderyn written in the first months of the war is, apart from his War Diary entries, his last prose attempt to record experiences and evocations that he had always invested with charged significance – often called 'prose poems' by him and his friends – but which soon fed into the clear, limpid strain of his verse once it had begun to flow in that same November.

Guy Cuthbertson includes it in his recent edition of Thomas's prose and suggests it is 'Thomas's last landscape essay'. Thomas ends the piece with a discussion of the etymology of the place name, mentioning 'One of the first Welsh melodies I ever heard was 'The girl of Penderyn parish' and that the village was once the home of 'Dick Penderyn... a kind of Dick Turpin'. These days Dick (now

*more often rendered Dic) is seen as a working-class martyr
– having been wrongfully hanged following an incident in
the Merthyr Rising of 1831.*

Except when I crossed it the river Neath was generally
hidden either by oak, ash or elder lining it or by the dry
and grey boulders on its wide bed. I'd for the most part
kept with it on the levels of the valley. The hills on either
side were sometimes cloven but for many miles unbroken.
They had a skyline usually of bare stone and ruddy
bracken, but, especially at a cleft, a great (part) of their
slopes down in the valley wore a fur of oak woods. Now
a colliery's precipitous smooth black terrace, now the
white bar of a house front, broke the autumnal mixture of
the woods.

Then I came to a village, and the river bed by the bridge
was warm and deep and the river, fresh from a waterfall,
poured out into the light under ash trees. As the river
was now little more than a brook, the hills of its valley
sides were now mountains, and preferred rocks upon their
slopes to woods. The mountains were broken on either
hand by the valleys of several traverses. Far ahead
Brecknock Beacons stood across the valley I was ascending
in a line of dark cones; where a light from between clouds
sailed across them the bare and uninhabited slopes glowed
a ruddy brown.

But the tops and the highest one visible was for ever
black. A lower hill intervened, cutting off all but the tops,
which showed above the ridge of it and looked like a flat
table, but gradually moved into position as something
like the butt of a tree sawn off straight and split down

the middle by a notch called The Wind's Gap. The nearer hill had a profile of rocks like a broad seat or platform and steps leading down from it; its upper slope ended in rock and nothing but rock like the curtain wall of a castle. On the other hand, that is on the left or to the west, the hills were less boldly featured expanses, showing a fin or two among tall trees at long intervals and far off a colliery with chimney smoking. There was now no valley, and not a yard of level clean ground between these hills. The river in one place ran black underground, and in another danced down a quarter of a mile of cascades white as milk. My road rose and fell towards the Beacons, over rough rushy common, or between ferny walls, past a white chapel and a farmhouse by a brook that ran over slabs under mountain ash berries. But I left the road and went down over the river and up beyond it towards that chair-like mountain, and along under the main steep of it I could see a pale road, a motor car crawling up on it towards the Beacons, racing a pony leaping upon the rough mountain over ditches, scattering sheep.

The fields down by the river were very green, enclosed, and protected by a few farmhouses and trees. But up above them all was open fern. Nothing bigger than a hawthorn grew there, except where I crossed the River Fellte, or rather the dry boulders of its channel, a few rocks sprinkled with silver lay about. Trees stood there faithfully. The rough ground was broken also by pits with pools at the bottom and the curly tailed foals shared it with sheep. It was crossed by tramlines from a quarry, so slight they seemed not so much to invade the mountain as to emphasize the calm mountain wilderness; the harsh stone piled at the quarry half a mile distant, and the dusty men passing me on the way to homes far off, added a touch of dreariness, the very least touch. It was made lonelier by the story of Mary Nant-y-Deri. She used to keep ponies in this mountain beyond Penderyn, and lived at her farmhouse alone in spite of warnings. One night she was found dead there. The house had been ransacked, but her money hidden under a basin escaped. An attempt had been made to burn the old woman, to pretend that she had set fire to her clothing and burnt to death, but her flannel would not burn. The murderer was never caught.

It was only when I had climbed some way that I saw Penderyn Church against the sky about three miles distant. My road was bending towards it, that is to the right, along under the hill like the motor road away from the Beacons. Chancel, nave, and square low tower in a row, and some neighbouring trees stood very clearly out on the ridge of a low hill. The hill itself to the left of the church has been cut by the quarry to a face like a wall: on the other side rose up a considerable dome called Penderyn Fach, for the most part bare even when it had not been quarried.

Very slowly that raw brown quarry became clearer. The road approached the main road at an acute angle. The land began to be hedged and green: there were sycamores and ash trees and a farm showing white among them. The road reaching the foot of the church had turned and crawled round it, and the village lay chiefly upon the road. Only a narrow lane went straight and steep up to the inn. The lane was full of mourners all in black except a baby who wore a long white shawl and was carried by the only man of the company. They were wandering slowly down admiring the mountain eastward. The rest of the male mourners were drinking and talking up above at the Red Lion opposite the church. The church, a plain building of harsh stone on the highest ground, was locked, but the grave digger was still at work filling up with bits of limestone the grave of a Morgan or Jones or Jenkins or Evans, another Gwenllian or David to be commemorated like the rest with a dark stone, which in its turn would be decorated by blackish lichen of liver shape. A few of the dead upon the slope had something more than a slab. Some angels and spire-like tombs were conspicuous against the sky. One of these greater stones bore many names, and I heard it said that two of them were brothers, young gentlemen who had gone to penal service for tarring and feathering and causing the death of an old man. They had died not long after leaving prison. One broad horizontal stone marked the grave of George Menelaus, a great ironmaster of Dowlais. The grass grew among the tombs thick and long, and frequently yellow brown flax with it. The ash trees which had been visible along beside the church loosely surrounded the churchyard. Nothing was here to remind me of August but Penderyn and the mountains, nothing to interfere with (it), nothing that did not give light and substance to the shadowy and tenuous beauty of the mere name Penderyn.

And yet it was little more than a name. its builders were dry mountain ones. Yet when I crossed the brook, the rustle of an overhanging aspen deceived me into thinking I heard water run. Between that sound and the rush of water there is not more difference than between the meaning of Penderyn to me and its meaning to an inhabitant.

Years before someone had waved his whip towards the mountains saying 'Penderyn is beyond that hill!' One of the first Welsh melodies I ever heard was that of 'The girl of Penderyn parish'. And once upon a time fresh years ago there lived a certain Dick Penderyn, a kind of Dick Turpin. So that evening the name was still pure music, perhaps more earthly than before, more definitely mountainous, perhaps the sweetest pace name in the world.

**

Four-and-Twenty Blackbirds, 1915

This collection of short stories, Edward Thomas's only attempt at a children's book, was aimed at the older reader. It was published with a dust jacket with a mounted colour plate by Betty Martin, which was also used as a frontispiece. Thomas would have liked the whole book to be illustrated but this never transpired. The book takes twenty-four proverbs from around the British Isles and makes them the basis of twenty-four tales, hence the title. Thomas's close friend, Edward Garnett, wrote a glowing reader's report for the prospective publishers, Duckworth, in which he enthused:

> *charming... absolutely perfect in style, full of clear, fresh colouring and most gay and ingenious in the simple twists of the story... The book ought to be a classic.*

Edward Thomas had enlisted in the Artists Rifles in July of that year. It is chilling to imagine him correcting the proofs of these 'most gay' children's stories in an army camp in High Beech, 'digging drains, carpentering, digging clay and spading it into a cart, with a bully over us' and writing with apparent nonchalance in a letter that 'apparently any man who will stand up and be shot is useful however hurried his training'.

One Swallow Doesn't Make A Summer

There was a poet in North Wales long ago named Rhys, who loved April because he loved sun, rain, and wind, separately and all together. As soon as April came he began to write poems, saying why April was better than March and May. One year, however, he cut his hand so badly in a briar bush by the river Alun that he could not write, yet he was sure that the poem which he made in his head on the first of April was better than any he had ever written down. He had found a swallow at the edge of the river, dead, killed by a hawk. First he had cried over the swallow. Then the sun had come out, and he made the poem. He had tried hard to write it down with his left hand, using a quill from the dead swallow's wing, dipping it in the blood of his wounded right hand. But he was too impatient. The first verse looked very bad, written slowly and awkwardly with the left hand, and he threw it angrily into the water. He had made up his mind what to do.

He went to a monk, an old man, and asked him to take down the poem from his dictation, though he knew in his heart that the poem was so good that he never would forget it. The monk did as he was asked, but Rhys left the poem with him in order that it might be copied out at leisure in his best handwriting and sent o the prince.

That night Rhys was taken ill; before he had seen another swallow he was dead. His last message was that the poem should be carried to the prince.

Now, the monk hated poems, and especially those that were written in Welsh instead of in Latin. And Rhys's poem seemed to him the most foolish poem that was ever written, even in Welsh, because every verse said that the dead swallow had brought the Summer on its wings and that now, since the bird was dead, Summer could not escape from Wales. This was ridiculous, it was a lie, said the monk. Summer was not a thing, said he. Besides, he added, Summer will come to all the wold, and not Wales only. Had this Swallow brought it from land to land, he asked. Moreover, he sneered, not a thousand swallows can make Summer if it is wet and cold. For this reason, and also because he hoped that he might have the poet's place of honour with the prince, the monk destroyed the poem, and wrote a very bad one of his own.

The monk's poem was contrary to Rhys's; at the end of every verse were the words: 'One swallow doesn't make a summer.' It pleased him so much that he sent it to the prince.

But the prince loved Rhys. When the monk's poem arrived he was still sorrowing for the poet's death, and the stuff changed his sorrow into anger. 'What bad verses,' he exclaimed, wishing more than ever that he had not lost his poet. The line, 'One swallow doesn't make a summer' particularly enraged him. 'Neither does one bad poem make a poet,' he cried, as he gave the manuscript to the goat to eat. The monk was disappointed. Nevertheless, whenever a swallow came in April and bad weather followed, somebody remembered the bad poem and the line: 'One swallow doesn't make a summer'; for the verse that Rhys tossed into the river was lost for ever, and there was nothing left of his poem to prove that the monk was wrong.

***

The Nearer The Bone The Sweeter The Meat

At Dynevor Castle in Caermarthenshire, high and stern above the River Towy and its fruitful meadows and quiet farm-folk, dwelt a prince who was very proud. His name was Urien. At the age of thirty he was lord of that land, its people, beasts, salmon, and corn. For his tall stature and strength and handsomeness, for his skill in war and hunting, for his black horse Arthur, and his sword Merlin, and his lance Uther, and for all his other great possessions, he was envied by many princes; but for his pride he was hated both by princes and by common men. He was not cruel; to children and animals he was often tender as a woman; but he was proud, and he looked like pride itself.

The bard Carvilios wrote poems in praise of Urien, and one of them excused his pride. "Urien" – so ran the poem – "Urien can love nothing that is not free as the north wind, as bright as mountain water, as read as mountain-ash berries, as white as snow, as black as the raven, as bold as the peregrine falcon, as swift as the stag, as musical as the poems of Carvilios, as beautiful as was Olwen his eighteen-year-old wife when she died. Therefore Urien is sorry for common men or women, with heavy motion, dull wit, hoarse voice, and no abounding beauty or strength or skill, and he cannot endure them. He has set his eyes on the hills: when he casts them down he frowns. Envy him not, for he is alone like the eagle on the cliff, like the sun in the heaven; and who envies them?"

Yet men hated Urien. Once he came into the chapel with his scarlet-hooded falcon upon his wrist, and, standing up, he listened a little while to the priest. He shifted upon his feet and his spurs rang with music sweeter than the bells at High Mass in the Cathedral at St David's. Outside the chapel door the horse Arthur heard the spurs, and he shifted upon his feet impatiently, and Urien heard him, and frowned, and turned and went out and rode away with hound and falcon.

This was the last time that Urien was seen by any man of the Towy valley. For on that day he rode far. He seemed to be following the white clouds that swept over the mountain tops swiftly towards the north. The black horse and its rider in green and gold with plume of white, the dappled hounds, the red falcon, were seen above Towy and Teivy and Severn, and none that saw them believed that they were man, horse, hounds, and falcon, such as dwell upon earth. They were like creatures out of a tale that poets sing: so swift were they, so light and beautiful.

But had Urien written down what befell him he would have told it differently. The horse fell dead of its speed. The falcons were found starved, and children robbed them of their silver bells. All the hounds except one leapt over a cliff, and were caught on the jutting holly-bushes and eaten by ravens. Urien crept at midnight into a den, where a hermit and a fox lived together. His one hound and he took up their abode with the hermit; the hound slew the fox, and Urien had to do penance for it.

In that land Urien was known to nobody. He grew old almost as soon as Cavall, the hound. Of his pride nothing remained but his way of standing up very straight in the den, where his head touched the roof of oak roots.

Urien and the hermit loved the old hound, Cavall. Sometimes when the two parted in the forest Cavall would stand stone-still, thinking, his tail slowly moving, his sad eyes looking from one to the other, and though both shouted, one for him to come on, the other for him to go back, he would be unable to choose which he would accompany, until both were disappearing from sight, and he ran first to one, then to the other, and made up his mind at last because he was tired of running and thinking. One day the two men quarrelled over the last bone of a stag which they had been living on for a week. The quarrel was ended by giving the bone to Cavall. The hound licked it and left it, tried a dozen ways of holding it, found a morsel here and another there, and at length gripped it with paws and teeth and began to grind. It was then that Urien broke the silence, by saying: "The nearer the bone the sweeter the meat." The two watched him until he fell asleep; a little afterwards they also fell asleep. In the morning Cavall was dead.

Many a time in after years Urien and the hermit remembered that evening and the saying, "The nearer the bone the sweeter the meat," and they smiled because Cavall had a quiet end, and because the saying was a true one, which men repeat down to this day in the land where Urien died, and in the Towy valley, and in many other places.

***

Soldiers Everywhere, 1915

This article was first published in The New Statesman on 8th May, 1915. It was Thomas's penultimate article, followed only by his piece about his friend Rupert Brooke which came out the following month. Guy Cuthbertson, who includes this piece in the second volume of Edward Thomas: Prose Writings: A Selected Edition, compares it to the essays in The Last Sheaf – 'Tipperary', and 'It's a Long Long Way', noting that 'Thomas was already a poet but not quite a soldier' when it was published. It is interesting that in this late essay, the soldier he chooses to write about is Welsh.

The first man I met this morning was a soldier. He was riding and shouting "Son of a bitch!" after a runaway horse which I expected to run me down in the narrow road. But the horse dislikes hurting anyone but an enemy, and as he approached me he slowed up. "Stop him" shouted the soldier in a Welsh accent. "Rise your hand; he won't come at you then". I raised my hand, and the horse stopped. The soldier rode cautiously towards him. when he was within a dozen yards he gave up threats and insults, saying very respectfully: "Come on, Thomas". The horse stood still, with his head towards the hedge. A few yards more, and the Welshman addressed him in an affectionate tone, almost endearingly: "Come on, Tom; come along". But as he leant out to seize the halter up went Tom into the air, twice his former length and half his height, with two legs, as it seemed, over one hedge and two over the other, yet without kicking anything. Then away he went like the wind, but with more noise, followed by the soldier's warning, "You wicked ———! I'll warm you when I get you!" After these stages had thrice been gone through the horse was caught, which gave the Welshman so much satisfaction that he forgot to perform his promise.

The railway carriage was almost packed by two sailors lying at length upon the seats, sober and tired out. I managed, however, to slip into one corner by the door, and a young farmer into the other, and so we travelled some distance. At each station, whenever someone was about to enter the carriage, the farmer winked and jerked his head towards the sailors: if necessary, he added: "Best leave them to have their sleep out." Thus the sailors were not disturbed until we reached a station near a big camp. The platform was crowded. Two navvies stumbled in upon us, good-humouredly protesting against the sailors changing position, but sitting down as good-humouredly. They began to talk about the camp. Bread was sixpence a loaf there at the canteen, and matches a halfpenny a box; their breakfast, dinner and tea on Sunday had cost them three and sixpence a head. One of them had picked up a fragment of some unidentifiable instrument with figures on it, and wanted to know if the sailors, or the farmer, or I could tell him if it was part of an aeroplane and what it was worth. The other navvy laughed when he read out the figures, 8 to 12, and explained that they meant "the time you have got to meet the young woman". The finder went on trying to read the maker's name. As he only had one good eye, he made slow progress. But he was proud both of the good and the other eye. That he had lost in the Boer War. The survivor, he said, was good enough for a soldier. He laid me five shillings that he could read as well with his one as I with two. He did not know that I had good sight and was accustomed to reading, and he lost the bet (but not the money). Three times, he said, he had offered to re-enlist. They were getting used to him. Last time he went the porter just shouted "Here's that one-eyed bloke again"; and the doctor just shouted back "Turn him out!" He was too indignant about this to be very sad. He and his mate were both past forty. They had the spirits of schoolboys, of unattached workmen.

At the big station these men and the sailors left the train. The sergeants of regulars came in and sat in opposite corners. A bulky cattle-dealer in a greasy box-cloth overcoat sat between them and me. An Army Medical private and a civilian sat on the other side, and in the fourth corner a great broad old man, who said nothing. The platforms were crowded with soldiers. "Soldiers everywhere", remarked the cattle-dealer, looking out sideways over his spectacles. "It's all right. If the German Emperor could see what's getting ready for him, he wouldn't smile again. The man must be mad! I said so right at the beginning of the war. There, look! there's some young ones!"

Here one of the sergeants spoke. He was trying to persuade an injured thigh into a comfortable position. He
was wretched. His grey eyes seemed incapable of seeing
things except as they were. "If you knew", said he, "what
I know, you wouldn't like to see those young ones. They
will get killed, most likely. We don't want many of their
sort in the trenches. They can't keep still and smoke.
They are too excited and restless, and keep bobbing about,
and they get shot. And don't you make a mistake: if some
of these men were to go out now, the Germans would die
of laughing".

"That's a fact", said the other sergeant. "Soldier's
clothes don't make a soldier".

"Quite true", said the cattle-dealer, disconcerted, but
glad to have a generalisation to agree with. From that
point onward he agreed with everything the sergeant said,
until he fell asleep, which he did in spite of the fact that
I did not put the window up for him. For the sergeant –
the un-wounded one: the wounded one did not speak
again – was truculent and three parts drunk. He was a
pioneer sergeant on his way up to see his colonel, hoping
to be made regimental sergeant.

The war, he said, was hell. Nobody who had been out
there once wanted to go a second time. It was hell: there
was no other word for it. After an interval the red cross
on the arm of the R.A.M.C. man – a meek, quiet young
man – roused him. "What did you join that for?" asked
the sergeant, grinning; "was it to shun the bullets?" The
young man had a bad voice, and, what with nervousness,
made no audible reply. But the sergeant did not mind; he
was set going now. He announced that it was every man's

duty – every man's – to go and have a taste of it. The upper classes had done their duty. The poor classes had done their duty. But the middle classes had not. They ought to be made to go. Varicose veins! Sprains! He had got sprains in both legs.

The civilian who wanted to agree with him, a man with half a mouthful of teeth like agates, said:

"Yes, and teeth too. You don't shoot with your teeth. That's what I say".

"But you eat with your teeth, don't you?" said the sergeant with his grin. He was not going to have any interruption. "I have done my share", he continued. "I was wounded in the Boer War. I was wounded on the Marne in this war. I have done my share, and others ought to do theirs".

The wounded sergeant looked at him, but only readjusted his thigh. The great broad old man looked at him, and, moreover, did not take his eyes off him, which, I think, was the reason why the sergeant began to feel the bit, and possibly why he got out at the next station. "I was a soldier before he was born", said the old man. "Some people don't know when to keep their mouths shut. He made a great mistake for a recruiter. He said right off that it was hell. Then he said everyone ought to be sent out for a taste. If he was in the Boer War, why doesn't he wear his medal? It's a crime not to in these times. Well, a man with no more sense than he has got will never make a regimental sergeant. He ought to be on the stage".

By the time we were all standing up to get out at the terminus the cattle-dealer woke, and, seeing the soldiers on the platform, said as before: "Soldiers everywhere. It's all right".

WALES IN THE POETRY OF EDWARD THOMAS
BY DR ANDREW WEBB

Edward Thomas's love of Wales is evident in his writing from the very start of his career in the late 1890s. Its appearance coincides with the three consecutive summers from 1897 to 1899 that he enjoyed with his father's extended family in the Ammanford and Pontarddulais areas of south-west Wales, and with the years, from 1898 to 1900, that he spent as an undergraduate at Lincoln College, Oxford, under the tutelage of the Welsh scholar and cultural figurehead O.M. Edwards. It was at this time that Thomas also developed an acquaintance with the Welsh-language poet Watcyn Wyn, and began a lifelong friendship with the bard, and later Archdruid, Gwili. Thomas's exposure to Welsh culture in these years lies behind diary entries like the one for 31 August 1899:

> Day by day my passion grows for Wales. It is like a homesickness, but stronger than any homesickness I ever felt – stronger than any passion. Wales indeed is my soul's native land, if the soul can be said to have a *patria* – or rather a matria, a home with the warm sweetness of a mother's love, and with her influence too.[1]

But it would be wrong to think of Thomas's love for Wales as a passing fad limited to the final years of the nineteenth century. Two years later, he wrote in a more matter-of-fact tone about 'patriotism of which I never felt a spark unless it be perhaps to love a few acres in Wales'.[2] In the same year, he wrote to O.M. Edwards, reminding him 'I am Welsh', and asking Edwards 'to suggest any kind of work which I could do far away from libraries, to help you and the Welsh cause'.[3] Over a decade later, in 1913, just before his own turn to poetry, and at a time of increased tension between European nations, Thomas wrote of Wales as a model for the troubled times: its 'national anthem', he suggests, is 'exulting without self-glorification or any other form of brutality', the symbol of a 'nation that knows, and would not rashly destroy, the bonds distinguishing it from the rest of the world'.[4]

Thomas's professed love of Wales sits oddly with his posthumous critical reception as a war poet, a guardian of Englishness, and the 'missing link' in an 'English line' of poetry stretching back to the Romantics. This is a trend that began in the foreword to the first edition of the *Collected Poems* (1920) in which Walter de la Mare declared that 'if one word could tell of his all, that word would be England'.[5] Certainly, there are well-known references to England in Thomas's writing, and his poetry is rightly read as part of an English literary tradition. But as Jeff Towns shows in this anthology, Thomas's work over two decades as a travel writer, essayist, literary critic, short story writer, reviewer, and anthologist also engages with the matter of Wales. It is unsurprising, then, to find numerous references and allusions to Wales not only in Thomas's prose, but also in his poetry, all of which was written between November 1914 and his fateful departure for the battlefields of France in January 1917. This essay will survey some of the ways in which Wales informs Thomas's poetry: the direct mentions of Wales, its Welsh settings, and its deeper engagements with Welsh folk and literary traditions.

There are five poems in which Wales is explicitly mentioned: 'Roads', 'Health', 'Words', 'The Child on the Cliffs' and 'Man and Dog'. The first of these, 'Roads', begins with a rare unqualified assertion for a Thomas poem, its speaker simply declaring 'I love roads'.[6] This simple opening immediately opens out into a complex exploration of the speaker's love of Wales, of the open road, and how both of these are changed by the immediate context of war. Quatrains contain short lines of two-three stresses each, lending the poem a fast pace and sense of movement. We learn that the speaker loves roads for 'the goddesses that dwell / Far along' them. But there is only one 'goddess' who is subsequently named:

Helen of the roads,
The mountain ways of Wales
And the Mabinogion tales[7]

Helen is a part-historical, part-mythical figure. Welsh wife of the fourth-century Roman Emperor, Macsen Wledig, she lent her name to the road, Sarn Helen, which connected forts in Carmarthen and Caernarfon. Her story is recounted in the classic Welsh medieval text, the *Mabinogion*, and is retold by Thomas in his 1911 anthology *Celtic Stories*, which features various translations from medieval Welsh texts, alongside Irish tales. Having established a Welsh context to the speaker's love of the open road, the poem branches out again. In a nod to the wartime context, it offers philosophical reflection on the relationship between roads and the relative short lifespan of those who use them: 'Roads go on / While we forget, and are / Forgotten like a star / That shoots and is gone'.[8] And yet the speaker suggests too that the road mysteriously depends for its own existence on the travellers who return to it: 'The hill road wet with rain / In the sun would not gleam / Like a winding stream / If we trod it not again'.[9] In this line, there are echoes of Thomas's travel book, *The Icknield Way*, one of the source texts for this poem:

> We may go or stay, but the road will go up over the mountains to Llandovery, and then up again over to Tregaron. It is a silent companion always ready for us, whether it is night or day, wet or fine, whether we are calm or desperate, wet or sick'.[10]

This brings us back to a Welsh setting. The association between love of the open road and Wales is no coincidence, given the time that Thomas spent walking in Carmarthenshire, the west of Glamorgan and what is now south Ceredigion. But the metaphor of roads also serves as a focal point for the poem's discussion of individual agency in the context of the First World War: a traveller in Wales drawn forever onwards by excitement at what 'the next turn may reveal' is confronted by the immediate historical context, the knowledge that for now 'all roads lead to France', as if the speaker's love of Wales must be put on hold until the war is over. Given the setting, though, and the allusions to Helen and the *Mabinogion*, we might equally argue that, for the speaker in this poem, all roads ultimately lead to Wales. It is Thomas's subsequent death in France that lends this poem its prophetic, tragic air, shifting the focus away from Wales.

The association between walking in Wales and recuperation is also present in 'Health'. Its speaker, bedridden in Hampshire thanks to illness, dreams of being able to 'ride or run or fly' to 'Wiltshire' or 'Wales'. As Edna Longley points out, in this poem Wales is a 'significant "horizon" of desire' for Thomas, a place associated in his mind with recovery and escape from the drudgery of hackwork as a literary reviewer for the London press. Indeed, it was often to Wales that Thomas travelled in order to cope with the bouts of melancholy or depression that periodically afflicted him.[11]

Wales is also directly mentioned in 'Words'. This poem explores the practice of writing poetry, and the extent to which a poet is the original author of the poem, or merely the conduit for a muse who acts through him. In one section, the poet-speaker calls on 'words' to 'choose me':

> Make me content
> With some sweetness
> From Wales
> Whose nightingales
> Have no wings [12]

On one level, this suggests the importance of Wales to

Thomas's formation as a poet, and to Wales as a source of inspiration. But there is more than meets the eye in this brief mention of Wales. While 'nightingales' of course allude to John Keats's famous ode, the specific mention of 'nightingales [with] no wings' appears inexplicable, until we realise that it is a riddle-like metaphor for the Welsh bards, the poetic songbirds of Wales. Thomas uses the term nightingale as shorthand for bard in his 1905 travel book, *Beautiful Wales*, where Huw Morus, the nineteenth-century, Welsh-language poet, is described as 'Eos Ceiriog', the nightingale of Ceiriog.[13] As this suggests, brief mentions of Wales in the poetry often open out into a deeper engagement with Welsh-language culture.

In 'The Child on the Cliffs', another poem that mentions Wales directly, the speaker and his mother lie on the south-facing Gower coast on a hot summer's day, a setting that undoubtedly draws on Thomas's own experience of family holidays in the area.[14] The child-speaker hears from beneath the sea 'the sound of the bell' from 'a chapel or church', a reference, as Sally Roberts Jones has rightly suggested, to the drowned wood of Coed Arian which lies between the Gower and north Devon coast.[15] It is also an allusion to the medieval Welsh legend of Cantre'r Gwaelod, in which a mythical expanse of Welsh land reclaimed from the sea was flooded again, thanks to the neglect of a sentry. But there is another allusion to Welsh folk material buried deeper in the poem: to the legend of Elidir, a folk tale from Gower first recorded by Gerald of Wales in which a young boy is led away by the 'tylwyth teg', the fairies. Thomas himself retells the story in *Beautiful Wales*, and its eerie, sinister atmosphere is also present in this poem.[16] There are suggestions of hallucination throughout: in the first stanza, the speaker remarks that 'things are strange today on the cliff'. The boy has eaten the root of a 'little yellow flower', which tastes like 'quinine'. Meanwhile, the 'sun shines so bright', and the boy seems disoriented, oddly fixated by the sounds made by 'the grasshopper'. The whole experience is uncanny and self-consciously 'strange'. In the second stanza, the speaker introduces images from medieval texts: he likens the grasshopper on a book to 'a green knight in a dazzling marketplace' and describes the breaking waves as feminine and seductive: their foam 'curls / And stretches a white arm out like a girl's'. The sound of the bell is merely 'sweet' to the mother, but to the boy, the sound draws him in, leading to the final stanza in which the child declares:

> Sweeter I never heard, mother, no, not in all Wales.
> I should like to be lying under that foam,
> Dead, but able to hear the sound of the bell,
> And certain that you would often come
> And rest, listening happily.
> I should be happy if that could be.

There is a sinister edge to the child's words here, as if the eerie, seductive setting and landscape is drawing the child away to its own death. Indeed, there is something un-childlike about the child and the way it speaks – as if indeed it is changeling. Here, then, we have a poem which explicitly mentions Wales, and which is clearly set in a Welsh location, but which draws on a deeper resource of

Welshness in its allusions to myth and medieval literature. This is a pattern that is repeated across much of Thomas's poetry.

In 'Man and Dog', written in January 1915, there is another, seemingly incidental, mention of Wales, which on closer analysis, reveals the poet's deeper engagement with the Welsh literary tradition. The poem describes the chance meeting in the woods between the speaker and an old man, who is accompanied by his dog. The speaker surmises that the man's mongrel 'kept sheep in Wales and scared / Strangers', and that his 'foxy Welsh grandfather must have paired / Beneath him'.[17] This is the only mention of Wales, but once again, it belies a deeper engagement with Welsh culture, for the poem is a retelling of a medieval Welsh englyn, 'Cân yr Henwr' (Song of the Old Man), from the ninth-century *Llywarch Hên* englyn sequence.[18] In its original Welsh form, 'Cân yr Henwr' is a dialogue poem in which an old man muses on his life, on his sons who have died in battle, on his old age, and on his own impending mortality. The ninth-century poem ends with a lament for his imminent demise, which is symbolised in the image of a leaf blown in the wind. In Thomas's 'Man and Dog', the speaker also meets an old man. Like his medieval predecessor, this old man talks about his sons who are fighting, this time at the Front in the First World War. He muses on his life as an itinerant labourer, 'navvying on dock and line', and in the army, 'a year of soldiering'.[19] He jokes about his own mortality. The closing image of the old man's departure also recalls the image from *Llywarch Hên*:

Stiffly, he plodded;
And at his heels the crisp leaves scurried fast,
And the leaf-coloured robin watched. They passed,
The robin till next day, the man for good.[20]

The image of the leaf blown in the wind is echoed in the twentieth-century poem. In this context, the image of the dog with its 'foxy Welsh grandfather [who] paired beneath him' is a nod to the poem's complex gene pool – its Welsh-language origins adapted into its present, English-language form.

While some poems mention Wales directly, others allude more subtly to Welsh culture. Thomas's poem 'The Ash Grove', written in early February 1916, mentions a Welsh folk song of the same name: the speaker recalls the fleeting memory of 'a girl sing[ing] / The song of the Ash Grove'.[21] As Longley suggests, while 'The Ash Grove' or 'Llwyn Onn' is a Welsh harp melody which exists in various versions, it is likely that the one by John Jones (1810-70) is the source for Thomas's poem. Regardless of the source text, it is clear from other, biographical sources that Thomas knew and recited Welsh folk songs, and it is likely that his familiarity with them derives from his upbringing in a London-Welsh home, their Welsh-speaking servants, and his friends and family back in south-west Wales. This Welsh folk song is linked, for the speaker, to the experience of learning 'what most I had desired, without search or desert or cost'.[22] Thomas's poem 'The Wind's Song' echoes the title of a Welsh-language poem of the same name: 'Canu y Gwynt', or 'Song of the Wind', which is found in *The Book of Taliesin*. Thomas was certainly familiar with the figure of Taliesin, having included a poem attributed to Taliesin in his 1907 anthology *Pocket Book of Poems and Songs for the Open Air*. Thomas's poem also alludes to 'Y Gwynt' or 'The Wind', the fourteenth century poem by Dafydd ap Gwilym. In Thomas's poem of the same name, the speaker suggests that 'there could be no old song so sad / As the wind's song; but later none so glad could I remember / As that same wind's song'.[23] Thomas's line here suggests that there is more than one 'song of the wind', a self-conscious nod towards the Welsh-language tradition that he has inherited.

Another motif to occur frequently in Thomas's poetry is that of a speaker who has a shared language with the birds and animals. While this motif is part of a common European medieval inheritance, it is likely that, for Thomas, it developed out of his reading of Welsh literature. In *Celtic Stories*, Thomas retells the story of 'Culhwch and Olwen', in which the character Gwrhyr, 'who knew all tongues of men and birds and beasts', helps Culhwch fulfil his quest, by talking to 'the Blackbird of Cilgwri', 'the Owl of Cwm Cawlwyd' and the 'Eagle of Gwernabwy'.[24] In Thomas's body of poetry, there are numerous instances in which the speaker is in the privileged position of being able to hear and interpret the language of birds. In 'The Unknown Bird', the speaker declares that 'I alone could hear him [the bird] / Though many listened'.[25] Similarly, in 'The Owl' we find that 'the bird's voice' is 'telling me plain what I escaped', 'speaking for all who lay under the stars, / Soldiers and poor, unable to rejoice'.[26] In 'I never saw that land before', the speaker wants to:

use, as the trees and birds did,
A language not to be betrayed;
And what was hid should still be hid
Excepting from those like me made
Who answer when such whispers bid.[27]

In 'She dotes', the female speaker 'dotes on what the wild birds say / Or hint or mock at', and she is 'trying to translate / the word the cuckoo cries to his mate'.[28] While none of these poems mention Wales directly, the motif of a speaker who can communicate with the birds is one that has its origins in the Welsh literary tradition, particular examples of which Thomas includes in his prose.

Another way in which Thomas's poetry is informed by the Welsh literary tradition is in its use of vatication or prophecy. Poems including 'No one cares less than I', 'As the team's head-brass' and 'It was upon' are concerned with the speaker's ability or otherwise to know what the future has in store. This aspect of his writing is rightly read through the lens of Thomas's immediate dilemma over whether or not to enlist, and his fate once the decision had been made. However, these poetic concerns also emerge out of an established tradition of vaticinatory verse within the Welsh-language poetic tradition. In 'This is no petty case of right or wrong', the speaker discusses the rights and wrongs of war with Germany until, 'dinned / with war and argument', he turns to a more magical way of predicting the outcome of the war:

> Two witches' cauldrons roar.
> From one the weather shall rise clear and gay;
> Out of the other an England beautiful
> And like her mother that died yesterday.
> Little I know or care if, being dull,
> I shall miss something that historians
> Can rake out of the ashes when perchance
> The phoenix broods serene above their ken.[29]

While this may be an allusion to the witches' cauldron from *Macbeth*, this alone would not account for the fact that there are two cauldrons, nor for one of the cauldron's association with rebirth. In order to understand the reference, we need to look beyond the English literary tradition. One of the cauldrons may be the 'Cauldron of Rebirth' from the Welsh story of Bran, retold by Thomas in *Celtic Stories*. In this story, any dead person placed in the cauldron will rise from it reborn. The Welsh take the cauldron to Ireland, thinking that it will guarantee them victory in their war with the Irish. Unfortunately, the cauldron is stolen, and the Irish use its magical powers of rebirth to defeat the Welsh. In this sense, the cauldron is a symbol of the unpredictability of the future, and in the immediate context of war, of not taking victory for granted. In Thomas's poem, the cauldron performs a similar function, suggesting that one vision of England has already died in the prosecution of the war thus far, while also serving to question readers' assumptions about the war's outcome.

There are other poems which, while they do not explicitly mention Wales or allude to its literary or folk traditions, nonetheless depict an identifiable Welsh setting. In 'The Mountain Chapel', written in December 1914, the first stanza's 'chapel' and gravestones, 'shrouded by a mountain fold' clearly suggest a Welsh location.

> Chapel and gravestones, old and few,
> Are shrouded by a mountain fold
> From sound and view
> Of life. The loss of a brook's voice
> Falls like a shadow. All they hear is
> The eternal noise
> Of wind whistling in grass.[30]

The stanza here echoes two prose accounts of Thomas's visits to mountain chapels which occur in *Beautiful Wales* and 'Penderyn'. In the latter essay, based on an October 1914 visit to the Cynon valley area, and the inspiration, as we shall see, for a number of his poems, Thomas writes of a 'plain building of harsh stone on the highest ground'.[31] In this quiet chapel which is given over to nature for most of the week, 'the grass grew among the tombs thick and long'. He likens 'the rustle of an overhanging aspen' to 'the rush of water' as he crosses a silent brook, a line that anticipates the poem's mention of the 'loss of a brook's voice'.[32] In *Beautiful Wales*, written almost a decade before, the narrator visits a mountain chapel graveyard where 'an ancient wind is ceaselessly remembering ancient things', a place where 'the gods – the gods that grow old and feeble and die – are there still, and with them all those phantoms following phantoms in a phantom land… which make Welsh history'.[33] These lines find echoes in the 'sound of any wind of the world / In grass-blades stiff', as well as the poem's closing observation that 'when gods were young / This wind was old'.[34]

'Over the Hills', written in January 1915, is also derived from Thomas's experience in Wales. Its speaker recalls searching for a path in the mountains beyond the 'horizon ridge', before stopping at a village inn for the evening. Longley makes the point that the phrase 'over the hills' occurs in a passage in *Beautiful Wales*: 'a mountain stream which many stones tore to ribbons, was with me for miles and to the left and to the right many paths ran with alluring courses for half a mile, like happy thoughts or lively fancies, and ended suddenly. The mountains increased in height as the sun sank... And in the end of the afternoon I came to a village I knew'.[35] If this suggests that Thomas's visit to Wales while researching *Beautiful Wales* was the inspiration for the poem, its closing image of a 'restless brook' and a 'mountain' would seem to confirm the Welsh setting. The speaker portrays a 'restless brook' which could not:

> turn back and climb the waterfall
> To the lake that rests and stirs not in its nook,
> As in the hollow of the collar-bone
> Under the mountain's head of rush and stone.[36]

This description of a lake nestling the 'hollow of the collar-bone / Under the mountain's head' is a brilliant and accurate description of Llyn y Fan Fach, high up on the Black Mountain in Carmarthenshire, a place where

Thomas used to walk with Gwili from his base in Ammanford, and a place he describes in *Beautiful Wales*.

The poem 'An Old Song II', written in December 1914, is another poem that is inspired by a Welsh setting. Along with 'A Child of the Cliffs', set on a Gower cliff top, it is Thomas's only seascape:

> The sun set, the wind fell, the sea
> Was like a mirror shaking:
> The one small wave that clapped the land
> A mile-long snake of foam was making
> Where tide had smoothed and wind had dried.
> The vacant sand.[37]

The poem goes on to incorporate lines from a verse and the chorus of the folksong 'The Maid of Amsterdam' – 'I'll go no more a-roving / With you, fair maid' and 'In Amsterdam, there dwelt a maid – Mark well what I do say'.[38] An October 1914 letter from Thomas, staying in Swansea, to his wife Helen, records a walk 'to the Mumbles up to Oystermouth Castle and back chiefly by the sands' during which he hummed tunes and sang songs that included 'The Maid of Amsterdam'.[39] Given this letter, and what we know of the area immediately around the Mumbles and Oystermouth Castle, it is likely that the poem is based on that experience, and that the seascape is a description of Swansea Bay.

In 'A Dream', written in July 1915, the speaker, accompanied by 'an old friend in dream':

Came sudden to a strange stream.
Its dark waters were bursting out most bright
From a great mountain's heart into the light.
They ran a short course under the sun, then back
Into a pit they plunged [40]

The poem depicts a dreamscape, the sources and setting for which are likely to be multivalent, and not related to a single place. Nonetheless, the 'mountain' and the way that the stream emerges from the mountain only to disappear underground again, suggest a particular Welsh location. In the essay 'Penderyn', Thomas describes how 'the river [Neath], fresh from a waterfall, poured out into the light under ash trees … in one place [it] ran black underground, and in another danced down a quarter mile of cascades white as milk'.[41] Indeed, several poems seem to echo the prose descriptions in the 'Penderyn' essay. The speaker in 'I never saw that land before' declares:

Great was the affection that I bore

To the valley and the river small,
The cattle, the grass, the bare ash trees,
The chickens from the farmsteads, all
Elm-hidden, and the tributaries
Descending at equal interval.[42]

Longley makes the connection between the poem and the passage in 'Penderyn' in which Thomas describes the Neath valley: 'Excepting when I crossed it, the river Neath was generally hidden either by oak, ash or elder lining it... Then I came to a village... As the river was now little more than a brook, the hills of its valley sides were now mountains... The fields down by the river were very green, enclosed and protected by a few farmhouses and trees'.[43] Thomas's visit to Wales in October 1914 also informs 'The Watchers'. Written at the end of April 1916, the speaker watches a 'horse and carter' from a room full of 'many cases of stuffed fish, vermin, and kingfishers', at an inn 'by the ford at the town's edge'.[44] Welsh inns feature in Thomas's 1902 collection of short sketches, *Horae Solitariae*, as well as *Beautiful Wales*, and the dedication for *The Icknield Way* was written at the 'Dolau Cothi Arms, Pumpsaint, Carmarthenshire'. But there is reason to suggest that it is his October 1914 visit to Wales, which lies behind the speaker's experience in 'The Watchers'. A letter to Helen from that month describes a stay at a room in a Welsh inn 'dignified by a black cock in a glass case as well as a fantastic heavy armchair, presumably for a President to sit in, a fretwork ship in a glass case, and a portrait of a pointer (I think).'[45]

While several of Thomas's poems contain direct reference to Wales, and while others allude to Welsh literature, culture and folklore, or are traceable to particular locations in Wales, it is also the case that the Welsh strict-metres tradition informs Thomas's poetry on a deeper, formal level. In an effort to pinpoint the difference between the poetry of Thomas and that of Robert Frost, Matthew Hollis identifies the experimental 'musical phrasings' that characterise the former's poetry. Longley offers more nuanced readings of Thomas's work, but neither she nor

Hollis entertain the idea that Thomas's innovations in poetic form are adaptations from the Welsh strict-metres tradition. From his correspondence, we know that Thomas's interest in the Welsh literary tradition included engagement with its strict metres' tradition. Elis Jenkins, writing in 1967, describes letters between his uncle, Gwili, and Thomas in which 'it is clear that Edward used to consult him about Iolo [Morganwg] and [George] Borrow, and the *Mabinogion*, and the Welsh metrical system'.[46] Jenkins even suggests that 'on the backs of one or two envelopes [from Thomas] were jottings about the rules of Welsh poetry.'[47] Other correspondence from Thomas shows that he was able to identify patterns of internal rhyme and alliteration in Welsh-language poetry.[48] Most significantly, it is clear that, in some of his poetry, Thomas adapts these patterns into English-language poetry. The opening lines of 'Head and Bottle' – 'The downs will lose the sun, white alyssum / Lose the bees hum' – suggest the influence of cynghanedd, in which the consonant sounds 'w', 'l' and 's' in the first half of the line – 'will lose the sun' – are repeated in the 'cyrch' – 'white alysum'- while there are internal half-rhymes in 'sun', 'sum' and 'hum'.[49] While these moments of 'direct' adaptation of a Welsh metre into English are rare in Thomas's poetry, it is certainly the case that Thomas frequently experiments with internal rhyme and consonant patterns to create innovative sound systems, formal techniques that he took from the Welsh-language tradition. 'The Green Roads', written in late June 1916, is a good example. From the opening lines, the originality and intricacy of its sound patterning is clear:

The green roads that end in the forest
Are strewn with white goose feathers this June,

Like marks left behind by someone gone to the forest
To show his track. But he has never come back.

Down each green road a cottage looks at the forest.
Round one the nettle towers; two are bathed in
     flowers.[50]

Thomas has set himself the task of writing a poem of un-rhymed couplets, where the first line ends with the word 'forest' and the second line contains an internal rhyme. This is a unique form. While this is not an adaptation of any particular Welsh metre, it does suggest a method of experimental writing that derives from his reading of Welsh poetry, and which employs in innovative ways its formal features. 'The Bridge' is another example.

I have come a long way today:
Over a strange bridge alone,
Remembering friends, old friends,
I rest without smile or moan,
As they remember me without smile or moan.[51]

This unusual form – a five-line stanza in which the second, fourth and fifth lines rhyme, there is internal rhyme in the first and third lines, and a refrain in the fourth and fifth – is repeated across the poem's three stanzas. The refrain in the final line has its origins in folk songs from both the English and Welsh traditions, while the internal rhyme in lines one and three is common to some forms of cynghanedd. It is also interesting to note that the poem echoes a passage in *Beautiful Wales* in which Thomas describes the experience of being alone on a bridge the ends of which were shrouded in mist.[52]

In some poems, Thomas's use of internal rhyme and alliteration completely subverts the traditional English form, turning the reader's aural experience of the poem into something else entirely. A good example is 'Rain', a poem written in the long-established English form of blank verse:

> Rain, midnight rain, nothing but the wild rain
> On this bleak hut and solitude and me
> Remembering again that I shall die
> And neither hear the rain nor give it thanks
> For washing me cleaner than I have been
> Since I was born into this solitude
> Blessed are the dead that the rain rains upon.[53]

In this first half of the poem, the iambic pattern and strong, unrhymed line-ends that we normally find in blank verse are disrupted by Thomas's use of repeated consonant sounds and internal rhyme. In particular, the repetition of the title word 'rain' three times in the opening line ensures that when the 'r' and 'n' sounds occur in subsequent lines, we hear an echo of the word 'rain'. Indeed, the word "rain" becomes the governing sound of the whole poem, dripping through its lines – present in 'remembering again', for example – in a way that reduces the aural significance of the strong line-ends and iambic pentameter of blank verse. In this way, Thomas uses techniques borrowed from Welsh-language poetry to transform a traditional English verse form.

To conclude, while this anthology reveals the extent of Thomas's engagement with Wales throughout his prose-writing career, it is clear that Wales also informs his poetry, all of which was written in the last three years of his life. The occasional direct mentions of Wales often open out into a deeper cultural engagement with Welsh folk or literary material, while a comparison of Thomas's poetry with his published prose and correspondence reveals the extent to which it features, or is inspired by, particular Welsh settings. On a more fundamental level, the innovative rhythms and sound patterns of Thomas's poetry reflect an engagement with the internal rhymes and consonant patterns of the Welsh strict-metres tradition, something that cuts to the heart of his achievement as a poet.

[1] Quoted in R. George Thomas, *Edward Thomas: a Portrait* (Cardiff: University of Wales Press, 1985), p. 80.

[2] Edward Thomas, Diary, 29 September 1901, National Library of Wales.

[3] Hazel Davies, 'Edward Thomas: Twelve Unpublished Letters to O.M. Edwards', *National Library of Wales Journal* 28, no. 3 (1994), pp. 335-345 (p. y43).

[4] Thomas, *The Happy-Go-Lucky Morgans* (London: Duckworth, 1913), p. 224.

[5] Walter de la Mare, 'Foreword' in Edward Thomas, *Collected Poems*, ed. by R. George Thomas (London: Faber and Faber, 2004), pp. 246-53 (p. 249).

[6] Edward Thomas, *The Annotated Collected Poems*, ed. by Edna Longley (Newcastle: Bloodaxe, 2008), p. 106.

[7] Ibid., p. 106.

[8] Ibid., p. 106.

[9] Ibid.. p. 106.

[10] Edward Thomas, *The Icknield Way* (London: Constable, 1913), p. 2.

[11] Thomas, *Annotated Collected Poems*, p. 82 and p. 226.

[12] Ibid., p. 92.

[13] Thomas, *Beautiful Wales* (London:, A. & C. Black, 1905), p. 5.

[14] Thomas, *Annotated Collected Poems,* p. 65.

[15] Sally Roberts Jones, 'Edward Thomas and Wales', in Jonathan Barker (ed.), *The Art of Edward Thomas* (Bridgend: Poetry Wales Press, 1987), pp. 75-84 (p. 81).

[16] Thomas, *Beautiful Wales*, p. 164 and p. 181.

[17] Thomas, *Annotated Collected Poems*, p. 57.

[18] Ibid., p.57. An Englyn is a traditional Welsh (and Cornish) short poem form, using quantitative metres involving the

counting of syllables and rigid patterns of rhyme and half rhyme.

[19] Ibid., p. 57.

[20] Ibid., p. 57.

[21] Ibid., p. 108

[22] Ibid., p. 108.

[23] Ibid., p. 118.

[24] Edward Thomas, *Celtic Stories* (Oxford: Clarendon Press, 1911), p. 95.

[25] Thomas, *Annotated Collected Poems*, p. 55.

[26] Ibid., p. 65

[27] Ibid., p. 120.

[28] Ibid., p. 132.

[29] Ibid., p. 134.

[30] Ibid., p. 43.

[31] Edward Thomas, *The Chessplayer and Other Essays* (Andoversford, Glos: Whittington Press, 1981), p. 26.

[32] Ibid., p. 26.

[33] Thomas, *Beautiful Wales*, p. 199.

[34] Thomas, *Annotated Collected Poems*, p. 43.

[35] Thomas, *Beautiful Wales*, p. 176.

[36] Thomas, *Annotated Collected Poems*, p. 53

[37] Ibid., p. 47.

[38] Ibid., p. 47.

[39] Quoted in Edna Longley, 'Notes', in Edward Thomas, *Annotated Collected Poems*, pp. 141-321 (p. 169).

[40] Thomas, *Annotated Collected Poems*, p. 96.

[41] Thomas, *The Chessplayer and Other Essays*, p. 23.

[42] Thomas, *Annotated Collected Poems*, p. 120.

[43] Thomas, *The Chessplayer and Other Essays, p. 24.*

[44] Thomas, *Annotated Collected Poems*, p. 119.

[45] Quoted in Edna Longley, 'Notes', p. 291.

[46] Elis Jenkins, "Edward Thomas: Some of his Welsh Friends," originally written in 1967, Ammanford Town History, accessed October 1, 2017, http://www.terrynorm.ic24.net/.

[47] Ibid.

[48] Edward Thomas, *Letters to Gordon Bottomley*, ed. R. George Thomas (Oxford: Oxford University Press, 1968), p. 67.

[49] Thomas, *Annotated Collected Poems*, p. 81.

[50] Ibid., p. 128.

[51] Ibid., p. 66.

[52] Thomas, *Beautiful Wales*, p. 111.

[53] Ibid., p. 105.

WALES IN THE LIFE AND WORKS OF EDWARD THOMAS A CHRONOLOGY

1878: Philip Edward Thomas born on March 3rd 1878 in Lambeth, South London, the eldest of six sons. His father, Philip Henry Thomas, was a native Welsh speaker from the South Wales Valley town of Tredegar, and his mother Mary Elizabeth was from nearby Newport. They both had numerous relatives spread across South Wales and amongst the Welsh communities around Swindon. Although his father had prospered through his work in the Civil Service and had moved to England he never forgot his Welsh roots. Edward would later speak of how he considered himself 'five eighths Welsh'.

1883: Edward first visited Wales age five, when his mother brought him to visit various relatives, mainly aunts, around Newport, Usk, and Swansea. Edward recalls the visit in his fragment of early autobiography *The Childhood of Edward Thomas* (not published until 1938), and it made a profound and lasting impressions:

> There were beautiful great rosy apples in the garden, and a well with a broad stone over it, and ivy and snails on the narrow paths. Then for the first time I thoroughly understood what wells, apples and snails were.... There also I first learned what a river was... The Usk was not too broad; it was winding; I heard the sound and felt the flood of it. Also I was told that a certain islet or peninsular ... was the site of King Arthur's Round Table. Either, ideas suggested by 'King Arthur and 'Round Table' even then, vibrated in my brain or they remained there...' This Holiday gave me most definite

and most pleasant of my early memories, together with some less definite ideas associated with Caerleon and Wales which afterwards increased, I might almost say magically, by the aid of things heard in home talk or read in books, and of a visit several years later.

1887: Edward makes his second visit to Wales, which was equally significant:

But my strongest and most often considered memory of this period was my second visit to Wales at the age of nine... I remember the names of the stations, 'Risca', 'Cross Keys'... There were long-horned shaggy cattle about. I saw the river Ebbw racing over stones...I saw chimneys and smoke and ruins and white-washed walls...I stopped at Abertillery ... and met Welsh people who spoke no English. Above all I remember a house lone on a hill with a parrot and a dark girl named Rachel, pretty, and dirty, who was down on her knees scrubbing the kitchen hearth ...That is all the stuff of abiding memory.

1888: Even when Edward holidayed with his Welsh grand-mother Rachel Thomas and her family in Swindon, Wales still permeated the households. Edward described it as 'little Wales', and he writes of how his Grandmother:

Read her Bible and sang hymns to herself, sometimes in Welsh. She also sang Welsh songs... in particular one that an old beggar used to sing at Tredegar... She first took me to church. Clad in uncomfortable clothes... layers of black. I felt everyone enjoyed being stiff, solemn, black, except myself... It was an inexplicable conspiracy for an hour's self torture. I was introduced to other women and discussed...To hide something from me they spoke in Welsh.

'at ten': from a manuscript titled 'Addenda to an Autobiography' held in the Berg Collection in New York Public Library, and recently published in Volume 1 Autobiographies, of the Oxford University Press *Edward Thomas Prose Writings*.

My early feeling for Wales culminated in my singing of Moore's 'Minstrel Boy', was clinched and fostered by it. I knew only of *Welsh* Harps. I supposed the minstrel boy with his wild harp slung behind him was Welsh and as I sung the song I melted and trembled with a kind of gloomy pleasure in being about to die for Wales, Arthur's and Llewelyn's Wales, the 'land of song'. While I shivered with exaltation repeating his words,

> Though each man else betrays thee
> One sword at least thy rights shall guard,
> One harp at least shall praise thee,
> it might have been my harp and my sword.

In his enthusiasm Thomas had obviously misconstrued Moore's 'Minstrel Boy' to be Welsh and not Irish.

1896: Thomas visits Mumbles and Swansea. Soon afterwards, three of Thomas's brothers, Reggie, Julian and Oscar, came to Ammanford to attend the Gwynfryn School, a small 'Academy' notable in South Wales not only for its experimental work in adult education, but for the wit of its bardic principal, Watcyn Williams, whom all Welshmen knew as Watcyn Wyn. [see Appendix 1.] Edward was a frequent visitor, and Watcyn Wyn became another great Welshman who befriended Edward.

1897: November: Thomas contributes an article 'Shadows of the Hills' to *The Speaker Supplement*. This appears to be his first published piece of prose set in Wales. Staying with Philip Treharne Thomas in Tynybonau, Pontarddulais, Thomas meets John Jenkins poet, theologian and educator. His Welsh bardic name was Gwili, the name of the river that flows from Pontarddulais to Ammanford. (see Appendix 1.)

1898: August: Edward is in Pontarddulais. He writes to his friend Harry Hooton:

'My dear Harry,
    The good Welsh people here have changed me into the animal I always potentially was. I eat and sleep, and my most serious work was yesterday – binding the sheaves of wheat in a strong sun; I really did work hard, and at the end had tea sitting round a cock of wheat with the reapers and binders.'

March: Thomas wins a history scholarship to Lincoln College, Oxford where his tutor is the eminent Welsh scholar Owen M. Edwards. Thomas felt very fortunate to have a Welshman as his tutor. The National Library of Wales possesses Thomas's ten letters to Owen M. Edwards. Hazel Walford Davies, in her introduction to the publication of these letters describes Edwards as 'arguably the greatest Welsh-language cultural figure at the turn of the century... to whose Welsh influence much in Edward Thomas's subsequent make-up as a writer can be traced'.

1899: June 20: Marries Helen Noble. She would remark that 'Wales, the native land of Edward Thomas was very dear to him'. Thomas himself comments in a diary entry, August 31, written whilst staying with relations in Pontarddulais that

Day by Day grows my passion for Wales. It is like homesickness, but stronger than any homesickness I have ever felt – stronger than any passion. Wales indeed is my soul's native land…a home with the warm sweetness of a mother's love, and with her influence too. Today, for example, what yearning thoughts filled my brain as Janet played the tune of *Y Ferch o Llandebie* and *Moli merched Cymru Ian!* And when I hummed the 'Gwlad! Gwlad!' of the national anthem, my heart broke with thoughts of what I might be and am not, of what I may be – Ah! The future in some bookish cottage in the pastoral Towy with Helen.

August 11th, 1899: Writes to his friend E.S. P. Haynes from Gwynfryn Ammanford.

Damn these bards! … They did not like it when I told them the Welsh would make Hebrews of themselves very soon, if they didn't take to some book other than the Bible and a little unnatural vice…. Still, my bard Gwili has just won a bardic chair with a poem on "Nature a witness of God," which was full of (incontinent) nymphs, Hylases and lascivious Satyrs, – that part, however, his judges described as "pompous"!

1900: Edward Thomas first uses the expression 'my accidentally Cockney nativity'. He obviously liked this whimsical, self-descriptive phrase, as he chose to use it twice. It occurs in this letter to his close friend Ian MacAlister sent from Ammanford in August:

After all Wales is good for me. In spite of my accidentally Cockney nativity, the air here seems to hold in it some virtue essential to my well-being, and I always feel, in the profoundest sense, at home.

And again, around the same time, and from the same place, he uses it in a letter to his tutor at Oxford, Owen M. Edwards :

As you may see I have altered my plans & come to Wales instead of Spain. Already this air, that seems to contain something essential to me, in spite of my accidentally cockney nativity, has done me good, so that I shall in the course of a few weeks probably be equal to an interview or anything else you might have to suggest.

January 15: Edward Thomas and Helen's first child is born; a boy, to whom they give the Welsh name Merfyn.

1901: Thomas writes to Edwards in a letter dated December:

I have just read your history of Wales, and I feel that I must thank you more plainly than I have done elsewhere. That such a critic & historian as myself should admire the book would not concern you, but I am sure that because I am Welsh you would be glad to know I love the book – It has made me regret very much that I have moved farther away from Wales. For it compelled me to wish that my small activities were usefully connected with Wales, which is now more than ever difficult. Still I should be glad if you could suggest any kind of work which I could do far away from libraries to assist you and the Welsh cause. First of all you will say I must learn Welsh from the beginning: – can you advise me as to a Grammar?

Summer: Thomas's younger brothers are still attending Watkyn Wyn's Gwynfryn School in Ammanford. Thomas spends time with them and Watkyn Wyn, and they become good friends. Watkyn Wyn helps and advises Thomas on the history of the Welsh language and literature.

December: Thomas writes to Ian MacAlister from Battersea:

> I was talking comfortably to the peasants and tinworkers of
> the Lwchwr valley, to one or two of the most famous Welsh
> bards, Watkyn Wyn and Gwili among others; but except
> perhaps in the case of Gwili, the people were to me only a
> sweet atmosphere in which I could most perfectly enjoy the
> legends and songs of Wales. The songs! I know some of them;
> they are part of my small, increasing stock of Welsh, and have
> taught me an interest in that branch at least of modern
> literature... The whole of Wales has become sacred ground
> to me for many reasons. In fact it is an ambition one day to
> add maybe only a gleam to this literature; my first attempt
> should, by the way, soon appear in a Welsh monthly – a
> translation in Welsh, by a Welsh bard of an article of mine in
> [the] Speaker of July, that seemed good to him.

1902: February: Thomas reviews *Wales* by Owen M. Edwards
in *The Academy*.

June: Thomas's second book *Horae Solitariae* is published
which he dedicates to Owen M. Edwards. This book contains
Thomas's first specific published references to Wales and
many of the essays are concerned with Wales and Welsh
themes. He had written to Owen M. Edwards declaring that
the essays were, '...most of them, only bound to Wales,
because my visits to Wales have been in an obscure fashion
their inspiration'.

July: Thomas writes to Owen M. Edwards, thanking him for
sending his new three volume edition of *The Mabinogion*.

October: Edward Thomas and Helen's second child is born;
a girl, who they name Bronwen. Eckert observes how this in-

dicates once again, 'Thomas's Welsh inheritance and love for the old Welsh names.'

1903: November: *Poems of John Dyer* is published as Number 4 in Owen M. Edwards's series *The Welsh Library*. Thomas provides the introduction, a task he had directly solicited from Owen Edwards in a letter sent in 1902:

> I have just noticed that John Dyer is to be included in your 'Welsh Library.' I know Dyer's work and the Towy valley well & have in fact made a rather particular study of him for years.

1904: October: Thomas is commissioned to write *Beautiful Wales* for A & C. Black. Edward Thomas and Helen spend a fortnight in Ammanford after which Thomas sets out on a long, solitary tramp across the middle of Wales, researching his book.

1905: October: *Beautiful Wales* is published in the popular *Black's Colour Book Series*. In his 'A Note on Edward Thomas' for *The Welsh Review,* September, 1945, Gordon Bottomley reveals that the book would appear to contain Thomas's first ever published poem. He writes;

> In *Beautiful Wales* there is a touching portrait of a young Welsh poet, born to obscurity, ailing, and briefly bound for oblivion; it is full of felicities, and one of the chief strokes is an English translation of a chosen poem, "She is Dead Eluned" It is a lovely thing perfect in every point; and one of its merits is that its beauty is not marred by its method suggesting a translator's hand – but a translator who is an accomplished master of free verse...the poem is demurely described as being "reduced to its lowest terms by a

translator"... I asked him who had done it for him; and if he thought the original had a great verbal beauty. He listened gravely, and looked sorry for me, as he asked me should I be annoyed or disappointed to learn there was no Welsh original. I stupidly asked "Then who wrote it" before I arrived at the idea the poem was his – he smiling at me the while. I urged with energy that he must write more verse of the kind; and that even a small volume of such pieces would have a success comparable with *The Shropshire Lad*. He was not interested: he only said "I shall never have a success comparable with *The Shropshire Lad:* I do not know how to do that trick again.

In the same month Thomas first met, and begins a long friendship with W. H. Davies. Thomas offered him support he could ill-afford and graciously invited Davies to share his small study cottage near Sevenoaks. Thomas wrote a glowing review of Davies's first book of poems, *The Soul's Destroyer,* in *The Daily Chronicle* which begins:

Mr William Davies is a Monmouthshire man. He has been active and passionate. He has been poor and careless and hungry and in pain...he has travelled: he knows Wales, London, America and Hell.

Thomas would describe Davies to W.H. Hudson as 'my East End Welsh poet' so perhaps he thought they were both 'accidentally cockney'. Thomas and W. H. Davies became close friends and Thomas helped and promoted him in his work and life. He would inscribe copies of his books to him including *The Tenth Muse*.

November: Thomas writes to Gordon Bottomley from Waun Wen, Swansea where he is staying with his schoolmaster friend, John Williams:

...although Welsh mutton is good my food is not altogether bracing. Also the merriest man I ever knew – Watcyn Wyn – the bard who wrote 'The Maid of Llandebie' and 'The Maids of Carmarthenshire' – is to be buried today: and on Sunday I am to be taken in my bowler hat and collar to a Welsh chapel.

1906: August: Thomas solicits friends to contribute towards a fund to replace W. H. Davies's broken, prosthetic wooden leg. Helen Thomas wrote of the incident:

This wooden leg got broken and Davies was anxious to obtain another, but had a morbid dread of any of the villagers knowing about it ...So under Davies's guidance Edward made a sketch of an appliance which he asked the village wheelwright to make, with-out of course telling him the purpose...and when the bill came back in it was for: 'Curiosity Cricket Bat – 5s. OOd.' The joke of which Davies enjoyed as much as we did.

1907: Thomas reviews the *Welsh Fairy Book* by Jenkyn Thomas in the *Daily Chronicle* in which he writes, '...the book comes in answer to a real need. There was no Welsh fairy book before, except Sir John Rhys's *Celtic Folklore: Welsh and Manx*, and that is far too expensive to be widely circulated'.

December: Thomas writes to his Literary agent C. V. Cazenove:

Then I thought of a book of extracts from prose and verse from Welsh writers – viz. translations from those who wrote in Latin and Welsh, And of those who wrote in English. This would mean quite an attractive book from a popular point of view as it would include Geoffrey of Monmouth, Gerald of Wales, the *Mabinogion*, the medieval Welsh poets and romances, some fairy tales, three out of four greatest religious poets (Herbert, Vaughan and Traherne), some great preachers and theologians etc. I should only include those who had at least one Welsh parent or whose families had been resident for at least two generations.

1908: February: Thomas writes to his friend A.D. Williams about Wales and his relationship to it:

The Welsh towns are either large villages like Tredegar or accidental mercantile and manufacturing congeries like Swansea and so far as I know the Welsh element in them is of no importance...You may be able to help me connect myself more definitely with Wales, with which I am flimsily connected now by birth, a few acquaintances, love of the country and a useless sentiment.

August: Thomas is appointed Assistant Secretary to a Royal Commission on Welsh Monuments but decides to live in London to facilitate his research in the British Museum Library and commits to commuting to Wales as and when needed. It seemed like a dream job to him, 'Congratulate me believe I have escaped' he told Gordon Bottomley. But although he did make a few visits to Wales, to Pennard Castle in Gower and Carreg Cennen, on Royal Commission business, the job was mainly desk-bound in London did not work out anything like he had hoped and he left in ill health after a few months.

October: Thomas writes the introduction to George Herbert's *The Temple* and *A Priest to The Temple* published as number 309 of the *Everyman's Library*.

November: Thomas visits Swansea on Royal Commission work.

1909: *The South Country* is published. Although it is the first in a series of books that the publishers, J.M. Dent, were calling *The Heart of England Series,* Thomas still feels the need to write of Taliesin and *The Mabinogion* and other Welsh vignettes occur in the text.

Thomas reviews Marie Trevelyan's *Folk-Lore and Folk-Stories of Wales* for the *Daily Chronicle,* in which he expresses regret that such material, 'of great significance is not more easily obtainable'.

1910: August: Edward and Helen Thomas's third child, another girl, is born. They call her Myfanwy.

September: Thomas spends a fortnight in the wilds of Cardiganshire and writes to Gordon Bottomley from Swansea;

> My Dear Gordon,
>   I have just had a fortnight in Wales mostly in the wild part of Cardiganshire & am going home tomorrow...Helen and the new baby are still very well I hear. The Baby's name is probably Helen Elizabeth Mevanwy (Myfanwy is the Welsh spelling but impossible in England). I prefer Olwen best but it is too near Bronwen.

1911: February: Thomas assists Edward Garnett with a petition for a civil list pension for W. H. Davies.

Celtic Stories is published (second and third editions followed in 1913 and 1918). The second edition has an additional 'Note on the pronunciation of Welsh names'.

September: Thomas experiences a severe nervous breakdown caused by overwork and financial worries. He is sent to West Wales to recover and to try and catch up on his writing commissions. He visits his friend John Jenkins, 'Gwili', who he describes somewhat unflatteringly in a letter to Gordon Bottomley;

> I've been staying... with the bard Gwili. I can't imagine what his poetry is like but it might be good. He is in many ways a coarse barbarian outwardly but with a real fineness of spirit as well as a crust of English culture. Oxford in 3 years didn't even teach him to eat silently. It taught him little Greek & to take his own boots off which his mother or some other women always used to do He is 39 & a boy, but fat and scant of breath. I only understand half he says because he laughs continually.

December: Thomas writes to Edward Garnett from Laugharne:

> The fact is I finished *Borrow*...so I'm going to have a look at Swansea, Newport and Caerleon again... If I had a few quiet months I could write a Welsh itinerary now, partly at any rate following Gerald as I have been a good while in his steps at St Clears, Whitland, Llawhaden, Haverfordwest, Camrose, Newgale, St. David's & Llanrhian, and I already know Caerleon, Newport, Neath, Swansea, Kidwelly and Carmarthen... Did you ever see Haverfordwest? A most fascinating dirtyish old town ... I want to do a book on Swansea which I know better than any other, but nobody wants it.

1912: September: *Lafcadio Hearn* (Modern Biographies Series) is published. Thomas dedicates the book to his friend Gwili.

The Pocket George Borrow is published (Authors for the Pocket Series). Passages from the works of Borrow were chosen by Thomas.

October: *George Borrow The Man and his Books* is published. The dedication to his friend E.S.P Haynes is dated 'Laugharne, Carmarthenshire 1911'. In the chapter on Borrow's *Wild Wales* Thomas is somewhat critical of Borrow's knowledge of Welsh Literature which, he hints, pales compared to his own:

> There is no evidence that he knew the great nineteenth century collections of Welsh manuscripts and translations. He says nothing of the "Mabinogion". He had apparently never heard of the pedestrian Iolo Morganwg. He perhaps never saw Stephens' "Literature of the Kymry". His knowledge was picked up anyhow and anywhere from Welsh texts and Lhuyd's "Archaeologia," without system and with very little friendly discussion or comparison. Wales, therefore, was to him as wonderful as Spain, and equally uncharted.

Thomas begins work on his novel *The Happy-Go-Lucky-Morgans* and he visits Swansea to gather material for his essay 'Swansea Village'.

1913: *Icknield Way* is published. Although wholly concerned with an English trackway, Thomas writes of Welsh influences on English landscapes, many associated with the itinerant Welsh drovers, who left 'Welsh ways all over England'.

September: *The Country* is published. Although largely concerned with England, Welsh themes and anecdotes litter the text.

December: *The Happy-Go-Lucky Morgans* is published, a novel set in London and Abercorran (Laugharne). Thomas writes that it is a story 'of Balham and of a family dwelling in Balham who were more Welsh than Balhamitish'.

1914: The Everyman edition of George Borrow's, *The Zincali, an account of the Gipsies of Spain,* is published with an introduction by Edward Thomas.

April: Thomas visits Wales with Merfyn and Bronwen. He reviews *The Life and Poems of Dafydd ap Gwilym* by Evelyn Lewes in the *Daily News,* which includes this attack on Welsh scholars:

> That there is not a volume of translations from Dafydd and the other half dozen Welsh poets which is worth mentioning in the same breath as Kuno Meyer's *Ancient Irish Poetry* is a reproach either to the devotion or ability of Welsh scholars.

June: 'Swansea Village' is published in *The English Review*

October: Thomas takes a cycling tour in Wales – it will be his last visit to Wales.

1915: July: Thomas enlists in the Artists Rifles. He writes to Helen, 'Some day I hope we shall live on Salisbury Plain *if it can't be Wales*'.

October: *Four-and-Twenty Blackbirds* is published. It contains 24 stories based on proverbs, two of which are set in Wales.

1917: April 9[th,] Easter Day: Edward Thomas is killed by a shell in the first hour of the Battle of Arras at 7.36 a.m.

Posthumous Welsh Responses

1917: June: *The Welsh Outlook,* Thomas Jones's monthly magazine, has a two-page obituary of Edward Thomas and a review of *An Annual of New Poetry,* published by Constable, containing eighteen poems by Thomas who used the pseudonym Edward Eastaway. The review ends:

> Mr Edward Easterway is the new comer to this company of poets but he should be very welcome. His vision is single enough; sometimes simple to the point of insignificance. But occasionally there is a touch of a living imagination, and always a fine responsiveness to the impulses and stirrings of nature.

W. H. Davies – Thomas's close friend, the poet W. H. Davies, was devastated by the death of his close friend and patron and was prompted to write this commemorative poem 'Killed in action (Edward Thomas)', which was included in his 1918 collection, *Raptures:*

Happy the man whose home is still
In Nature's green and peaceful ways
To wake and hear the birds so loud,
That scream for joy to see the sun
Is shouldering past a sullen cloud

And we have known those days, when we
Would wait to hear the cuckoo first,
When you and I, with thoughtful mind,
Would help a bird to hide her nest,
For fear of other hands less kind

But thou, my friend, art lying dead
War, with its hell-born childishness,
Has claimed thy life, with many more
The man that loved this England well
And never left it once before.

1920: *Poems* by Gwili is published, a small book of his English poems. It includes his long memorial poem, 'Edward Eastaway'. [See Appendix 1.]

1924: *Wales,* a cheaper version of *Beautiful Wales*, is published in a smaller size with the full text but fewer illustrations. This book remained in print for years and was issued without illustrations as a paperback by the OUP in 1983. This from the Press catalogue:

Edward Thomas writes... 'of a hidden Wales', where 'an ancient wind is ceaselessly remembering ancient things', of the seasons and of the Welsh countryside, of farmhouses 'smelling of bacon and herbs and burning sycamore and ash'.. and above all of the mysterious Welsh people.

1926: *Chosen Essays* is published in a fine limited edition by Wales's Gregynog Press. The selection was made by Ernest Rhys, who, as a proud Welshman, includes a good amount of Thomas's Wales-based prose. The introduction by Edward Garnett is a paean to Thomas. He questions the general neglect of Edward Thomas and describes the book as being, 'selected, illustrated, printed and published in Wales as a tribute to Thomas from his countrymen'.

Selected Poems is published by The Gregynog Press. It is a limited edition of Thomas's poetry, selected and introduced by Edward Garnett.

1928: *The Last Sheaf – Essays by Edward Thomas* is published. It contains three essays set in Wales, 'Swansea Village', 'Glamorgan' and 'The Pilgrim'. The introduction, by Thomas's friend Thomas Seccombe is based on the memorial letter he wrote to *The Times* on Edward's death in 1917.

1937: Helen Thomas comes to Swansea to talk about and read Thomas's poems to the Swansea Literary Society. She visits and stays with Vernon and Gwen Watkins at their home in Pennard, Gower. A warm friendship develops between them. Helen gives Vernon the fine Hoppé portrait photograph of Thomas which takes pride of place in his study. She gives Gwen an exquisite patchwork handbag that she had crafted herself, made from swatches of old fabric from Thomas's favourites pieces of his young daughters' worn out summer frocks.

Helen also met Gwili's descendent Elis Jenkins and inscribed his copy of her own memoir *As It Was* with these words, 'Wales, the native land of Edward Thomas, was very dear to him'.

Edward Thomas: a Biography and a Bibliography is published, by Robert P. Eckert. It is the first biography and bibliography of Thomas. Eckert writes;

> He developed a love for the Welsh country, its people and its legends, its crags and hills, its winding lanes, its apple trees and its white rivers, that he never lost. It made him grateful for his Welsh inheritance, gave him an understanding of its temperament.

October: Geoffrey Grigson writes a review of Eckert for *John O'London's Weekly*, which is headlined, 'MORE ABOUT EDWARD THOMAS A WELSH POET WHO WROTE OF

ENGLAND'. Grigson begins with a scathing attack on Welsh writers by quoting, 'Mr. H. E. Bates said the other day that sex in Welsh novels was rather like decayed cheese'. Then Grigson adds his own voice to the criticism,

> And not only sex, and not only novels. There is almost a school of exudative, cheesy Welsh verse. There are scores of exudative, cheesy Welsh short stories, squashed up with rhetoric and violence. These Welsh rabbits (you will have understood I am not Welsh), this decayed Caerphilly, has certainly to do with some part of the Welsh nature, or some part of common nature which manages more easily to squeeze out to the surface if one is born in Wales.

He ends grudgingly by concluding: 'Edward Thomas is a smallish writer'.

Gwili Cofiant a Phregethau by E Cefni Jones, a life of Gwili is published. It contains a section on Edward Thomas, including a photograph and a letter from Edward to Gwili. [see Appendix 1.]

1938: *The Childhood of Edward Thomas* is published. It contains descriptions of his holidays to Wales as a young boy.

1939: John Moore's *The Life and Letters of Edward Thomas* is published by Heinemann. The introduction is by David Lloyd George, who writes:

> I am interested and attracted by him and his work, firstly because he was a Welshman, secondly, because he was a poet and thirdly, because he was a lover of Nature and the countryside.

August: Gwyn Jones's periodical, *The Welsh Review*, includes a long article on Edward Thomas by James Guthrie of the Pear Tree Press, who had published Thomas's first book of poetry, *'Six Poems by Edward Eastaway'*, in 1917. The article is illustrated with a woodcut by Guthrie's son, Robin, depicting Thomas out walking.

1940: June: Gordon Bottomley, the poet, dramatist and close friend of Edward Thomas, visits Cardiff University to lecture to the English Society on 'Poetic Drama in the late Thirties'. R. George Thomas, who went on to become the pre-eminent Edward Thomas scholar and editor, was there and reports that Bottomley spoke only 'briefly and with restrained feeling' about Thomas. However R. George also recounts that Bottomley was 'delighted to learn that Thomas's friend Gwili had been librarian and war-time teacher in the University'. However, he was somewhat surprised that the College Library did not possess a complete set of Edward Thomas's published works. Perhaps to spur them on, Bottomley made his first generous gesture when in June 1940 he gifted to the Library the original manuscript of *Beautiful Wales*. When making the gift he said:

> After treasuring this for 35 years I grow old and private possessions are in danger of destruction by enemy action. I am happy in transferring it to the greater safety of the University of Cardiff... to represent a great Welshman in his own ancestral quarter of Wales.

And just a few weeks later Bottomley gifted 238 letters from Thomas along with other important manuscripts and ephemera which became the basis for the Library's now extensive Edward Thomas holdings.

1941: Alun Lewis writes his memorial poem to Edward Thomas, 'All Day It Has Rained' which ends with the lines:

> To the Shoulder o' Mutton where
> Edward Thomas brooded long
> On death and beauty – till a bullet
> stopped his song.

1946: Dylan Thomas's BBC programme *Welsh Poetry* is broadcast in which he includes a section on Edward Thomas beginning:

> Now we come to the 20th century. From Edward Thomas, who was killed in France in 1917, to Alun Lewis, who died in India in 1944, there sprang to life a whole new body of poetry written by Welshmen. I do not think there was, in common between these poets, anything but a love of poetry and of their own country.

He then introduces his reading of 'The Child on the Cliffs' with these words, 'Here is a poem written in Wales', before reading Thomas's earlier poem 'The Owl'. He concludes the broadcast by quoting Alun Lewis, but mistakes Thomas's age, 'Edward Thomas was twenty-five years old when 'a bullet stopped his song'. Thomas was of course 39 – the same age that Dylan Thomas was when he died in New York in 1953.

1949: July 29: Dylan Thomas again broadcasts on Edward Thomas for the BBC Welsh Home Service's 'Arts Magazine'. Dylan would read nine poems by Thomas; 'The Owl', 'The Sign-Post', 'The Child in the Orchard', 'Snow', 'The Child on the Cliffs', 'The Unknown Bird', 'To-night', 'Sowing', and ending with 'Lights Out'.

The Welsh poet and critic A.G. Prys-Jones, reviewing the 1949 edition of Edward Thomas's *Collected Poems* in the *Western Mail,* describes Thomas as, 'a proud and solitary Welsh poet'.

1964: R. S. Thomas edits *Selected Poems of Edward Thomas* for Faber. He writes in his introduction:

> As he grew up, Edward sought out the Celtic tales and legends for himself, and later went on a walking tour of Wales. This he recorded in prose. It was a time of renewed interest in Celtic literature.

1965: *The Green Roads*, a selection of poems by Edward Thomas for young readers, is published by Bodley Head. It is edited by Eleanor Farjeon who also contributes an introductory essay, 'Walking with Edward Thomas', in which she observes:

> Still more he loved the traditions of the earth you were treading together; the past of the ancient earth of Kent and Wiltshire, or of his native Wales, which he loved better still.

1967: The *Anglo-Welsh Review*'s Winter issue contains an article by Alun John entitled, 'Edward Thomas: Anniversary Considerations'. It is a rather churlish and mean summing up – he speaks of, 'claims made from time to time that [Thomas] was a Welsh poet' and ends by dismissing Thomas, 'After all he was a shy self-effacing person who left no prose masterpiece and who was, even for those who greatly admire him, only a fine minor poet'. Damning with faint praise indeed.

1971: *Triskel One: Essays on Welsh and Anglo-Welsh Literature* is published by Christopher Davies, Wales. It contains Leslie Norris's essay 'The Poetry of Edward Thomas'. Writing of Thomas's war poem, 'As the Team's Head-Brass', Norris observes:

> The verb topple, seems to suggest not merely the turning of the earth under the plough, but the overthrow of the world.
>
> *The horses started and for the last time*
> *I watch the clods crumble and topple over*
> *After the ploughshare and the stumbling team.*
>
> Here too, the texture of the verse is wonderfully suggestive, the pattern of sounds in 'start' and 'last', 'clods', 'topple' and 'ploughshare', 'crumble' and 'stumbling' remind us of the Welsh use of sound-pattern and internal rhyming, as well as making palpable the very movement of the horse.

1978: *Poetry Wales* produce an 'Edward Thomas' special number, edited by John Powell Ward containing Alun John's article 'Edward Thomas and Wales'.

1980: The Edward Thomas Fellowship is established with Myfanwy Thomas as president. The Fellowships describes itself thus,

> Here you will find information about the poet, essayist and country writer Edward Thomas (1878-1917). The Edward Thomas Fellowship exists to promote knowledge and appreciation of his life and work.

1986: Faber publishes in their *Student Guides Series* Professor Stan Smith's monograph on Edward Thomas. Although written from his Marxist viewpoint it is nevertheless a study that emphasises Thomas's Welshness. Smith states categorically, 'There is after all one major complication to the concept of Edward Thomas as *the* English poet: *his Welshness'*. The italics are Smith's.

1987: *The Art of Edward Thomas* is published by Seren, edited by Jonathan Barker. It contains Sally Roberts Jones's informative essay 'Edward Thomas and Wales'.

1992: The National Library of Wales makes a significant addition to its Edward Thomas holdings. From America they acquire, Thomas's early correspondence with his first mentor, James Ashcroft Noble (the father of his future wife Helen), together with Thomas's diaries for 1900-1912 and 1915, and 300 letters to Helen dated from 1896-1917. Thomas's grandson also gifts two remarkable pocket books from 1914-1916 containing drafts of over fifty of his poems. Writing in the *Times Literary Supplement* about this major acquisition, Daniel Huws, the Keeper of Manuscripts at the National Library of Wales (and a published Faber poet), writes:

> When he was young, Thomas spoke of Wales as 'my soul's native land' …At several times of crisis it was to Wales that he withdrew. There, at Laugharne, he picked himself up after the severe breakdown of 1911. During the long withdrawals…there were long almost daily letters between Edward and Helen and they are some of their best. In 1910 Edward stayed at Tregaron and walked some of the remotest parts of Wales. Two extracts from letters convey some of the flavour (in the first is the germ of a later poem):
>
>> These mountain farms have a chapel smaller than themselves for each group of a dozen or so. They are just like one-roomed cottages with a fire place at one end for God to sit by on winter nights. People, usually women

and children, were haymaking in the little green fields among the rushy brown hillsides. Only one man passed me riding a pony & leading another. I could see him at some of the rises miles ahead. They ride the ponies as if sitting on a gate – I mean without any of the pomp of English horseriding:& they wear trousers and usually bowler hats.

1994: Twelve previously unpublished letters to Owen M. Edwards are published in the *National Library of Wales Journal*. They are edited with notes by Hazel Walford Davies.

1995: *Edward Thomas – Selected Letters* is published, edited by R. George Thomas.

2013: Andrew Webb's *Edward Thomas and World Literary Studies Wales Anglocentrism and English Literature* is published by the University of Wales Press. The book makes a strong case for the importance of Wales and Welsh history, culture and landscape in the life and work of Thomas.

February: Edward Thomas's poem 'Words' is selected by the *Guardian* for the 'Poem of the Week' section. In her long introduction to the poem, Carol Rumens makes much of the 'Welshness' of this poem and singling out Thomas's friendship with Gwili, she writes, 'Thomas may have known little of his forebear's language but he certainly heard Welsh spoken, and with Gwili's help, he made notes on Welsh verse-forms'.

2016: Newly discovered photographs by Edward Thomas are used in a new edition of *In Pursuit of Spring*. Cardiff-based photographer Rob Hudson found the images buried in the Cardiff University Edward Thomas archive. This remarkable set of photographs were taken by Thomas on a 130-mile bicycle ride from London to the Quantock Hills in Somerset in 1913 when he was researching for the book.

2017: *Under the Same Moon: Edward Thomas and the English Lyric*, by Edna Longley, is published. Despite the book's title the afterword is entitled *Archipelagic Thomas,* and in it Longley comments on Andrew Webb's work and reconsiders her opinions of Thomas's notions of nationality.

Heather Cobby contributes a very telling article in the *Journal of the Friends of the Dymock Poets No. 16.* 'Two Thomas's and *hiraeth'* examines the similar but divergent versions of this uniquely Welsh concept as it manifests itself in the writings of Edward Thomas and R.S. Thomas. Cobby quotes the University of Lampeter's 2016 definition of *Hiraeth;*

> Homesickness tinged with grief or sadness over the lost or departed. It is a mix of longing, yearning, nostalgia, wistfulness, or an earnest desire for the Wales of the past.

And goes on to quote Thomas's daughter Myfanwy on her observations of how this mix of emotions affected her father;

> I am sure that my father's feeling of searching for something, of not belonging, came from a yearning – *Hiraeth* (a beautiful, untranslatable Welsh word) – to belong to Wales, but that he could not honestly ease his way in, as it were, without being born and reared there.

Edward Thomas: A Life in Pictures by Richard Emeny is published by Enitharmon. It is a handsome, well-illustrated book. Wales is conspicuous by its almost total absence.

AFTERWORD

And I have known the sombre Cenfig water among the sands where I found the wild goose feather with which I write.

Beautiful Wales, 1905

I came to Edward Thomas quite late. My mother was Welsh; she came from a coal-mining family in a very small village, Ynysddu, in Monmouthshire. She had gone to London as a teenager to enlist in the WRAF at the start of the War, and met and married a cockney squaddie. She never returned to live in Wales. I grew up in the East End of London, but I spent most of my summer holidays running wild while staying with my Welsh grandparents in Ynysddu. My grandfather and all of my mother's three younger brothers worked at the coalface down the local pit. But my mother was bookish and encouraged a love of literature in me. She introduced me to Welsh writers, being especially proud to tell me of William Thomas, Islwyn, the Welsh bard who was born in Ynysddu. She read Kate Roberts, and, when I heard about a Welsh poet who had influenced Bob Dylan to change his name, she gave me FitzGibbon's biography of Dylan Thomas to read. In 1967, when I came to think about further education, I chose to go Wales, to Cardiff, to train to be a teacher.

At Cardiff College I was lucky to be taught by some very good lecturers – two of them were also poets – avuncular John Stuart Williams, who was head of English, and young urbane John Idris Jones, who had recently joined the staff after teaching in America. John Idris was a big fan of Edward

Thomas, but it was another lecturer, Mrs Jessie Thomas who was married to Dr R. George Thomas, the Professor of English at Cardiff University, who would have a profound effect on me. R. George Thomas was the pre-eminent Edward Thomas scholar. He was a passionate enthusiast for preserving and nurturing Edward Thomas' literary reputation. Edward Thomas's daughter Myfanwy wrote this about him in her 'Foreword' to Helen Thomas's book *Letters to Helen,*

> Mother, after her first meeting with R.G.T. was bright-eyed and happily amazed at how well the Cardiff professor knew and understood the complexity of Edward's nature; She was overjoyed and buoyant knowing he was the man she could trust to write about her husband.

George Thomas was also an assiduous book-collector. He was passionate about Edward Thomas as a writer but also obsessive about collecting his work. He single-handedly amassed a remarkable and extensive Edward Thomas archive of books, letters and manuscripts, which he eventually gifted to Cardiff University. He then set about soliciting more gifts from family and friends of the poet. As a result Cardiff University Library now has a magnificent and important Edward Thomas Collection.

Mrs Thomas arranged for her husband to come and lecture us on Edward Thomas's life and work as an extra-curricular special event. For me this memorable lecture was something of an epiphany, and Edward Thomas joined my list of favourite writers. I began searching out and buying paper-backs and cheap used copies of his books to carry with me and read.

I qualified and left Cardiff. Marriage took me further west to Swansea, where, in 1970, I opened a second-hand book-shop called *Dylans Bookstore,* in homage to the town's most famous literary son. I began to add all the other Welsh Thomases to my list of 'house authors' and Edward Thomas was one of them.

One of my first serious customers was a remarkable local collector, a retired schoolteacher named Elis Jenkins. His small semi-detached house in a suburb of Neath was like a side-gallery at the V & A. He collected the rarest books on Welsh and local history alongside fine Welsh porcelain and paintings. More interesting from my point of view at least, he was a nephew of John Jenkins, the bard Gwili. Elis was very proud of this connection and 1967 to commemorate the fiftieth anniversary of Thomas's death he wrote a detailed memoir of Edward Thomas and his Welsh friends that was published in *The National Library of Wales Journal*. In his article Elis described his treasured copy of Edward's third, and very rare book the 1902 edition of *Rose Acre Papers*, which was inscribed, 'To Gwili, wishing the book were better'. I coveted that book in a most un-Christian way – he could keep his ox and his donkey – I wanted that book! And many of the other Edward Thomas rarities, which he gloatingly enjoyed showing me, whenever I visited, usually to sell him something unusual on ceramics or the Neath Valley.

After Jenkins's death the bulk of his library was sold to an old Cardiff bookseller John Parker. I called on John not long after I started in the trade and we became good friends and I began to buy most of the good books that came his way. One Saturday evening I picked up the phone and Parker began reeling off a list of rare, local history and ceramics books that he had just acquired. "Were you dealing with folk by the name of Jenkins", I enquired hopefully. John's reply was incredulous, "Why yes – How the devil do you know that?" Only Elis Jenkins had books such as these on his shelves. I was knocking at Parker's door within the hour. All I could think of on the drive over was the inscribed *Rose*

Acre Papers. He opened the door into a hallway the floor of which was knee deep in books, the study was the same. I gave the books a cursory glance and asked "What did you pay?" He played his card; mumbled a figure. I offered his figure plus £200. He accepted. I loaded all the books into my car, virtually sight unseen, and headed west down the M4 feeling pretty pleased with myself.

It was a great collection, and the *Rose Acre Papers* was there. As were all the other Edward Thomas rarities I had lusted after for so long. I kept them all in my collection for a good while until I decided to offer it for sale. My passion for Edward Thomas had brought me into contact with other booksellers who were Edward Thomas aficionados; Stephen Frances Clark of Clearwater Books, Paul Gibb from Tiverton and his long-time running mate, Veronica Watts and Joan Stevens. We were general booksellers and bought whatever books of interest came our way, but we all pursued Edward Thomas with a special, albeit benign competitiveness. It was Paul Gibb who sold me a copy of *The Last Sheaf,* the uncommon posthumous collection of Edward Thomas's essays, where I was to discover Edward's remarkable essay *Swansea Village*. Reading it had a profound effect on me and increased my admiration for him as writer. It became a favourite and still is, and I often dream of publishing it in an elegant, illustrated, small, finely printed edition.

Our Paterfamilias, Alan Hancox, was a much loved bookman, and a great book-collector. Melvyn Bragg described him as being, "harmoniously domesticated, serene in his eccentricities, even the flow of white hair is just as it ought to be. Conjure up a Bookman and step forward A. Hancox". For a while Alan was the Director of The Cheltenham Literary Festival and his shop became a focus of literary life in the town. Alan's first literary love was Edward Thomas. He always had a well-stocked shelf of his books in his elegant shop, and he issued regular catalogues of Edward Thomas rarities. We all fed his habit like bookish drug dealers because he could not resist adding to his own collection. Hancox was, of course, interested in my collection. I sent him a brief catalogue of the collection, and he replied, keen to buy.

With my collection gone to a new and very appreciative home, Edward Thomas became a kind of house author, I always had a few titles in stock, I always had a few customers too, and I have to say that Edward Thomas, by and large, attracted a good class of reader and collector, focused but courteous, and as keen to talk about Edward Thomas as to buy his books. But they needed constant gratification and it was a decade or so before the next exciting cache came my way.

One day I received a telephone call from the widow of Theodore Roethke, the American poet and friend of Dylan Thomas. Beatrice Lushington as she had become, lived in Hastings and had been recommended to me by her neighbour, Rhiannon, who happened to be the daughter of the great Welsh editor, publisher and poet Keidrych Rhys – another good friend of Dylan Thomas. Just the day previously, Rhiannon Rhys had happened to visit my shop in Swansea and had noticed a striking reproduction image of Dylan Thomas, framed and hung behind my desk. The photograph had been taken in the graveyard in Laugharne in 1952, just a year before Thomas would end up buried there. The photographer was John Deakin, a Soho low-life, sometime lover of Francis Bacon, with a louche reputation; but he was a genius with a camera in his hand. I greatly admired his work. I greatly desired this image. I had wanted it from the very first time I ever saw it.

Beatrice had telephoned me because, by the kind of synchronicity that I cherish, she happened to have a rare and remarkable original print of the very same photograph, and she invited me to call and discuss the print. We made an appointment I drove down to Hastings and after some negotiation I bought the photograph. As I made to leave, Stephen, her second husband, intercepted me. Stephen Lushington was a long-retired, dedicated teacher and an extremely well-read book-lover. He was also a much-respected reader of poetry, indeed he was one of the readers in Westminster Abbey when the memorial stone to the First World War poets was unveiled by Ted Hughes in 1985, the service ending with his readings of two Edward Thomas poems. He explained that they were downsizing. Could I, would I, not just buy the photograph but also buy and remove Stephen's library; some 3,000 books, that filled to overflowing a downstairs circular study. I descended with some trepidation and my first impression was that, post-internet, what I saw before me was a booksellers' worst nightmare; shelf-full after shelf-full of tired old editions of the classics, many unreadable due to outdated content, others unreadable due to condition. But I had warmed to the couple upstairs and wanted to help, so I took a closer look.

I am glad I did. My first discovery, nestled away in a corner, was a small, neat, two-volume, 1817, third edition of Jane Austen's *Pride and Prejudice* in a nice contemporary calf binding. Not a first edition, but any lifetime printing was highly desirable. Next, a cursory look inside a grubby first edition of Virginia Woolf's *The Waves*, revealed an interesting hand-written postcard in her distinctive purple ink, praising 'young Lushington', (Stephen himself, now 90) for having the audacity to recite from her work at his school speech-day. I knew that would be easy to place. And then to my surprise – a cache of Edward Thomas books.

I should not have been surprised; I recalled in an instant that Stephen Lushington's father, Franklin Lushington, had been Edward Thomas's commanding officer when Edward, just 39 years old, was one of the first to fall on the first day of the battle of Arras. Edward had survived little more than two months in France. On his death, Major Lushington wrote this letter to Helen, Edward's widow, in which he chose to sanitise the exact nature of Edward's death to spare her further grief.

April 10th, 1917.
Dear Mrs. Thomas,

You will have heard by now from Mr. Thorburn of the death in action of your husband. I asked him to write immediately we knew about it yesterday, but delayed writing myself until the funeral, from which I have just returned.

I cannot express to you adequately in words how deep our sympathy is for you and your children in your great loss. These things go too deep for mere words. We, officers and men, all mourn our own loss. Your husband was very greatly loved in this battery, and his going has been a personal loss to each of us. He was rather older than most of the officers and we all looked up to him as the kind of father of our happy family.

He was always the same, quietly cheerful, and ready to do any job that was going with the same steadfast unassuming spirit. The day before his death we were rather heavily shelled and he had a very narrow shave. But he went about his work quite quietly and ordinarily as if nothing was happening. I wish I could convey to you the picture of him, a picture we had all learnt to love, of the old clay pipe, gumboots, oilskin coat and steel helmet.

With regard to his actual death you have probably heard the details. It should be of some comfort to you to know that he died at a moment of victory from a direct hit by a shell, which must have killed him outright without giving him a chance to realise anything, – a gallant death for a very true and gallant gentleman.

We buried him in a little military cemetery a few hundred yards from the battery: the exact spot will be notified to you by the parson. As we stood by his grave the sun came and the guns round seemed to stop firing for a short time. This typified to me what stood out most in your husband's character – the spirit of quiet, sunny, unassuming cheerfulness...

Yours very sincerely,

Franklin Lushington

(Major Comdg. 244 Siege Battery, R.G.A.)

When he got back to the UK, Lushington visited Helen in person and spent time with her. After his visit she wrote to a friend: 'He told me there was no wound and his beloved body was not injured'. Until quite recently this was the accepted version of Edward's death but his latest biographer, Jean Moorcroft Wilson, in the course of her research, discovered a letter in an American archive in which Lushington writes that Edward was 'shot clean through the chest'. Arras went on to claim close to 160,000 British casualties.

On his return to civilian life Franklin Lushington wrote a memoir of his war using the pseudonym Mark Severn. *The Gambardier: the Experiences of a Battery of Heavy Artillery on the Western Front during the First World War* was first published by Ernest Benn in 1930. Edward Thomas is featured as 'Thomas Tyler' and this is what his commanding officer wrote:

Among the subalterns Thomas Tyler alone was reliable and helpful. He was old enough to be Shadbolt's father and before the war, had achieved a name for himself as a writer. A great lover of the countryside and all of God's clean and pleasant things, it must have been hell for him to live and fight in the mud and foulness and never-ceasing din of war, his only relaxation at night the battery gramophone grinding out foxtrots and the barrack room jokes of Hickling and Lewis. He carried on quietly and patiently until he was killed about two months later. His serene and kindly presence did much to alleviate the squalid miseries of life for his companions.

The Lushington Edward Thomas books included many later books by and about him, many with evidence of the warm friendship which grew up between the two families, books warmly inscribed to Stephen by Helen and Myfanwy. But the real treasure was tucked inside a small, later reprint of *The Heart of England* by Edward Thomas. It was inauspicious to look at, a 1932, Dent edition, edited and illustrated by Eric Fitch Daglish. Tipped onto the front paste-down was the original autograph letter from Edward Thomas to Henry Nevinson asking permission to dedicate the first edition of the book to him. Nevinson was a remarkable man; a British War correspondent during the Second Boer War, and World War I, a campaigning journalist exposing slavery in Western Africa, a socialist political commentator and suffragist (as was Edward's wife Helen). When Edward came down from Oxford, Owen M. Edwards arranged for him to meet a number of Fleet Street editors and Nevinson at the *Daily Chronicle* was the only one to give Edward continuous reviewing work. He would later recommend Edward to write the A. & C. Black *Colour Book* on Oxford – Edward's first serious literary commission, for which he was paid a much needed £100.

Edward's letter was on printed note paper headed 'The Weald, Nr Sevenoaks', and dated 6.12.06.

Dear Nevinson,

May I dedicate to you a book called The Heart of England which I have written this year? It contains my best work plus a good deal of my worst as it is done in haste. But I know you will forgive that, and it would give me great pleasure and satisfaction to thank you, in this ethereal way, for your exquisite and lasting kindness. I still hope you will come down.

Yours

Edward Thomas

With the letter was a small postcard printed, with Henry Nevinson's name and Hampstead address. It is dated Sept 14th 1932 and addressed – Lushington at Pigeon Hoo, Tenterden, Kent. Nevinson had written:

Henry W. Nevinson, Friend of Edward Thomas.
The better part of Discretion is Valour.

Perhaps this is the most apt epitaph for Edward Thomas.

After some brief and cordial negotiations I bought the library and took it back to Swansea.

Stephen later wrote his own account of his father's life and the interactions with the Thomas family which was published in the newsletter of The Edward Thomas Fellowship. [see Appendix 2]

Around the time I acquired the Lushington library my most stalwart Edward Thomas customer was a wonderful man called Tim Wilton-Steer. I met him at a Book Fair in the Hotel Russell, where he visited every month when he was not away travelling with his job in international publishing. He only called on a small handful of booksellers who were party to, and empathised with, his obsession with the life and writings of Edward Thomas. Tim had great passions for many things – he was fit and energetic, played real tennis with a mad vigour, loved to travel to exotic places, loved a fine cigar and good brandy, but his passionate devotion to Edward Thomas was above all else.

Over the years I knew him, Tim bought almost all the exceptional Edward Thomas items that came my way; and he stretched his finances to the limit reaching for rare signed and inscribed books and autograph letters, but was also unstoppable in hoovering up any and every variant printing, foreign translation, magazine, periodical, newspaper or piece of ephemera that was in anyway related to Edward Thomas. I arranged for him to come to Swansea and talk on Edward Thomas in 2014 when I was programming literary events at the Dylan Thomas Centre and he delivered a magnificent talk on *The War Poetry of Edward Thomas*. The audience in the Centre were spellbound.

I offered the Lushington Edward Thomas books to Tim at what I thought was a fair price, but he reluctantly declined. They ended up being bought by a leading London bookseller.

Sadly, not long after, Tim died. Sometime later I visited Hilary, Tim's widow, who I had met when she and Tim came to Swansea. I spent an afternoon at their London home, left alone in what the family referred to as the 'Edward Thomas Room'. It was a big room and it was packed with an amazing collection, larger and more obsessively all-embracing than I could ever have imagined. Endless shelves with what seemed like at least a dozen (or more) variant printings of almost every Edward Thomas title; together with small collections of books by all his literary friends; biographical and critical books; as well as literary magazines, ephemera, photographs and prints. It was too much to take in, and when I opened the first edition of Horae Solitariae and saw Edward's small but beautiful, loving inscription to his wife I had to stop. Before leaving I spoke with Hilary about what might happen with the collection and offered what advice I could, but at that time no decisions had been made.

My most recent Edward Thomas acquisition also came out of blue, earlier this year – the centenary year of Edward's death. I received an email from a legendary London bookseller and litterateur, John Byrne, who for many years had worked and held court at Bertram Rota's Covent Garden bookshop. John is now gracefully semi-retired but enjoys facilitating the efficient handling of spectacular literary collections. John was sent in my direction by the National Library of Wales. He had delivered to them Edward Thomas's correspondence with W. H. Hudson, which were the jewels in a very fine Edward Thomas collection he was handling. When John asked the Library where in Wales he might find someone interested and appreciative of the rest of the extensive Edward Thomas collection and Welsh interest books, *Dylans Bookstore* was suggested.

The collection had been assembled over many years by Geoffrey Woolley, a proud Welshman who had died in 2010. He was born in Tredegar (where Edward Thomas's father was born) the son of a colliery owner. He was educated at Clifton College and Caius College, Cambridge, where he read English (when F.R. Leavis joined the faculty). After serving in the Second World War he became a journalist, first on the *Monmouth Beacon* and then the *Western Mail*. After moves to other provincial papers he finally joined *The Times*. In 1953 he became editor of the famous 'Letters Page'. He was to preside over it with consummate magisterial skill and tact for more than 30 years.

But Geoffrey was also a cultured, dedicated and accomplished book collector. With John Byrne's help I eventually made arrangements to go and see the sections of his library that might fall into what John had decided was my remit, and I drove down to Geoffrey's splendid home near Brighton. On arrival I met Geoffrey's partner and was guided to tables piled high with good Welsh topography, largely concerned with Monmouthshire, and some unusual Anglo-Welsh literature, including a fine Arthur Machen collection. Then John took over, and with great ceremony and the odd flourish on the way, he led me upstairs, where in a long book-lined passageway I was instructed to examine and appraise the 'lower seven shelves only'. I felt John might fit me with blinkers to prevent my covetous eyes from wandering. But I was more than satisfied with the Edward Thomas collection which filled the seven permitted shelves. John had told me that the holy grail of Edward Thomas collecting, the Pear Tree Press's *Six Poems by Edward Eastaway* (1916, only 100 copies printed) had already gone. I was disappointed, but had handled the book just once and felt grateful for that. Besides, what filled the shelves in front of me was wonderful enough. Just about all the books by and about Edward Thomas were present, largely in first edition, along with periodicals, ephemera and books by his literary friends. But of real note were several books from Edward's own library with his signature and brief notes – 5 out of 8 volumes of his set Wordsworth Poems; and a battered and well read copy of Trench's *On the Study of Words* and a collected edition of *The Plays of Massinger* all with his neat signature and date of acquisition. And there was a fine presentation copy of his biography of Swinburne, with a very warm inscription to Theodore Watts-Dunton, Swinburne's friend and patron, who had helped Edward so much with his book.

A deal was struck that satisfied all parties involved and we packed the books into my car, but just before leaving John came bounding into the room clutching a small red volume and demanding I immediately write a supplementary substantial cheque. The book was *The Tenth Muse* with an oh-so-sweet inscription from Edward to W. H. Davies. I haggled weakly and wrote the cheque. Back in Swansea it was a real joy to catalogue the books, many of which revealed hidden extras in the way of newspaper cuttings, ephemera and manuscript notes. Some of the books quickly found new homes, especially when I took a stall at Cardiff University's Edward Thomas Centenary Symposium.

At the Cardiff Conference I met Dr. Andrew Webb from Bangor University, whose book *Edward Thomas and World Literary Studies* I had recently read, and which, as already mentioned, in many ways prompted this book. I also met Jeremy Mitchell, the treasurer of Petersfield Museum. It was very gratifying when he approached, read my name tag, took a step back and said 'So you're the source of so many of Tim's Books! I find your invoices in so many of them'. It became apparent that the family of Tim Wilton-Steer had decided to gift Tim's Edward Thomas collection, in its entirety, to Petersfield Museum. It was to be housed in a newly expanded Edward Thomas Study Centre, which was part of the revamped old County Police Station. I was invited to the opening day celebrations which were to take place within the huge gothic splendour of nearby St Peter's Church.

The drive down to Petersfield took me through some of Edward's favourite walking country. The programme for the day looked very interesting – a stellar line up of Edward Thomas aficionados – Edna and Michael Longley, Edward's recent biographer Matthew Hollis, Richard Emeny, the Chairman of the Edward Thomas Fellowship and Guy Cuthbertson who had recently edited Edward Thomas prose 'Autobiographies' for the OUP (the TLS Book of the Year). None of these speakers disappointed and Michael's reading was deeply moving; echoing and resonating around the towering ecclesiastical gothic space. As a bonus, at the end of the conference the Centre bought an interesting, unpublished biographical manuscript about Edward from the Woolley Collection, which has now joined the other 1800 items in the collection.

With hindsight it was the synchronicity of buying the Lushington and Woolley Collections, reading Andy Webb's book and meeting him at The Cardiff Centenary Edward Thomas Conference, hearing his lecture, and then the subsequent opening of the Wilton-Steer Memorial Collection, that prompted this book. Somehow the thoughts and emotions these events engendered in me, grew into a feeling that Edward Thomas's 'Welshness' was being overlooked, and after living in Wales for 50 years I had developed my own deep feelings for Wales. I had developed my own *Hwyl* and *Hiraeth*. I had recently read Jean Moorcroft Wilson's, 2015 life of Edward Thomas – *From Adlestrop to Arras*. The first page of the first chapter has a passage which I will quote because it struck such a chord;

> Origins fascinate most people, especially their own. They were of more than usual interest Edward Thomas... His engagement to the past began... aged 5, with a visit to his parents' native home of Wales. It was here he conceived a 'passion for Wales' which never left him. Inspired by his own ancestors and partly by the country's colourful history... Thomas's own London birth...seemed to him an 'accidentally Cockney nativity'.

I can empathise with all these notions and conjectures. I have felt them too. Like Edward Thomas, I feel that I too had experienced 'an accidentally Cockney nativity'. These are the thoughts that inspired me to compile this anthology which I hope in some way brings Edward Thomas's work back to Wales.

APPENDIX 1
THE WELSH FRIENDS OF EDWARD THOMAS – WATCYN WYN, JOHN JENKINS (GWILI), AND OWEN M. EDWARDS

In February 1902 Edward Thomas wrote a laudatory review of Owen M. Edwards's *Wales* in the *Academy* magazine. He manages not only to praise the author, his Oxford tutor, but also to sing the praises of his two other great Welsh friends and influences, Watcyn Wyn and Gwili.

Watcyn Hezekiah Williams, 1844–1905. Known as Watcyn Wyn – Schoolmaster, poet, and preacher.

Wyn was born in 1844 at Ddolgam, in the Llynfell valley, Carmarthenshire.. It was a remote, rural community in which many old Welsh folk-customs survived. He was brought up, the second of a family of ten, on his father's farm of Cwm garw Ganol, near Brynaman. At the age of eight he began work in one of the local coal mines that were opening in the region. He worked, chiefly as a collier, with occasional periods of attendance at various local schools, until the age of twenty-seven. Later in life he would insist that the best school he attended was the one held by his fellow colliers in the bowels of the earth. This was a Welsh school, with no trace of the unspeakable "Welsh Not"' (at this time pupils were banned from speaking Welsh during school hours). In his own words:

> Every lunch time we had a class for reading or writing in Welsh, or making a speech, or composing a verse or singing a song.

Literary competitions were held and the compositions were written in chalk on a piece of stone. it was at one of these that he had his first eisteddfod success for crafting a verse on the subject Y Ci Kipar [the dog Kipar]—with a box of matches as the prize.

In 1870 he married Mary Jones of Trap, Carreg Cennen; but her death in less than a year led him to quit his home and occupation, and in 1872 he entered the school of his relative, Evan Williams of Merthyr. His progress was rapid, and he was soon able to give assistance in teaching. In 1874 he decided to become an independent minister. He returned home and began to preach at Gibea Chapel, and, after a little preliminary training, was admitted to the Presbyterian College at Carmarthen in 1875. After he qualified and having left the college in 1879, he married Anne Davies of Carmarthen, when, instead of seeking a pastorate, he took a post as a teacher in a private school at Llangadock. In 1880 he and a friend moved to Ammanford and founded the 'Hope Academy'. In 1884 Watkyn took sole charge, and in 1888 he moved to new premises which he adapted for school purposes, He named his school 'Gwynfryn' and he was to teach here for the rest of his life fashioning the institution as a preparatory school for those about to enter the dissenting ministry or other professions. He was ordained an independent minister in 1894.

Edward Thomas wrote to Gordon Bottomley from Swansea on November 23rd, 1905. He was not having a great time and shared a catalogue of his woes with his friend ending

> The merriest man I ever knew – Watcyn Wyn – the bard who wrote *The Maid of Llandebie* and the *Maids of Carmarthenshire* is to be buried today: and on Sunday I am to be taken in my bowler hat and collar to a Welsh chapel in the town.

Edward had included both these songs by Wyn (which had been translated from the original Welsh versions by Gordon Bottomley) in *Beautiful Wales* and he comments to Bottomley, 'I shall rejoice over Wales just because it includes these songs'.

After the death of his wife Watcyn Wyn was cared for by his daughter Mary who gave up her own life in order to dedicate all her time to her beloved father. She kept house for him and also kept a Day-Book for visitors to write in. It is a remarkable gathering of poems, quotes, and drawings by the good and the great of Welsh literature and politics who thronged to the Wyn's door. Gwili writes two poems for her, but a real interest is a full page humorous drawing by Edward Thomas's brother signed 'Oscar Thomas Clapham London' But the real surprise in the album is this fine autograph poetic quotation by Edward Thomas, who inscribes a favourite extract from a favourite poet – Shelley's *Ode to the West Wind*. It is signed and dated 'Edward Thomas 19 viii 98 Oxford'

***

John Jenkins (Gwili), 1872 – 1936. Welsh Poet and Teacher
John Jenkins, who is better known by his bardic name Gwili (after the local river), was born in Hendy, Carmarthenshire in 1872. He was educated at the Baptist College after which he taught at Watcyn Wyn's Gwynfryn school in Ammanford for eight years. It was during this time, around 1897, that he met and became good friends with Edward Thomas. Apart from being a gifted poet Gwili went on to become one of Wales's foremost theologians gaining a doctorate in literature from the University of Oxford. Thomas learned much of what he knew of Wales – its folklore, literature, topography and natural history, from Gwili, who also

accompanied Thomas on walking and fishing trips around West Wales. Gwili is the canny angler described in Thomas's essay 'Digressions on Fish and Fishing' as a 'superannuated preacher of some rigid sect in Wales, who had exchanged quite naturally his symbolical crook for rod and line'.

In 1937 a Welsh biography of Gwili was published – *GWILI Cofiant a Phregethau* by E Cefni Jones. It has a section on Edward Thomas, including a photograph and a letter from Thomas to Gwili. The following is a translation of the passage:

Edward Thomas

We have already referred to him, and to his visits to Gwili in Hendy and Ammanford. In September 1897 Edward Thomas, was grieving with Gwili over the death of Ben Bowen, who died on August 16th, 1903, and the whole of Wales were in tears of despair after him. Edward was staying in the south in *Gwili Cottage*. The following days Gwili and Edward Thomas visited interesting local places, paths that were to become well trodden by the two of them. "I remember", Gwili said in an article in the *News Chronicle*, "a long journey made by Edward Thomas, and another friend, on a moonlit night, to the Golden Grove, the discussion we had, as we made our way through the brushwood, of past inhabitants who wandered these ancient tracks long Grongar Hill. It is to these journeys that I attribute his edition of the works of John Dyer, and his interest in the Towy Valley and its literary radiations. "Such was his enthusiasm that he persuaded his friend Thomas Seccombe, author of *Age of Johnson*, to make a summer journey to Carmarthen and then on by bicycle up to Llandeilo, and onward to Carreg Cennen, and to meet us there. "The conversation we had that day by the Castle was very interesting, Seccombe was cursing Robertson Nicoll for cutting his *Hanes Llenyddiaeth Saesneg (History of English Literature)* to nearly half its intended size. I teased him after he confessed that he had forgotten everything about the connection between Taylor and Dyer and the Valley he was travelling through; Edward Thomas and he had great enjoyment laughing about *The Parson* – the nickname they had given me. I will never forget that sunny day, and I see from Seccombe's words to remember Edward Thomas, in the *Times Literary Supplement,* that our day at Carreg Cennen is also sealed in his memory".

A large number of the letters Edward Thomas wrote to Gwili from the year 1897 onwards, are available, and kept as sacred treasures with the family. Edward Thomas's father was from Tredegar, and he moved to London having secured a post in the Marketing Board. It was there that he brought up and educated six sons, Edward being the eldest of them. A correspondent of the *News Chronicle* noted on 1st July, 1931:

The interest in Edward Thomas and his works is increasing, and the various editions of his essays and poems, have appeared during the last few years, culminating in the beautiful selections of the Gregynog Press, which are now widely known. Reference has been made previously to the time spent by Edward Thomas in Wales, and to his Welsh associations generally... He used to stay with Philip Trehearne Thomas, but his greatest friend during his Welsh 'holidays' was Gwili, himself a keen student and lover of Nature. I remember hearing of Gwili and Edward tramping over the Black Mountains, and finally reaching Dryslwyn. Edward Thomas was trying to get into conversation with the Welsh dairymaid of the farm at which they had called, but she turned to Gwili and asked in Welsh, 'What's this Cockney trying to say?' These visits must have been when Edward Thomas was a student in Lincoln College, Oxford. Readers of Thomas's essays will recall one in which *Gwili Cottage* and its kitchen are described with the felicity characteristic of a lover of old things. It was in this kitchen that he spent most of his time when at Pontardulais, fondly handling the old brass candlesticks, which stood on the mantelpiece, and blowing the fire with the old studded bellows. He was so attracted to them, that when he moved to *Rose Acre Cottage* (his first home after marriage), he had bought himself a pair of candlesticks and a bellows from a second-hand dealer in London.

The following is an interesting letter that Edward Thomas wrote to Gwili's mother, in September 1904, after one of his visits to *Gwili Cottage*:

My dear Mrs Jenkins

Since I got back home, I have been puzzling how I might best thank you for all the pleasure I received at Pontardulais from you and your daughters. I wanted to thank you prettily, so as to show you I was indeed grateful. But I could not do it, I could merely say "Thank you" very heartily. Well, I thought that was not enough, and I gave up trying to tell you how grateful I was, and how affectionately I think of you all, and decided to send you these flowers instead; they, I am sure, will thank you very prettily, unless they have faded by the time they reach Hendy. They are very few; if you think they are too few, remember that we have not enough flowers in London, so we cannot spare many even for our best friends; if we did not keep some back, I do not know how we should live.

I expect Sarah Ann is reading this for you, and I hope she will not forget that I thought of her too, when I sent the flowers, and Bronwen too. Perhaps they will wear one each, may they, if the flowers are alive on Sunday. I should like to think of Lizzie and Sarah Ann and Bronwen wearing flowers to chapel, if such gay things are permitted.

I hope this bright hot weather will not torment you very much, though it does serve as an excuse for staying indoors in that cosy kitchen "cooch" of yours, singing your lovely Welsh. Please ask Gwili always to let me know how you all are when he writes to me; and to let me know when the kitchen is bright in the late autumn, because of the falling of the poplar trees by the door, before midday.

Ever yours gratefully,

Edward Thomas

In *The Annual of Poetry* of 1917, which contains the works of some of the major English poets for that year, there are eighteen poems by Edward Eastaway. As has been noted, the early death of Edward Thomas was a bitter and difficult blow for Gwili, and there is nothing more tender in his English Songs than his poem in remembrance of his fond friend._

EDWARD EASTAWAY

"They are lonely
While we sleep, lonelier
For lack of the traveller,
Who is now a dream only."

I miss thee in the dim and silent woods
Where Gwili purled for two who loved her well
Her rippling sweetness through her shrivelled reeds;
And where we played at fishing with our hands,
Or garnered nuts that fell from out their cups,
A voluntary shower; or climbed the bridge,
A gipsy hand to help us gain the road.

The river murmurs still; the hazels pelt
Into the stream their golden affluence.
It is October, and the woods are dim,
And lovely in their loneliness – but thou
Hast travelled west, my Edward Eastaway,
And to these silent woods wilt come no more.

I miss thee on th' undesecrated moor
That shelters Llyn Llech Owen, where the cry
Of curlews give us welcome, and the Lake
Of legend led thy dreaming spirit far
To some grey Past, where thou again couldst see
The heedless horseman gallop fiercely home,
And the well drown the moorland with is spate.
Again I cross through sedges, and the gorse
Burns like the bush of Horeb unconsumed.
The golden lilies in their silver bed
Rustle, and whisper something faint and sad.
Can some maimed wanderer from the fields of France
Have lingered by these waters on his way,
And murmured to the lilies and the reeds
That thou hadst passed along another road
Far to the west, where Llyn Llech Owen woos
No longer, and where lilies are unheard?

And most of all I miss thee on the road
To Carreg Cennen, and the castled steep
Thou lovedst in all weathers, and the cave
Thither we wandered in thine Oxford days,
When there were hours of gladness in thy heart
That seemed a hoard thy childhood had conserved,
When song burst out of silence, and the depths
Of thy mysterious spirit was were unsealed.

Thither we sauntered in the after-years,
London cares had made thy Celtic blood
Run slow, and thou had'st sought thy mother Wales
Full suddenly – for all too brief a stay.
Lore of the ages, music of old bards
That would have soothed the ear of Golden Grove
And its great exile priest, and brought delight
To Nature's nursling bard of Grongar Hill,
Beguiled the footsore pilgrims many an eve,
Past Llandyfân and Derwydd, past Glyn Hir.
It is October, but thou comest not
Again, nor hast returned since that wild night
When we were on this road, late lovers twain,
And thou said'st, in thy firm and silent way,
That all roads led to France, and called thee hence
To seek the chivalry of arms.
To-night,
The road is lonelier – too lonely far
For one. I turn toward set of sun, since thou
Hast journeyed west, dear Edward Eastaway.

from *Poems* by Gwili. 1920

Owen Morgan Edwards, 1858 – 1920. Writer, publisher and scholar

The Welsh scholar, Hazel Walford Davies, who is currently engaged in writing a new biography of Owen M. Edwards has this to say about the importance of Edwards to Thomas:

O.M. Edwards and Oxford confirmed intellectually what Wales herself, through, the friendship with Gwili and John Williams, the schoolmaster of Waun Wen Swansea, had already made the young Edward feel on the pulse.

Edwards was born in Llanuwchllyn, Merionethshire, in 1848, the eldest son of Owen and Elizabeth. Originally intended for the ministry, his education began at the local church school, and continued at Bala Theological College. He then took a more secular path and at Aberystwyth he read English and History. After a year at Glasgow University in 1884, he entered Balliol College, Oxford and his brilliant career as a historian began. He travelled in Europe, but then returned to Oxford, this time to Lincoln College, where he took up his post as a Fellow and Tutor. However, it became apparent that, more than just an historian, he was a fine all-round man of letters. He published his popular survey *Wales* (in *The Story of the Nations* series) in 1901. The book and its author had a profound effect on his student Edward Thomas who had arrived at Oxford under Edwards tutelage in 1898.

Owen M. Edwards's real interest lay in promoting Welsh culture particularly the indigenous Welsh folk culture, in both the Welsh and English language. To facilitate this he founded, edited, and contributed to many important Welsh periodicals in particular *Cymru* and its English counterpart *Wales*. Edwards had also set to work to reprint considerable selections of classic Welsh Literature, notably in his two series of classic reprints *Cyfres y Fil* and *Welsh Library Series* – Edwards had sent Edward Thomas his three volume edition of the *Mabinogion* and then commissioned him to edit the volume on the Welsh poet, John Dyer.

Edwards would go on to publish many books in Welsh, the most influential being *Cartrefi Cymru*, which came out in 1896. This book encapsulated Edwards's deep-rooted feelings about the importance of the hearth and the home in Welsh folk-culture, an idea explored in depth by Professor M. Wynn Thomas of Swansea University, in his book *The Nations of Wales*, 1890-1914 (UWP 2016), Professor

Thomas describes it as his 'great ideologue of the '*gwerin*', adding that the book 'became virtually a classic overnight'.

Although *Cartrefi Cymru (The Homes of Wales)* is written in Welsh, Edward Thomas seems to have been deeply influenced by the book and to have shared similar ideas to those of his tutor and one can only assume that the two men discussed in depth the ideas around Edwards' notion of *y werin*, which M. Wyn Thomas defines as;

> ...the seminal self-aggrandising Nonconformist concepts of *y werin* (the naturally cultured and devout rural 'volk')

When Edward Thomas's second book, *Horae Solitariae*, came out in 1902, Thomas dedicated it to Owen M. Edwards. Andrew Webb has pointed out some remarkable similarities between O.M. Edwards's book and Thomas's. He notes that *Horae Solitariae* shares with *Cartref y Cymru* a strong love and respect for rural Welsh culture, particularly as manifested in pastoral hospitality and the sanctity of the 'hearth and home'. Webb also points out the similarity of O.M. Edwards's passage in *Cartrefi Cymru* in which he describes a Welsh hotel, where he takes shelter from the storm, and enjoys not only its roaring fire and food but that 'there were books also. That is the difference between a Welsh hotel and other hotels', comparing it to Thomas's essay, 'Inns and Books', in which Thomas's narrator shelters from a storm in the Merlin Arms and describes various books in the parlour. Edward Thomas seemed throughout his short life to experience 'Hiraeth' – that Welsh word, with no real English equivalent, for a certain homesickness and yearning for the security of a much loved, specific place. A phenomena that Jeremy Hooker explores in his edited selection of Thomas's short stories *The Ship of Swallows* (Enitharmon 2005).

APPENDIX 2
AN UNSIGNED REVIEW OF *THE HAPPY-GO-LUCKY MORGANS,* FROM *THE WELSH REVIEW*, NOVEMBER 1914

Mr. Edward Thomas is well-known as a writer of distinction and a literary critic of acute insight and catholic tastes. As a Swinburnian critic his ability and authority are generally recognised, and his Borrovian studies have gladdened the heart of every lover of that human and enigmatic nomad – George Borrow. In this book the author appears in a new literary role – that of the writer of romance – and the volume has all the grace, charm, and love of the highways and byways of letters which we have learnt to associate with the author's work.

The story – what there is of it – is "of Balham and of a family dwelling in Balham who were more Welsh than Balhamitish." There, in Abercorran House, dwelt the Morgans – father, mother, five sons and the daughter Jessie: as careless, irresponsible and delightfully Bohemian a set of people as one could wish to meet in a year's reading. Even to say that they are irresponsible and Bohemian is to do them some injustice. For the epithets are too definitive and exact, and the Morgans, as they flit across these pages, are indefinable and almost indefinite characters. They are shadowy without being unreal or vague. Their elusiveness is not the elusiveness of objects seen in twilight or through a haze, but the elusiveness of fairies and fairy-land. Every wise man has known fairies, though none but fools attempt to define them. They belong to those things in life which are too large or too small for our definitions. The Morgans belong to the same category. And so true is this about the Morgans that one cannot at all times be quite certain whether Mr. Thomas set out to write a story, fairy-like and romantic, or to propound an allegory. There is so much suggestiveness, – so fine a criticism of life (not, of course, of the inartistic, speculative, pedagogic order) in the volume, that one feels that the story has only just fallen short of being both an excellent romance and an excellent allegory. This ambiguity may or may not have been intentional, but in so far as it exists it creates a mild misunderstanding between author and reader. And even the unmistakably human and mundane properties of Ann – the permanent servant of whom it was said that they also rule who only serve and wait – tend to rather aggravate than to clear up the misunderstanding.

This, however, is but a slight blemish, and microscopic fault-finding is ungrateful where there is so much to please. Those who will go to the book for the mere pleasure of reading a tale will find a story well and imaginatively told; and for those who delight to delve beneath the surface there is here rich ore. The writer is on the side of the poetry of life and underneath the serenity of his style there burns volcanic fires of revolt against everything that makes for the materialism of men. And no Welshman who wishes to see his people as they appear to a just and friendly observer should miss reading "The Happy-go-lucky Morgans."

APPENDIX 3
STEPHEN LUSHINGTON'S MEMOIR OF HIS FATHER, FRANKLIN LUSHINGTON, AND EDWARD THOMAS

This memoir was first published in the *Newsletter of the Edward Thomas Fellowship* in 1997.

It was eighty years ago, Easter Monday 1917, that Edward Thomas was killed on the opening day of the battle of Arras. My father Franklin Lushington, a young man of 24, commanded the battery of Siege Guns in which Edward served and died. In his unpublished account of two world wars he wrote of Edward:

"He was a quiet scholarly man, a little older than the rest of us, with a manner at once open and withdrawn. His approach to life's problems was simple and direct. Poetry and gunnery might be poles apart, but each could be made to yield their secrets if tackled honestly and with humility. Edward had lost the youthful arrogance and affectation that betrays uncertainty. He was sure of himself and of his world and the knowledge of this shone through him as light shines through glass. His willingness to do all things for the general good rather than for himself alone, coupled with an innate modesty and goodness of heart, endeared him to us all. Yet behind it one felt a certain reserve, a kind of hidden melancholy that may have been due to loneliness. For his was a spirit beyond the common run and he may well have felt lonely at times among us. Edward loved England and the English countryside and all that pertains to an outdoor life.

North of the valley of the river Scarpe stands Vimy Ridge, whence the ground, downland, unfenced and almost treeless, drops abruptly towards the city of Arras and the Douai plain. South and east of the town lie a number of large caves and quarries from which in the seventeenth century the chalk was quarried for the rebuilding of the city. It was in one of those quarries, on the outskirts of the little village of Achicourt, that we went into action for the coming battle. On the day of our arrival a lorried ammunition column was driving through the main street when it was caught by a German concentration. In an instant the blazing exploding lorries turned the village into an inferno and, when the German guns lifted, there was nothing left of it but heaps of brick rubble and burning wood.

It was now our turn. For half an hour the shells rained into the quarry. One plunged into the ground at Edward's feet but failed to explode. "Edward" Tom said that night in the mess, "you obviously bear a charmed life. No doubt you will be the only one of us to survive the war".

There was much to be done in the short month before the battle. For in addition to all the normal routine work connected with taking up a new position in the line, the laying out of the telephone system, the selection of observation posts, the registration of targets, the building of dugouts and shelters, the dumping and counting of ammunition, the new battery was still only half trained.

Easter Monday, April 9th 1917, dawned cold and wintry. Heavy black clouds in the eastern sky portended snow and bad weather. They hung like a menace of evil over the tortured land on which the shells were falling with a slow and languid monotony as if even they were weary of this endless business of destruction. In the packed trenches long lines of haggard faced men, bayonets fixed and gas masks at the alert, waited impatiently for zero hour. In the gun positions shells were being fused and final preparations made to launch that storm of metal which was to move before our infantry from trench to trench, from stronghold to stronghold.

I looked at my watch. Edward should be at the O.P. by now. Why hadn't he rung me up? An instant later the air was rent by a swelling thunder of sound, stunning, ear-splitting, deafening. The battle of Arras had begun.

We were having breakfast when the signaller at the O.P. telephoned that Edward was dead, killed by a chance shell a moment before the barrage fell. Soon after it was reported that we had taken all our objectives. At midday we ceased fire. The enemy was out of range.

It began to snow. Outside the quarry, on the track leading up towards the front of the cavalry were moving up, little men on hairy unclipped horses, muddied to the hocks; coming towards them under the falling snow were the stretcher bearers carrying Edward's body, trudging unsteadily down the rough track."

It was my father's job to write to Helen about Edward's death and his letter led to a long family friendship which he valued very much. Later I was privileged to be part of this and as I approach my own 80th birthday I remember Helen as one of the warmest, most genuine and delightful people I have ever met.

Eighty years ago Edward was a poet of less than three years; in the army he kept his poems to himself and was most anxious not to appear different or superior both in his early days in the ranks and in his last months as an officer. The MS of two of his poems was written on a page torn from an army notebook with gunnery calculations scrawled at the top, the lines written straight on as if they were prose, so that his companions should not know they were poems. One of these was 'Lights Out', a long time favourite of mine, so that it was a particular pleasure for me to read it in Poets'

Corner, Westminster Abbey, on November 11th 1985 at the dedication of the Memorial to World War I Poets.

What a change in his reputation and standing as a poet between those years! From the edition of 1920 published by Selwyn & Blount, with its sensitive and sympathetic introduction by Walter de la Mare; twelve years later recognition from F.R. Leavis in New Bearings in English Poetry; both early signposts to a public not yet ready to open its arms. But his greatest, steadiest, most tireless supporter was Helen who must have realised before she died how wonderfully her efforts had borne fruit.

Edward's apprenticeship to prose was wearying but not in vain; when he came to write poems he had learnt that words need wooing, not ravaging, in fact he addresses them in the poem of that name as if it is not he who is using them, but they him, and it is this poem that Walter de la Mare quotes in his 1920 introduction. When I was lecturing in Modern Poetry at Goldsmith's College Summer School in 1970, 'Words' was one of the poems which interested students the most. I was offered the job by the head of University College London because he had heard me give a reading.

But it is the personal memories that I value most. Helen, and later Bronwen, came to visit us at Pigeon Hoo, Tenterden, and I bicycled to stay with Helen at Starwell Farm, Chippenham, where she cooked me scrambled eggs mixed with tomatoes and gave me a copy of Middleton Murry's book 'Keats & Shakespeare'. I have too a copy of Dover Wilson's 'The Essential Shakespeare' inscribed "To Stephen Lushington, a fellow-enthusiast, from Helen Thomas, Sept 1932". I was fifteen and flattered by the description! Years later I paid at least one longer visit to Helen and Myfanwy at Bridge Cottage, and later still brought my young daughter and her friend for a day out. Helen loved young people, and they immediately took to her warm and natural welcome.

When Eric Anderson, then Head master of Eton, was appointed Rector of Lincoln College, Oxford, Edward's old college, I sent him one of the cards of ET's poems with a woodcut by Yvonne Skargon to congratulate and wish him well. In his reply of 27 April 94 he wrote "Your card brought me good news since I did not know, I am afraid, that Edward Thomas (one of my favourite poets and my wife's) was a Lincoln man."

I should like to end these rambling thoughts by quoting a letter Edward wrote to H.W. Nevinson ninety years ago. Helen gave me the original which I treasure.

The Weald, Sevenoaks 6.12.06
Dear Nevinson,

May I dedicate to you a book called The Heart of England which I have written this year? It contains my best work plus a good deal of my worst as it is done in haste. But I know you will forgive that, and it would give me great pleasure and satisfaction to thank you, in this ethereal way, for your exquisite and lasting kindness. I still hope you will come down.

Yours
Edward Thomas

BIBLIOGRAPHY

Primary Sources

Thomas, Edward, *A Language Not To Be Betrayed: selected prose of Edward Thomas*, ed. Edna Longley (Manchester: Carcanet, 1981).
- *The Annotated Collected Poems*, ed. Edna Longley (Newcastle: Bloodaxe, 2008).
- *Beautiful Wales* (London: A. & C. Black, 1905).
- *Celtic Stories* (Oxford: Clarendon Press, 1911).
- *The Chessplayer and Other Essays* (Andoversford, Glos: Whittington Press, 1981).
- *The Childhood of Edward Thomas* (London: Faber and Faber, 1938).
- *Chosen Essays* (Newtown: Gregynog Press, 1926).
- *The Country* (London: B.T. Batsford, 1913).
- Diary, 29 September 1901, National Library of Wales.
- *Four-and-Twenty Blackbirds* (London: Duckworth & Co, 1915).
- *George Borrow, The Man and His Books* (London: Chapman & Hall, 1912).
- *The Happy-Go-Lucky Morgans* (London: Duckworth, 1913).
- *Horae Solitariae* (London: Duckworth & Co, 1902).
- *The Icknield Way* (London: Constable, 1913).
- *The Last Sheaf* (London: Jonathan Cape, 1928).
- *Letters to Gordon Bottomley*, ed. R. George Thomas (Oxford: Oxford University Press, 1968).
- *Letters to Helen*, ed. R. George Thomas (Manchester: Carcanet, 2000).

- *Light and Twilight* (London: Duckworth & Co, 1911).
- *A Pilgrim and Other Tales,* ed. R. George Thomas (London: Dent, 1991).
- *The Pocket Book of Poems and Songs for the Open Air* (London: E. Grant Richards,1907).
- *The Pocket George Borrow* (London: Chatto & Windus, 1912).
- *The Poems of John Dyer* (London: T. Fisher Unwin, 1903).
- *Rest and Unrest* (London: Duckworth & Co, 1910).
- *Selected Poems* (Newtown: Gregynog Press, 1927).
- *A Selection of Letters to Edward Garnett* (Edinburgh: The Tragara Press, 1981).
- *The Ship of Swallows: a selection of short stories,* ed. Jeremy Hooker (London: Enitharmon, 2005).
- *The South Country* (London: Dent, 1909).

Secondary Sources

Barker, Jonathan, ed. *The Art of Edward Thomas* (Bridgend: Poetry Wales, 1987).

Berridge, Anthony, ed. *Letters of Edward Thomas to Jesse Berridge* (London: Enitharmon, 1983).

Cooke, William, *Edward Thomas: A Critical Biography* (London: Faber and Faber, 1970).

- *Edward Thomas: A Portrait* (Youlgrave: Hub, c. 1978).

Coombes, H., *Edward Thomas* (London: Chatto, 1956).

- *Edward Thomas: A Critical Study* (London: Chatto, 1973).

Cuthbertson, Guy, 'Edward Thomas Prose Writings', Vol. I., *Autobiographies* (Oxford: O.U.P., 2011).

- & Lucy Newlyn, *England and Wales*, Vol. II. (Oxford: O.U.P., 2011).

Davies, Sir Alfred T., ed. *"O.M." (Sir Owen M. Edwards): a memoir* (Cardiff & Wrexham: Hughes, 1946).

Davies, Hazel, 'Edward Thomas: twelve unpublished letters to O. M. Edwards', *National Library of Wales Journal* 28, no. 3. (1994) pp. 335-345.

de la Mare, Walter, 'Foreword' in *Edward Thomas Collected Poems,* ed. R. George Thomas (London: Faber and Faber, 2004) pp. 246-53.

Eckert, Robert P., *Edward Thomas: a Biography and a Bibliography* (London: Dent, 1937).

Edwards, Owen M., *Cartrefi Cymru* (Wrexham: Hughes, 1896).

– *Wales* (London: T. Fisher Unwin, 1901).

Emeny, Richard, Jeff Cooper, *Edward Thomas, 1878-1917: towards a complete checklist* of his publications (Blackburn: White Sheep Press, 2004).

– *Edward Thomas: A Life in Pictures* (London: Enitharmon, 2017).

Farjeon, Eleanor, *Edward Thomas: The Last Four Years* (Oxford: O.U.P., 1958).

– ed., *The Green Roads: Edward Thomas Poems for young readers* (London: Bodley Head, 1965).

Gant, Roland, ed., *The Prose of Edward Thomas* (London: Falcon Press, 1948).

Hollis, Matthew, *Now All Roads Lead to France: The Last Four Years of Edward Thomas* (London: Faber and Faber, 2011).

Jenkins, Elis, 'Fiftieth Anniversary of the Death of Edward Thomas (1878-1917): Some of his Welsh Friends', *National Library of Wales Journal* 15, no.2. (Winter 1967) pp. 147-56.

Jones, Sally, 'Edward Thomas and Wales', in Jonathan Barker (ed.) *The Art of Edward Thomas* (Bridgend: Poetry Wales Press, 1987) pp. 75-84.

Jones, E. Cefni, *GWILI Cofiant a Phregethau* (Llandysul: Gwasg Gomer, 1937).

Kirkham, Michael, *The Imagination of Edward Thomas* (Cambridge: C.U.P., 1986).

Moore, John, *The Life and Letters of Edward Thomas* (London: Heinemann, 1939).

Motion, Andrew, *The Poetry of Edward Thomas* (London: Routledge & Kegan Paul, 1980).

Ralph, Maud, ed., *Dylan Thomas: The Broadcasts* (London: Dent, 1991).

Rhys, Ernest, *Wales England Wed* (London: Dent, 1940).

Roberts, David, *Minds at War* (London: Saxon Books, 1996).

Sacks, Peter, ed., *The Poems of Edward Thomas* (New York: Handsel Books, 2003).

Severn, Mark, (pseudonym of Franklin Lushington) *The Gambardier* (London: Leonaur, 2007 reprint).

Smith, Stan, *Edward Thomas* (London: Faber and Faber, 1986).

Stephens, Meic, ed., *The New Companion to the Literature of Wales* (Cardiff: U.W.P., 1998).

Thomas, Helen, *As It Was & World Without End* (London: Faber and Faber, 1956).

–   *Under Storm's Wing* (Manchester: Carcanet, 1988).

Thomas, M. Wynn, *The Nations of Wales: 1890-1914* (Cardiff: U.W.P., 2016).

–   ed., *Edward Thomas Collected Poems* (Oxford; O.U.P 1978).

Thomas, R. George, *Edward Thomas* (Writers of Wales) (Cardiff: U.W.P., 1972)

–   *Edward Thomas: A Portrait* (Oxford: O.U.P., 1985).

–   ed., *Edward Thomas Selected Letters* (Oxford; O.U.P., 1995).

–   ed., *Edward Thomas Collected Poems and War Diary 1917* (London: Faber and Faber, 2004).

Webb, Andrew, *Edward Thomas and World Literary Studies* (Cardiff: U.W.P., 2013).

Wilson, Jean Moorcroft, *Edward Thomas: from Adlestrop to Arras* (London: Bloomsbury, 2015).

Periodicals

Anglo-Welsh Review
Journal of the Friends of the Dymock Poets
Newsletter of The Edward Thomas Fellowship
National Library of Wales Journal
New Welsh Review
Poetry Wales Magazine
Welsh Outlook

A Carnival of Voices

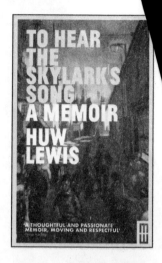

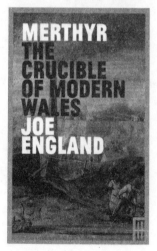

PARTHIAN

www.parthianbooks.com